The 105 Best Investments for the 21st Century

Other Books by Richard J. Maturi

Stock Picking: The 11 Best Tactics for Beating the Market

Wall Street Words

Divining the Dow

Money Making Investments Your Broker Doesn't Tell You About

Main Street Beats Wall Street

The 105 Best Investments for the 21st Century

Richard J. Maturi

McGraw-Hill, Inc.

New York   San Francisco   Washington, D.C.   Auckland   Bogotá
Caracas   Lisbon   London   Madrid   Mexico City   Milan
Montreal   New Delhi   San Juan   Singapore
Sydney   Tokyo   Toronto

Library of Congress Cataloging-in-Publication Data

Maturi, Richard J.
    The 105 best investments for the 21st century   /   Richard J. Maturi.
        p.   cm.
    Includes Index.
    ISBN 0-07-040939-0
    1. Investments.   2. Finance, Personal.   3. Economic forcasting.
  I. Title.   II. Title: One hundred and five best invesments for the
21st century.
  HG4521.M363   1995
  332.6—dc20   94-39884
                                                     CIP

1 2 3 4 5 6 7 8 9 0 DOC/DOC 9 0 9 8 7 6 5 4

ISBN 0-07-040939-0

The sponsoring editor for this book was David Conti, the editing supervisor was Paul R. Sobel, and the production supervisor was Donald F. Schmidt. It was set in Palatino by McGraw-Hill's Professional Book Group composition unit.

Printed and bound by R. R. Donnelley & Sons Company.

This publication is designed to provide accurate and authoritative information in regard to the subject matter covered. It is sold with the understanding that the publisher is not engaged in rendering legal, accounting, or other professional service. If legal advice or other expert assistance is required, the services of a competent professional person should be sought.

                —from a declaration of principles jointly adopted by a committee
                  of the American Bar Association and a committee of publishers

As we approach the 21st century, we must look to the next generation to lead our country. In the spirit of that vision, I dedicate this book to my sons, Craig and Matthew, who will become the leaders of tomorrow. May they grow in wisdom as life unfolds before them.

Contents

Preface

We live, work, and invest in a dramatically changing world. Global competition, the historic tearing down of the Berlin Wall and collapse of the Iron Curtain, the emergence of Third World countries as fierce economic competitors, and the formation of the European Economic Community and North American Free Trade Agreement all work to change the investment playing field.

It is no longer possible to purchase 'Blue Chip' stocks and hold them for the long-term without periodic portfolio reassessment. Investors who staked a portion of their portfolios in International Business Machines Corporation (NYSE: IBM) in the late eighties or early nineties saw the value of their holdings drop precipitiously, to less than a third of its original value in the span of under three years.

Unfortunately, this grim scenario repeated itself all too often with other stocks and market sectors. In today's volatile economic and political environment, there's no longer any such thing as a 'Blue Chip' investment. Each investment must be continually scrutinized for future prospects in light of ever-changing realities.

With that in mind, I have pulled together a portfolio of investments positioned to perform well as we move into the 21st century. This book includes a wide variety of investment options that promise to provide diversification and unique opportunities to prosper as changes in both the domestic and international political and economic arenas unfold in the years ahead. Some of these investments will perform better than others in certain economic environments. Be sure to adjust your portfolio mix as the economic playing field changes.

As with any investment strategy; investing for the 21st century requires periodic reassessment as company, industry, national, and international circumstances change. Forget about the so called 'Blue Chips', stake your fortune in companies and other investments geared to perform well in the 21st century.

Each chapter will provide tips on where to find investment information, the suitability of the investment for conservative/aggressive investors, tax implications (where applicable), and investment track records. More importantly, an analysis of each of the spotlighted investments will delve into why and under what circumstances these investments are expected to outperform the market.

In the following pages you will find growth companies, special situations, beaten down stocks, turnaround situations, and other unique investment opportunities.

This book goes well beyond looking at past performance to find future winners. It uses specific key investment yardsticks such as cash flow, market niches, management talent, and insider ownership to narrow the list of candidates.

There's a wealth of investment options contained within these pages. Sit back and prepare yourself for the 21st century. Investors desiring to keep appraised of "The 105 Best Investments for the 21st Century" are invited to avail themselves of the new "21st Century Investments" newsletter special offer at the end of this book.

Acknowledgments

I extend my thanks to the following who were kind enough to allow reprint of charts and illustrations: Blanchard & Company, Inc., Kruse International, Krause Publications, Platinum Guild International, Inc., R.M. Smythe & Company, Inc., The Bank of New York, Value Line Publishing, Inc.

Richard J. Maturi
Cheramie, Wyoming

The 105 Best Investments for the 21st Century

1
Top Industrial Stocks

To be sure, ferreting out the top industrial, consumer, and service stocks can be a daunting task. Undoubtedly, others will come up with their own candidates that appear to be attractive stocks at a particular moment in investment time. This book, however, takes the investment perspective one step further, looking ahead to anticipated events in the twenty-first century to determine which companies and stocks will out-perform their industry and market-sector counterparts.

Each of the following industrial candidates, and those investments in the chapters that follow, has its own unique set of characteristics and circumstances that makes it well positioned for impressive gains. Needless to say, many of these companies will share some qualities, such as savvy management, solid product or service territories and markets, niche products, strong financials, etc. You can use the techniques and guidelines illustrated in this book for discovering other strong candidates for superior performance in the twenty-first century.

One caution is in order, however. While I present historical data and ratios, I caution against using past performance as the only guideline for uncovering top investment prospects. These historical numbers tell where the company, mutual fund, or other investment has been, but not necessarily where it is headed. In the same respect, there will be many other investments not covered here that may sport better historical performance numbers but lack the right combination of markets, products or services, economic climate, management talent, and/or financial wherewithal to be a top performer in the years ahead.

The discussion also indicates whether or not the company offers a dividend reinvestment program (DRIP). DRIPs are a convenient way to compound your investment gains and to purchase stock at lower costs and even at a discount from market price.

In these first three chapters, I have divided up the stocks into the somewhat arbitrary industrial, consumer, and service categories. Granted, it could be argued that Rubbermaid Incorporated could be classified in the industrial category rather than the consumer category in which I chose to place it. Likewise, a case could be made to classify R. R. Donnelley & Sons Company as an industrial firm rather than a service company, as I have classified this commercial printing firm. Regardless of where you decide to classify a particular company in your own analysis efforts, the main point is that the company must stand poised to deliver solid revenue and earnings gains, and thus higher stock prices for its shareholders.

The industrial sector of America's economy is enjoying a resurgence that promises to speed up as we enter the twenty-first century. Years of capital improvements, combined with a renewed emphasis on quality improvements and enhanced productivity, have worked to make American industry competitive once again on a global scale.

Some of these companies have undertaken to make their own systems and operations more efficient and productive by means of capital improvements and new management techniques. On the other side of the same coin, others manufacture equipment and products that aid business customers in their efforts to reduce costs and improve their bottom lines.

The following companies represent a diverse cross section of America's industrial strength. From business forms to machine tools to industrial coatings to quality control instrumentation, they work to produce world-class, competitive products that can go up against any produced in the world. As required by the new global competitiveness, their products are backed by excellent service capabilities and a desire to find innovative solutions to customer problems and special needs.

INDUSTRIAL STOCKS	INDUSTRY
Cincinnati Milacron Inc.	Machine Tools
Giddings & Lewis, Inc.	Automated Industrial Systems
Pall Corporation	Filtration Products
RPM, Inc.	Industrial Coatings
The Reynolds and Reynolds Company	Business Forms
X-Rite, Incorporated	Quality Control Instruments

☆1 CINCINNATI ☆ MILACRON INC.

CINCINNATI MILACRON INC.
4701 Marburg Avenue
Cincinnati, OH 45209
513-841-8100

Stock exchange: NYSE
Ticker symbol: CMZ
DRIP program: Yes
Ownership:
  Institutional: + 66%
  Insiders: + 10%

Industry Review.   The machine tool industry is on the rebound from an early 1990s downturn. Increased economic activity, both domestically and abroad, bodes well for this sector. In addition, U.S. machine tool companies have made giant strides in competitiveness against Japanese and other countries' machine tool manufacturers, which had captured a large share of the domestic U.S. market in the eighties. Now running lean and mean, companies such as Cincinnati Milacron stand to benefit as the global economy improves.

Company Profile.   Cincinnati Milacron ranks as a leader in the machine tool industry. It serves its worldwide markets from 15 facilities in the United States as well as plants in Canada, Mexico, Austria, France, Germany, Great Britain, Japan, and The Netherlands. Its machine tool equipment product lines are state of the art, utilizing computer controls and advanced applications software.

The company operates three business segments: machine tools (48 percent of revenues); plastic machinery (38 percent); and industrial products such as metal-working fluids, precision grinding wheels, and metal-cutting tools (14 percent). In recent years, the company has shuttered outmoded plants and relocated other machine tool operations for more efficiency.

Adding diversity to its operations, the Ferromatik acquisition boosts the company's presence in the plastics machinery market. Cincinnati Milacron is the largest U.S. producer of injection molding machines. A major 1992 modernization and expansion program at the firm's Mt. Orab, Ohio plastics-processing machinery facility doubled the company's capacity for injection molding machines, substantially shortened production lead times, and reduced manufacturing costs. All of these operating benefits combine to strengthen Cincinnati Milacron's status as an industry low-cost producer.

Management Talent. Chairman and Chief Executive Officer Daniel J. Meyer, President and Chief Operating Officer Raymond E. Ross, and operating vice presidents have years of solid industry experience. They exhibit the courage and talent to reposition the company with strategic plant closings and other disposals, facility and equipment modernization, acquisitions, and new product introductions.

Financial Status. A 1993 offering of common shares allowed the company to pay off high cost debt, improve financial flexibility, and have capital for key acquisitions. Operating efficiencies and higher revenues are working to substantially boost cashflow. Cashflow per share has been improving dramatically, from a deficit in 1991 to nearly $2 per share in 1993. Look for increased cashflow, as the global economy heats up in the years ahead.

DRIP Details. The company's dividend reinvestment plan is at no administration or commission charge to the shareholder. It allows for additional purchases of company shares in amounts ranging from $25 to $1000 per month. Information may be obtained by writing to: Mellon Bank, N.A., Dividend Reinvestment Services, P.O. Box 444, Pittsburgh, PA 15230-0444.

Particular Strengths. Management has embarked on an aggressive acquisition and new-product-introduction program. Recent acquisitions include Valenite Corporation, a leading producer of expendable industrial-metal-cutting products, and the Ferromatik plastics injection-molding-machine business from Klockner Werke A.G. in Germany. Cincinnati Milacron has a strong overseas presence capable of benefiting from a European and Far East economic recovery. In addition, its technologically advanced and diversified product line makes the firm a leading competitor in both the machine tool and plastics machinery markets.

The Ferromatik acquisition represents a major step toward the company's goal of establishing a manufacturing and distribution base in Germany to serve European and other key overseas markets.

The new "Wolfpack" design program seeks to produce a steady stream of world-class products, superior in performance, competitive in price, and capturing increased market share. In excess of 60 percent of recent sales derive from products not in the company's line five years ago.

Financial statistics (figures in millions, except per-share amounts):

	1990	1991	1992	1993
Revenues	$805	$754	$789	$1,029
Net income (loss)	(24)	(100)	22*	(102)†
Earnings (loss)/share	(.95)	(3.67)	.77*	(3.16)†
Dividend/share	.72	.63	.36	.36
Long-term debt	157	156	154	108
Stock price range/share:				
High	21⅜	15¼	18¼	29⅝
Low	8⅞	6⅝	10⅞	18¼

*Includes extraordinary tax benefit from loss carryforward of $5.4 million or 19 cents per share.

†Includes nonrecurring charges of $47.1 million for machine tool consolidation, $22.8 million for disposition of subsidiary, $52.1 million in accounting changes, and an extraordinary loss of $4.4 million for early extinguishment of debt, totaling $3.86 per share.

Investment Assessment.   As extraordinary charges for write-downs and plant disposals disappear from Cincinnati Milacron's year-to-year financial comparisons, the company's per-share earnings will turn up significantly. The company's growing worldwide manufacturing and distribution capabilities portend increased market share. Look for higher stock prices and a boost in the dividend payment, as the economy picks up and Cincinnati Milacron captures additional market share from weaker competitors.

Cincinnati Milacron is a solid, well-managed company prepared to make the necessary operating and financial adjustments to compete successfully on a global basis in the twenty-first century.

☆ 2 GIDDINGS ☆ & LEWIS, INC.

GIDDINGS & LEWIS, INC.
142 Doty Street
P.O. Box 590
Fond Du Lac, Wisconsin 54935
414-921-4100

Stock exchange: NASDAQ
Ticker symbol: GIDL
DRIP program: No
Ownership:
   Institutional: + 90%
   Insiders: + 1%

Industry Review.   Like Cincinnati Milacron, Giddings & Lewis operates in the machine tool industry, serving industrial customers such as
the automotive, aerospace, construction, defense, appliance, energy,
and electronics industries through the design and manufacture of high-
precision, automated industrial systems. The machine tool industry is
on the rebound from an early 1990s downturn. Increased economic
activity both domestically and abroad is good news for this sector. In
addition, U.S. machine tool companies have made giant strides in competitiveness against Japanese and other countries' machine tool manufacturers, which had captured a large share of the domestic U.S. market
in the eighties.

Company Profile.   Giddings & Lewis is well positioned to benefit
from the trend in industrial companies to upgrade their operations
with high-tech automated systems. For example, its "smart" manufacturing system for Harley Davidson constructs motorcycle frames in a
four-machine setup, and its automated machining systems produce
medium and heavy truck engine components for Mercedes-Benz. The
firm manufactures its industrial systems, integrated transfer lines, and
automation measurement and control products in 14 facilities in the
United States, England, Germany, and Scotland.

The more than 100-year-old company divides its business into four
operating groups: automation technology (contributing 32.5 percent of
revenues), integrated automation (40.4 percent), automation measurement and control (8.2 percent), and European operations (18.9 percent).
An important factor in the company's revenue and earnings growth
prospects, Giddings & Lewis' presence in the European market continues to expand. From less than 14 percent of company revenues in 1990,
European operations expanded to nearly 20 percent by the end of 1993,
with European segment bookings up in excess of 25 percent in 1993.

The company sports a broad line of products serving a diversified
customer base. Examples include an engine-block production system
for the new Ford Sigma engine plant in Spain, a manufacturing system
integrating many non–Giddings & Lewis machines for the Republic of
China on Taiwan, machining systems for General Electric, MRI equipment for the health care industry (the firm's largest subcontract order
ever), a large vertical turning center for the Metropolitan Transit
System in Washington, D.C., and automated machine tools for a U.S.
manufacturer of heavy capital goods.

Management Talent.   Giddings & Lewis completed its search for a
new Chairman and Chief Executive Officer in July 1993, after William J.
Fife, Jr.'s resignation. Joseph R. Coppola, a Giddings & Lewis Board of

Directors member since 1989, brings veteran industry experience to the firm's top position, having served as Senior Vice President/ Manufacturing Services at Cooper Industries and possessing nearly 20 years' experience in a variety of manufacturing management positions with General Electric Company.

Financial Status. The company is in the enviable position of having achieved debt-free status in the second quarter of 1993. This is especially impressive since the company took on substantial debt with the acquisition of Cross & Trecker, a company almost twice Giddings & Lewis' size, in late 1991. In less than two years, the firm paid off approximately $156 million in acquisition debt. It nearly doubled its cashflow per share, from $1.06 per share in 1991 to almost $2.00 per share in 1993. This trend promises to continue in the years ahead, with higher revenues, increased operating efficiencies, and the elimination of long-term debt.

Particular Strengths. Giddings & Lewis seeks to serve specific customer needs with customed-designed and -produced machinery and equipment. This market segment offers the opportunity for less competition and higher margins than are to be found in traditional machine tool sales. In pursuit of this goal, the firm has beefed up research and development expenditures dramatically since 1990. In 1993, Giddings & Lewis invested in excess of $60 million in research and development activities, compared with less than $25 million just three years earlier.

The firm's debt-free position gives it added flexibility to take advantage of market opportunities, as by making strategic acquisitions, introducing new product lines, and expanding current or entering new markets.

Financial statistics (figures in millions, except per-share amounts):

	1990	1991	1992	1993
Revenues	$243	$327	$623	$517
Net income (loss)	20	22	36	44*
Earnings (loss)/share	.92	.95	1.16	1.31*
Dividend/share	.08	.08	.11	.12
Long-term debt	00	51	68	00
Stock price range/share:				
High	10⅝	15⅛	25¾	29¾
Low	6⅛	7⅞	14¾	19½

*Includes $8 million, or 23-cents-per-share gain on Russian contract collections, and changes in reserves for plant closings.

Investment Assessment. Giddings & Lewis continues to make good inroads into key overseas markets. Its strong financial position and emphasis on research and development make it a solid long-term player in the global machine tool and automated industrial systems business.

Earnings have been on an uptrend since the firm became a public company again in 1989, rising to $1.31 per share in 1993 from only $.83 per share in 1989, even with substantially more shares outstanding. Disappointing revenues and earnings for 1994 caused investors to flee the stock, giving it all the more room to rebound sharply as conditions improve.

☆ 3 PALL CORPORATION ☆

PALL CORPORATION
2200 Northern Boulevard
East Hills, New York 11548
516-484-5400

Stock exchange: NYSE
Ticker symbol: PLL
DRIP program: Yes
Ownership:
    Institutional: 68%
    Insiders: 10%

Industry Review. Pall Corporation manufactures fluid filters and equipment for use in the aerospace, biomedical, and fluid-processing markets. The continued global recession and a decrease in military and aerospace markets combined to yield relatively flat industrywide revenues in the early 1990s. On the plus side, growing use of more sophisticated filtration products in the health care and food processing industries promises revenue growth in the years ahead. Likewise, there should be further growth in certain overseas markets such as England, Spain, France, and Japan as the world economy improves.

Company Profile. Pall Corporation is the world leader in the technology of fluid filtration. Its products aid companies in the biomedical, food and beverage, film, magnetic tape, electronics, aeropower, and chemical and petrochemical industries to remove microscopic contaminants in their manufacturing processes.

The company operates three industry segments: health care (contributing 51 percent of company revenues), aeropower (26 percent), and fluid processing (23 percent). In light of changing market dynamics, Pall Corporation has been restructuring its operating segments and product lines. Health care has grown from 38 percent of company revenues in fiscal 1992 to over 50 percent at the end (July 31) of fiscal 1993.

Consolidation of aeropower facilities and the shedding of unprofitable fluid-processing operations contributed to the greater emphasis placed on the health care segment. Pall maintains manufacturing facilities in Connecticut, New York, Florida, Puerto Rico, the United Kingdom, and Japan. In addition, offices and warehouses in Canada, China, France, Germany, Italy, Singapore, South Korea, and Switzerland round out its global operations.

The company's customer base is diverse, with no customer accounting for more than 10 percent of annual revenues. Approximately 43 percent of revenues derive from the Western Hemisphere, while the balance comes from Europe (42 percent) and the Pacific Basin (15 percent). More than 70 percent of the products sold overseas are also manufactured at overseas facilities, largely eliminating the effect of currency fluctuations on overseas profits. The firm's overseas plants, offices, warehouses, and research and development facilities also help the company to better supply and service overseas customers.

Since 1978, Pall has increased its share of the potential world market for its filtration products from 8.5 to over 13 percent.

Management Talent. Chairman and Chief Executive Officer Maurice G. Hardy has been a company officer since 1972. Eric Krasnoff was elected to the positions of President and Chief Operating Officer in July 1993, after having served in other company-officer capacities since 1986. From 1951 to July 1992, Eric's father, Abraham, Chairman Emeritus and Director, served as a senior officer of Pall Corporation and Director. Management has successfully guided Pall into its industry leadership position.

Financial Status. The company has cut its long-term debt in half, dropping it to $24.5 million at the end of fiscal 1993 from $59 million a year earlier. A strong working-capital position of nearly $200 million, including more than $100 million in cash, cash equivalents, and short-term investments, gives Pall Corporation plenty of operating flexibility.

It uses forward exchange contracts to minimize the effects of currency fluctuations. Over the past two years,the Board of Directors has authorized the repurchase of $65 million of the company's common stock. The Board also has voted three stock splits since January 1991.

The company's cashflow per share makes solid gains each year, having risen from $1.07 per share in 1990 to an estimated $1.65 per share in 1993.

DRIP Details.   Pall Corporation's dividend reinvestment program pays all fees and commissions on company shares purchased through the plan. The DRIP plan allows for the purchase of additional shares in amounts from $25 to $5000 per month. Contact Investor Communications at 800-645-6532.

Particular Strengths.   The company's shift away from less-promising markets in aeropower and defense to the high-growth areas of biomedical and selected-fluid processing segments will improve the company's revenue and earnings base. For example, several years back, Pall did not serve the world's blood banks. Today, with a line of innovative products, Pall has been selected as the exclusive supplier for blood filtration by the American Red Cross.

Extensive worldwide production, distribution, and research and development facilities give Pall Corporation the competitive edge over smaller and less financially sound competitors. Backing up its drive for new products, research and development expenditures have risen to over $40 million in fiscal 1993, from less than $31 million two years earlier.

Financial statistics (figures in millions, except per-share amounts):

For fiscal year ended July 31	1990	1991	1992	1993
Revenues	$565	$657	$685	$687
Net income (loss)	66	80	93	78
Earnings (loss)/share	.57	.69	.79	.68
Dividend/share	.18	.21	.26	.31
Long-term debt	56	52	59	24
Stock price range/share:				
High	12.46	20.12	24.09	23.16
Low	10.04	8.71	16.50	16.38

Investment Assessment.   The earnings drop in fiscal 1993 was mainly attributable to downsizing the military portion of the aeropower segment, a move designed to strengthen the company's long-term revenue and earnings prospects and better utilize company resources.

"Pall fits neatly into the overall growing emphasis on improved environmental standards and product purity globally. It has the most sophisticated technology in the industry. None of its competitors has the breadth of product line that Pall possesses," says Bradley E. Turner, Director of Gradison-McDonald Asset Management in Cincinnati, Ohio.

Pall's strong worldwide franchise and concentration on growth markets will deliver higher revenues, earnings, and stock prices.

Turner also likes Pall for its consistent performance. It has produced growing revenues and earnings per share for over 45 years, through every type of economic environment. "Pall is uniquely positioned to benefit from long-term industry fundamentals," says Turner.

☆ 4 RPM, INC. ☆

RPM, INC.
2628 Pearl Road
P.O. Box 77
Medina, Ohio 44258

Stock exchange: NASDAQ
Ticker symbol: RPOW
DRIP program: Yes
Ownership:
    Institutional: 42%
    Insiders: 6%

Industry Review. RPM, Inc. operates in two major, very attractive markets: specialty chemicals for the industrial maintenance industry, and do-it-yourself consumer products. As such, its revenue stream is virtually recession-resistant. The neverending battle to preserve the nation's infrastructure provides continual demand for RPM's specialized waterproofing products and corrosion-control coatings. Likewise, the trend toward consumer do-it-yourself projects in home maintenance, automotive repair, and hobby and leisure areas continues its double-digit growth.

Company Profile. RPM, Inc. is a leading manufacturer of specialized industrial chemicals and coatings (55 percent of revenues) for corrosion control, industrial waterproofing, and maintenance. It rounds out its product line and diversification with consumer do-it-yourself products (45 percent).

Management employs an aggressive acquisition strategy, seeking out companies with strong products lines and dominant market positions. In fact, the company generates a large percentage (over 30 percent) of its growth through key acquisitions. For example, in October 1993, RPM expanded into a major new market with the acquisition of Stonhard, Inc.—$100 million in revenues; a major player in the industrial and commercial flooring segment—in a $200 million deal involving a combination of cash, stock, and assumed debt. In another major 1993 market move, RPM acquired Dynatron/Bondo Corporation, an automotive-repair-products supplier with $45 million in annual revenues.

RPM has achieved consistent growth over the years. The fiscal year ended May 31, 1993, concluded the company's forty-sixth consecutive year of record revenues, earnings, and earnings per share. For the 10 years ended fiscal 1993, revenues and earnings have increased at compounded rates of 16 and 17 percent, respectively.

Cash dividends have increased for 19 consecutive years, and the Board of Directors has voted numerous stock splits. Shareholders have done well holding RPM stock over the years. An investor savvy enough to have purchased 1000 shares at the initial offering price of $8 per share in 1964 had an RPM portfolio at the end of fiscal 1993 of 82,537 shares worth more than $1.5 million, and generating $40,000 in annual cash dividends. This extraordinary return does not even factor in the effects of participation in the company's dividend reinvestment (DRIP) plan.

Management Talent.   RPM takes an entrepreneurial attitude toward the running of its subsidiaries. When looking for strategic acquisitions to bring into the RPM fold, it takes a long, hard look at existing management expertise. Most acquisitions include provisions to keep former management, and ties their overall compensation package to continued high-performance results. Each operating company maintains direct control over day-to-day operations and decision making. Planning, from capital expenditures to new-product introductions, is done jointly with the home office corporate management and individual division officers.

Thomas C. Sullivan has been Chairman and Chief Executive Officer of RPM since 1971 (his father founded the original company, Republic Powdered Metals). President and Chief Operating Officer James A. Karman has served in those positions since October 1982. The RPM team has proven itself adept at seeking out strategic acquisitions and successfully integrating them into part of the RPM team.

Financial Status.   RPM uses a combination of cash, stock, and debt to finance acquisitions, helping to keep leverage down to a manageable level. Even with the fiscal 1993 Stonhard and Dynatron/Bondo acquisitions, long-term debt had dropped nearly $50 million by the end of fiscal year 1994's first quarter, due to the retiring of $130 million of debt and the redemption of all outstanding 6.75 percent Convertible Subordinated Debentures due 2005. This move not only strengthens the balance sheet but adds operating flexibility and cuts interest expenses.

Working capital stands at a little under $190 million, and the company generates cashflow at around $1.35 per share. A solid cash position and strong cashflow provide adequate funds for increased cash dividends. RPM has boosted its cash dividend payout by a compounded annual rate of 14 percent over the last 10 fiscal years.

DRIP Details.   The company's DRIP program permits additional investment in company shares, at no administrative or commission cost to the shareholder, in amounts between $25 and $5000 per month. A whopping 71 percent of RPM shareholders participate in the DRIP program. According to a 1992 National Association of Investment Clubs survey, RPM ranked as the fifth most popular stock held by individual investors, and the eighth most profitable investment held by individuals over the years. Contact the company for DRIP information.

Particular Strengths.   As discussed earlier, one of the main keys to RPM's impressive performance has been its successful acquisition strategy. Look for this track record to continue. The company operates small plant facilities at near-capacity levels, ensuring maximum efficiency. An overseas presence (12 percent of annual revenues) provides market diversification and distribution opportunities for new acquisitions and product lines.

Financial statistics (figures in millions, except per-share amounts):

For fiscal year ended May 31	1990	1991	1992	1993
Revenues	$445	$500	$552	$626
Net income (loss)	28	32	34	39
Earnings (loss)/share	.63	.68	.73	.83
Dividend/share	.35	.40	.44	.47
Long-term debt	146	114	239	221
Stock price range/share:				
High	$12\frac{1}{8}$	$15\frac{1}{2}$	$18\frac{1}{2}$	$19\frac{3}{8}$
Low	$8\frac{3}{8}$	$10\frac{7}{8}$	$12\frac{5}{8}$	$16\frac{1}{4}$

Investment Assessment.   RPM's fiscal 1994 started out with record revenues and earnings for the first nine months ended February 28, 1994. Sales increased 6 percent, while earnings jumped 42 percent. Shareholders should continue to earn impressive overall returns by investing in RPM's solid and well-managed business. Based on financial results for 1993, RPM joined the ranks of the elite *Fortune* 500 for the first time, with a ranking of 491st in sales and 265th in profits. Its 10-year total return to shareholders, of 18.3 percent compounded, earned an 88th place ranking.

Look for RPM to improve on this stellar record. (See Fig. 1-1, the RPM. Inc. stock chart.)

RPM, INC. NDQ-RPOW

RECENT PRICE	P/E RATIO	(Trailing: 20.5 Median: 17.0)	RELATIVE P/E RATIO	DIV'D YLD	VALUE LINE
18	18.9		1.29	3.1%	529

TIMELINESS 2 Above Average (Relative Price Performance Next 12 Mos.)
SAFETY 3 Average (Scale: 1 Highest to 5 Lowest)
BETA .90 (1.00 = Market)

1997-99 PROJECTIONS

	Price	Gain	Ann'l Total Return
High	30	(+65%)	16%
Low	19	(+5%)	5%

Insider Decisions

	N	D	J	F	M	A	M	J	J
to Buy	0	0	0	1	0	0	0	0	0
Options	0	0	1	0	2	0	0	0	0
to Sell	0	1	1	0	0	0	0	0	0

Institutional Decisions

	4Q93	1Q94	2Q94
to Buy	37	38	47
to Sell	21	36	31
Hld's(000)	18277	19479	19791

Options: CBOE

Splits noted on chart: 5-for-4 split, 3-for-2 split, 12.0 x "Cash Flow" p/sh, 25% div'd

Shaded areas indicate recessions. Relative Price Strength.

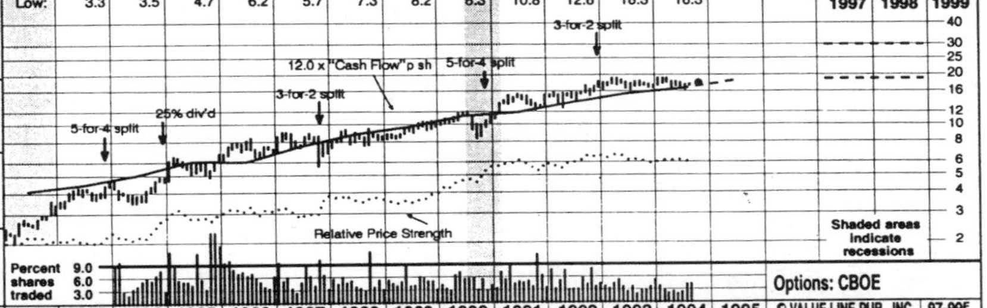

Target Price Range 1997 1998 1999

Per-share statistics

	1978	1979	1980	1981	1982	1983	1984	1985	1986	1987	1988	1989	1990	1991	1992	1993	1994	1995	© VALUE LINE PUB, INC. 97-99F
Sales per sh A	3.12	4.10	4.61	4.68	4.91	5.15	5.70	6.92	6.63	7.52	8.13	8.92	10.51	10.73	11.70	13.22	14.37	17.15	20.75
"Cash Flow" per sh	.26	.30	.35	.40	.37	.43	.51	.62	.51	.62	.74	.82	.99	1.14	1.14	1.28	1.38	1.55	2.10
Earnings per sh B	.18	.21	.23	.26	.26	.28	.31	.37	.37	.41	.51	.58	.66	.67	.72	.79	.89	1.00	1.50
Div'ds Decl'd per sh C■	.06	.06	.07	.08	.08	.11	.14	.18	.21	.24	.29	.33	.40	.40	.45	.47	.51	.55	.80
Cap'l Spending per sh	.03	.06	.10	.08	.08	.11	.11	.18	.12	.25	.15	.21	.25	.35	.36	.39	.45	.30	.40
Book Value per sh D	1.17	1.32	1.49	1.63	1.76	2.02	2.19	2.90	3.06	3.25	3.49	3.81	4.17	4.43	4.70	5.05	5.54	6.40	9.00
Common Shs Outst'g E	24.11	24.65	24.82	25.37	25.37	25.41	27.05	29.36	38.66	42.04	42.17	42.32	46.61	47.18	47.32	56.75	56.75	58.00	65.00
Avg Ann'l P/E Ratio	9.1	9.8	8.7	11.3	9.1	11.6	13.0	13.5	17.0	18.6	15.7	14.8	15.6	17.4	19.9	21.4	20.0		16.0
Relative P/E Ratio	1.24	1.42	1.16	1.00	1.00	.98	1.21	1.10	1.15	1.24	1.30	1.12	1.16	1.11	1.21	1.26	1.23		1.25
Avg Ann'l Div'd Yield	1.6%	1.9%	3.2%	2.6%	3.5%	2.4%	2.8%	3.6%	3.3%	3.1%	3.6%	3.8%	3.5%	3.4%	3.1%	2.8%	2.9%		3.3%

Company financials

	1984	1985	1986	1987	1988	1989	1990	1991	1992	1993	1994	1995	97-99F
Sales ($mill) A	154.2	203.2	250.7	290.5	342.0	376.1	444.8	500.3	552.1	625.7	815.6	995	1350
Operating Margin	12.0%	12.4%	12.4%	15.0%	15.3%	14.6%	14.6%	14.1%	16.0%	16.1%	15.6%	16.5%	16.5%
Depreciation ($mill)	3.1	4.3	6.6	8.3	9.6	10.1	12.2	14.4	19.4	21.4	25.9	25.0	35.0
Net Profit ($mill)	8.4	10.7	12.6	15.9	21.4	24.2	27.7	31.9	34.5	39.4	52.6	65.0	100
Income Tax Rate	39.0%	40.5%	34.6%	45.6%	37.8%	38.3%	38.3%	38.4%	39.8%	40.4%	40.2%	42.0%	42.0%
Net Profit Margin	5.4%	5.3%	5.0%	5.5%	6.2%	6.4%	6.2%	6.4%	6.2%	6.3%	6.5%	6.5%	7.4%
Working Cap'l ($mill)	52.1	54.9	64.3	67.2	88.9	93.3	122.4	129.7	162.8	172.9	227.0	480	400
Long-Term Debt ($mill)	39.6	41.8	61.8	76.1	75.4	77.0	145.2	114.5	238.9	220.9	233.0	430	350
Net Worth ($mill)	54.5	64.4	109.6	118.2	136.4	147.0	161.0	206.3	221.8	239.1	314.5	370	585
% Earned Total Cap'l	10.4%	12.1%	9.8%	9.8%	11.8%	12.2%	10.5%	11.3%	9.0%	10.1%	10.8%	9.5%	11.5%
% Earned Net Worth	15.4%	16.7%	11.5%	13.4%	15.7%	16.5%	17.2%	15.4%	15.5%	16.5%	16.7%	17.5%	16.5%
% Retained to Comm Eq	8.2%	8.9%	8.8%	5.4%	7.3%	7.9%	6.6%	6.2%	7.1%	7.1%	7.2%	8.0%	8.0%
% All Div'ds to Net Prof	47%	47%	56%	60%	53%	56%	54%	57%	60%	57%	57%	55%	53%

BUSINESS: RPM, Inc. mfrs. protective coatings, incl. paints, sealants, roofing membranes, & furniture & auto touch-up products. Brands: Alox, Alumination, Bondex, B-I-N, Carboline, Day-Glo, Floquil, Geoflex, Martin Mathys, Mohawk, Rust-Oleum, Talsol, Testor. Makes decorative fabrics & wallcoverings. Acq'd Kop-Coat, 1/90; Rust-Oleum/Europe, 6/91; Day-Glo Color, 11/91; Martin Mathys, 5/92; Sentry Polymers, 10/93; Rust-Oleum/U.S., 6/94. For. oper., 12% of sales. '94 depr. rate, 9.8%. Estd. plant age, 4 yrs. Has 4,500 empls.; 23,950 shrldrs. Insiders own 4.8% of stock (8/94 Proxy). Chmn./C.E.O.: Thomas Sullivan, Pres./C.O.O.: James Karman. Inc.:Ohio. Add.: Box 777, 2628 Pearl Rd, Medina, OH 44258. Tel.: 216-273-5090.

Figure 1-1. RPM, Inc. stock chart. (Copyright 1994 by Value Line Publishing Inc. Reprinted by permission; all rights reserved.)

☆ 5 THE REYNOLDS ☆ AND REYNOLDS COMPANY

THE REYNOLDS
  AND REYNOLDS COMPANY
115 South Ludlow Street
Dayton, Ohio 45402
513-443-2000

Stock exchange: NYSE
Ticker symbol: REY
DRIP program: Yes
Ownership:
  Institutional: 65%
  Insiders: 25%

Industry Review. While the office equipment and supplies industry looks to experience moderate growth in the years ahead, innovative companies serving some niche market needs, such as Reynolds and Reynolds, should outpace the competition and gain market share. The emergence of new or expanded opportunities in Europe, Mexico, and Latin American and South American countries, in the wake of the European Economic Community (EEC) and North American Free Trade Agreement (NAFTA), promises to boost the revenues and earnings of those companies that aggressively pursue these growing, lucrative markets.

Company Profile. Like other office-supply companies, the Reynolds and Reynolds Company supplies business forms to general business markets. What gives Reynolds and Reynolds a unique market niche is its additional focus on supplying business forms and turnkey computer systems to the automotive (vehicle dealerships, auto repair shops, auto parts stores, etc.) and health care industries. With both automotive and health care companies under pressure to reduce back-office costs and to do a better job with critical financial information, the firm stands to benefit from its efforts to upgrade and streamline computer information systems.

The company operates 13 businesses from manufacturing facilities in the United States and Canada, while the computer systems segment services customers through a network of over 600 service and support personnel in 175 offices worldwide. In addition, the Reyna Financial Corporation subsidiary provides financing for the company's computer systems. Approximately $7\frac{1}{2}$ percent of revenues derive from sales outside of the United States.

While the business forms sector continues to maintain market share and improve operating income, the computer systems segment has been providing strong growth in both revenues and earnings. For the fiscal year ended September 30, 1993, computer systems revenues came in at over $300 million and operating income rose to $54.6 million. By comparison, only two years ago this segment contributed under $250 million in company revenues, and less than $24 million in operating income.

Record revenues and improving gross profit (an impressive 34 percent) point to solid performance in the years ahead. New-product introductions and key acquisitions also figure in the greater market penetration of Reynolds and Reynolds.

Management Talent.   Chairman, President, and Chief Executive Officer David R. Holmes heads a management team that is dedicated to being number one in customer service and achieving record revenue and earning results. The firm already has garnered recognition with rankings in *Business Week*'s list of the 1000 most valuable companies and *Financial World*'s listing of the top 200 growth companies.

The 1993 annual report focuses on Reynolds and Reynolds' goal of becoming the best in the industry: "We are evolving beyond satisfying our customers to absolutely delighting them and creating customers for life."

Financial Status.   Twelve consecutive quarters of record income from operations (through the first quarter of fiscal 1994 ended December 31, 1993) has significantly enhanced Reynolds and Reynolds' already substantial financial prowess. In late 1993 the company refinanced its long-term computer systems segment debt, to take advantage of favorable interest rates. The computer systems debt now stands at a minimal 13.2 percent.

In fiscal 1993, cashflow exceeded $60 million, or around $3.55 per share. Management used available funds to repurchase $17 million in common stock and to acquire three companies. The Board of Directors increased the quarterly cash dividend from 13 to 15 cents per share, the sixth cash dividend rise since 1989.

DRIP Details.   Reynolds and Reynolds' DRIP program permits additional purchase of company common stock in amounts ranging from $100 to $1000 per quarter, at no cost administrative to the shareholder. For information, contact the Corporate Secretary at 513-443-2000.

Particular Strengths.   The company's thrust into computer systems for automotive and health care firms promises to keep revenues and earnings on their upward path. An improving product mix (as the computer services segment expands) will contribute to even greater gross margins and bottom-line earnings. Reynolds and Reynolds' strong cashflow and impressive financial standing will open up new market opportunities such as the 1993 acquisition of the Atlanta-based COIN Inc., a company with one of the larger installed bases of customers in the automobile dealership industry.

Financial statistics (figures in millions, except per-share amounts):

For fiscal year ended September 30	1990	1991	1992	1993
Revenues	$630	$632	$645	$697
Net income (loss)	27	25	39	33
Earnings (loss)/share	1.17	1.07	1.67	1.53
Dividend/share	.40	.42	.45	.52
Long-term debt	133	111	94	128
Stock price range/share:				
High	$12\frac{1}{4}$	$18\frac{5}{8}$	$25\frac{5}{8}$	$43\frac{5}{8}$
Low	$5\frac{7}{8}$	8	$16\frac{3}{4}$	$20\frac{3}{4}$

Investment Assessment. Look for strong earnings comparisons in the years ahead, particularly since fiscal 1993 results included an 86-cents-per-share nonrecurring charge to reflect the effects of accounting changes. Reynolds and Reynolds entered fiscal 1994 with a record backlog. With a broadened customer base in diversified industries, the company looks to achieve double-digit revenues and earnings gains in the foreseeable future.

☆ 6 X-RITE ☆
INCORPORATED

X-RITE INCORPORATED
3100 44th Street, SW
Grandville, Michigan 49418
616-534-7663

Stock exchange: NASDAQ
Ticker symbol: XRIT
DRIP program: No
Ownership:
    Institutional: 13%
    Insiders: 43%

Industry Review.   X-Rite Corporation provides quality control instruments to a variety of markets including aerospace, automotive, graphic arts, medical, microfilm, packaging, and photographic. As such, it serves a diversified customer base. A return to a more vibrant economy will boost overall precision-industry shipments.

Company Profile.   X-Rite, Incorporated sports a wide variety of quality control products to help its customers improve quality and productivity. It manufactures proprietary instruments involving advanced electronics and optics technologies for use in light and color measurement. The firm operates from an office and manufacturing facility near Grand Rapids, Michigan with a "clean room" and atmospherically controlled assembly operation.

An industry leader, X-Rite has generated higher revenues every year for more than a decade. Its 10-year compound sales growth rate exceeds 23 percent. Earnings have grown steadily, with the exception of a slight dip in 1988.

Management Talent.   Ted Thompson has been President and Chief Executive Officer since 1976. With growth, the company has hired and promoted new talent. The vice presidents of finance, engineering, and operations have all held their respective positions since 1983.

Testimony to the company's management depth is the fact that it has qualified for inclusion in *Forbes* Best Small Companies in America for the last three years running (1991, 1992, and 1993).

Financial Status.   The company maintains a strong, debt-free balance sheet, with the last long-term debt disappearing back in 1986. Working capital has improved dramatically in recent years, rising from less than $15 million in 1988 to over $28 million in 1993, including in excess of $14 million in short-term investments. Return on equity has consistently scored in the double-digit range over the past decade and has surpassed 20 percent the past two years.

Operating cashflow for each of the past three years totaled more than $5 million, and is more than sufficient for those capital and research and development requirements needed to keep the company on the cutting edge of technology. In addition, the more than $14 million in short-term investments in the company coffers provide plenty of operating flexibility and opportunities for market expansion.

Particular Strengths.   X-Rite invests heavily in research and development in order to meet customer requirements. The company owns eight U.S. patents protecting current products. Research and development expenditures have risen to over $2.5 million from less than $1.5 million in 1990. The firm's enhanced products lines and manufacturing efficiencies work to improve gross profit to nearly 70 percent.

Making its instruments more efficient for customers and attacking the huge automotive market, X-Rite introduced portable hand-held color-measuring devices for use on metallic paint surfaces in 1990.

A 1993 product introduction received good market response from paint manufacturers and large retailers. The new Mix-Rite system accurately matches and mixes household paint to the exact specifications of retail consumers.

In late 1993, X-Rite signed its largest contract in the firm's history, inking an agreement to supply custom spectrophotometry instruments in 1994 and 1995 to E.I. DuPont de Nemours and Company under a two-year, $10 million contract. To put the contract in the proper perspective, X-Rite's largest previous contract, back in 1991, amounted to only $2.5 million, and revenues for 1993 totaled a tad over $39 million.

X-Rite is the dominant leader in proprietary quality-control color-measuring devices. With more than 16 million existing colors, only the finest precision instruments can detect those critical variations needed to reproduce the exact color desired by manufacturers. The firm's heavy emphasis on research and development and new-product introductions keeps it ahead of the competition. It controls more than 85 percent of the medical market in which it competes, more than 33 percent of the graphics art market, and is the lead player in the film market, supplying every major film manufacturer worldwide.

Export sales, which account for over 30 percent of annual revenues, are handled by an independent dealer network in more than 60 countries. Strengthening its overseas presence in 1993, X-Rite formed a wholly-owned subsidiary, X-Rite GmbH in Germany, to enhance European sales opportunities.

Financial statistics (figures in millions, except per-share amounts):

	1990	1991	1992	1993
Revenues	$24	$29	$36	$39
Net income (loss)	4	5	7	8
Earnings (loss)/share	.36	.45	.68	.72
Dividend/share	.06	.07	.12	.16
Long-term debt	—	—	—	—
Stock price range/share:				
High	7¼	14⅞	33¼	27
Low	4	5½	11¼	17½

Investment Assessment.   X-Rite represents a well-managed company with solid growth potential and attractive margins. It has paid cash dividends every quarter since 1977 and more than doubled its annual payout since 1991. Look for new stock market highs in the wake of continued solid operating performance.

The next chapter will delve into opportunities in consumer stocks. Search out your own industrial candidates that will benefit from changes in the economic environment as the global economy expands.

2
Top Consumer Stocks

The consumer sector of the U.S. economy is poised to rebound, as the economy picks up steam and people become less concerned about their job security and start loosening their purse strings. Those companies in tune with changing demographics (age, race, income levels, etc.), consumer tastes, preferences, and brand loyalties will be positioned to benefit from rising consumer spending patterns.

An increased emphasis on expanded product lines, quality/price relationships, customer service, upscale shopping—and conversely, discount shopping—will challenge consumer-oriented companies in the decades to come.

More competition from both domestic and overseas companies, and industry consolidation, will also come into play. Companies willing to adjust to new markets, competition, and customer dynamics stand ready to remain or replace industry leaders. The following candidates possess the management talent, financial resources, product and market franchises, and market savvy to be top consumer performers in the twenty-first century. In the same vein, they are anticipated to outperform their industry counterparts in the stock market.

CONSUMER STOCKS	INDUSTRY
Albertson's Incorporated	Grocery store
American Greetings Corporation	Greeting cards
McCormick & Company, Incorporated	Food processing/seasonings
PepsiCo., Inc.	Soft drinks
Rubbermaid Incorporated	Household products
Tootsie Roll Industries, Incorporated	Food processing/candy

As indicated, the companies cover a wide range of products and services, from food products to greetings cards.

☆ 7 ALBERTSON'S ☆ INCORPORATED

ALBERTSON'S INCORPORATED	Stock exchange: NYSE
250 Parkcenter Boulevard	Ticker symbol: ABS
P.O. Box 20	DRIP program: NO
Boise, Idaho 83726	Ownership:
208-385-6200	Institutional: 43%
	Insiders: 13%

Industry Review. The grocery store industry in which Albertson's operates has traditionally been a low-margin business with intense competition. New forms of competition from such outfits as WalMart and warehouse clubs are also adding to the pressure on traditional grocery stores. The trend promises to continue in the late nineties, and will even intensify as we move into the twenty-first century.

The grocery stores are not sitting still, however. Many are fighting back with a variety of tactics: more efficient floor-space usage; the introduction of upscale, higher-margin products; superstore concepts, with large bakery, deli, and sushi and cappuccino bars; strict cost control; enhanced information systems; raised inventory turns. All these are methods being employed by grocery stores across the nation to capture market share and earn a decent return.

As in real estate, location is a key to a successful grocery store operation. Differences in regional economic factors can play a big role in the divergent performances of otherwise similar grocery chains, or even between stores within the same chain.

Company Profile. Albertson's Incorporated operates in excess of 650 retail grocery stores located in 19 western, midwestern, and southern states stretching from Washington to Florida and from Montana to Arizona. Up to 50 more stores are scheduled to open in 1994 and in each of the next five years. In addition, management plans to remodel another 200-plus existing stores. The company's geographically diffuse base helps to insulate it from negative regional economic pressures. Albertson's thrust into the high-growth Seattle, Washington, Florida, and Texas markets postures the firm for future revenues and earnings prospects.

With the acquisition of over 70 Jewel Osco stores in 1992, Albertson's ranks as the sixth largest retail food/drug chain in the nation. The company's stores include a full line of conventional grocery items and a wide variety of specialty departments. Over 270 of its stores fall into the superstore category, offering over 30,000 items. In comparison to many competitors, Albertson's runs a modern shop, with more than 90 percent of its stores having been opened new or remodeled within the past 10 years. It runs an everyday low-cost marketing strategy that draws in customers, keeps volume levels high, and costs down, making it a tough competitor in every market it enters.

Management Talent. Gary G. Michael, Chairman and Chief Executive Officer, moved up to those positions in 1991 after having previously served as the firm's Executive Vice President and Chief Financial and Corporate Development Officer since 1983. John B. Carley, President since 1984, assumed the duties of Chief Operating Officer in 1991. Other top management positions are filled with veterans possessing years of company and food and drug industry experience.

Financial Status. Albertson's superior financial posture gives it a decided edge over less fortunate competitors. Strong earnings and cashflow are helping to pare down long-term debt taken on with the Jewel Osco acquisition and a $517 million stock repurchase program resulting from the founder's death.

Cashflow provided by operations approaches $500 million, and adequately provides for capital expenditures to keep stores and distribution facilities upgraded. Healthy cashflow has allowed the Board of Directors to raise the cash dividend for 23 consecutive years.

Particular Strengths. Albertson's is capitalizing on the synergies stemming from the Jewel Osco acquisition, which provided an efficient distribution network to key markets. The company also has been beefing up its capabilities with an expansion of its Fort Worth, Texas, distribution center in late 1992, a new distribution facility opened in Arizona in mid-1993, and another operation in Florida which came fully on-line in March 1994.

The expanded warehouse network enables Albertson's to stock approximately 80 percent of store products from company inventory. Removal of the middleman supplier translates into higher margins.

The company's shift to more superstores with full-service, one-stop shopping will improve per-sale customer sales and increase profit margins, both of which already rank among the highest in the industry.

Financial statistics (figures in millions, except per-share amounts):

For fiscal year ended February 3	1991	1992	1993	1994
Revenues	$8,218	$8,680	$10,174	$11,284
Net income (loss)	234	258	269	340
Earnings (loss)/share	.88	.97	1.02	1.34
Dividend/share	.24	.28	.32	.36
Long-term debt	159	143	508	665
Stock price range/share:	1990	1991	1992	1993
High	$18\frac{7}{8}$	$25\frac{3}{4}$	$26\frac{5}{8}$	$29\frac{5}{8}$
Low	$12\frac{1}{8}$	$16\frac{1}{4}$	$18\frac{3}{8}$	$23\frac{3}{8}$

Investment Assessment. Albertson's has all the right cards (distribution network, grocery/drug product mix, modern stores, superstore/combination store improving mix, rising margins, decreasing costs, regional diversification, and financial strength) in place to improve upon its already impressive record.

The company has the momentum to generate even larger earnings gains in the years ahead, as less strong competitors fall by the wayside. Knowing as we do that the stock market tends to reward industry leaders with higher price/earnings ratios, we can be sure that Albertson's will continue to pace the industry both in revenue and earnings growth.

☆ 8 AMERICAN ☆ GREETINGS CORPORATION

AMERICAN
GREETINGS CORPORATION
One American Road
Cleveland, Ohio 44144
216-252-7300

Stock exchange: NASDAQ
Ticker symbol: AGREA
DRIP program: Yes
Ownership:
  Institutional: 77%
  Insiders: 64%*

*Insiders control 67 percent of the votes.

Industry Review. The greeting card, gift wrap, and related consumer products industry is dominated by several large companies, with a number of smaller card companies targeting specific markets. In order to maintain market share and margins, the larger companies have had to go beyond the traditional cards (birthday, anniversary, etc.) and offer a wider variety of cards for more diverse occasions. Efforts have also been placed on improving the efficiency of their operations.

There are at least five social trends at work that play right into the hands of the greeting card industry. First, the large baby-boom generation is fast approaching its peak greeting-card-buying years. Second, another demographic trend comes into play with the aging of the nation. The existence of more and larger extended families will translate into more card sales opportunities as Americans live longer. Third, the trend toward multiple marriages, divorces, etc., creates new opportunities for card sales. Fourth, the buying pattern change that has women purchasing more cards and other personal communication products in chain drug stores, supermarkets, and mass retail outlets greatly expands the number of card distribution outlets and eye-contact, point-of-purchase locations for impulse shopping. Fifth, recessionary times, and tight consumer pocketbooks, have failed to dent the sale of high-margin greeting cards. In fact, the price of the average retail greeting card continues to escalate.

Company Profile. American Greetings Corporation ranks as the second-largest greeting card company in the nation (with approximately 35 percent of U.S. industry sales) and as the largest publicly traded greeting card company. It has been an innovator in introducing new product lines and moving into related business ventures.

Greeting card and gift wrapping operations are located in a dozen manufacturing and distribution facilities in the United States, plus a number of offices and operations facilities in England, France, and Mexico. In addition, the company manufactures its own display fixtures as well as custom fixtures for other retailers, and manufactures and distributes metal picture frames and hair-care accessory products. It also distributes a line of candles, paper party goods, and other personal communication products.

American Greetings maintains a number of distribution channels including drug stores, mass merchandisers, supermarkets, stationery and gift shops, variety stores, military post exchanges, combination (carrying a variety of food, drug, and general merchandise items) stores, and department stores.

Greeting cards make up 65 percent of annual company revenues. Sales outside of the United States generate approximately 17 percent of yearly revenues.

New-product rollouts, acquisitions, and streamlined manufacturing and distribution keeps American Greetings' revenues and earnings on a solid uptrend.

Management Talent.   Irving Stone, Founder and Chairman of the Executive Committee, still keeps tabs on new card designs, but day-to-day operations are headed by Chairman and Chief Executive Officer Morry Weiss and President and Chief Operating Officer Edward Fruchtenbaum, both long-time company employees with plenty of industry know-how. Equally if not more important in a creative company such as American Greetings, the firm's employee rolls include hundreds of artists and designers. The company also has garnered trademarks of famous characters such as Strawberry Shortcake®, Care Bears®, and Holly Hobbie®, as well as the rights to use the likenesses of Ziggy® and others.

Financial Status.   American Greetings' streak of expanding revenues and earnings stretches back to 1988, and has helped to improve its financial status. For fiscal 1993 (ended February 28), record results helped to pare long-term debt 35 percent to $169 million, from $256 million a year earlier. Fiscal 1994 proved to be another record year, with earnings rising to $1.77 per share (before the effects of an accounting change were reflected) from $1.56 per share. American Greetings again slashed long-term debt, this time by over 50 percent to under $90 million.

Working capital in the $600 million range provides plenty of cash for capital expenditures, new product introductions, acquisitions, and heavy display and marketing efforts (a key to success in the greeting card business). Cashflow per share has increased dramatically, from less than $2 per share in 1991 to around $3 per share in 1994.

DRIP Details.   American Greetings' DRIP program permits additional purchase of company common stock through the automatic reinvestment of dividends; however, it does not allow for additional cash purchases. There is no administrative or commission cost to the shareholder for stock purchases. For information on the dividend reinvestment program, write to: American Greetings Dividend Reinvestment Plan, c/o Society National Bank, Corporate Trust Division, P.O. Box 6477, Cleveland, OH 44101-1477.

Particular Strengths.   Creativity, financial prowess, and key acquisitions make American Greetings a force to be reckoned with in the greeting card and related consumer products industry. Management runs a highly efficient operation, from satellite communications between the home office and outlying facilities to distribution through a global network of nearly 100,000 retail outlets in more than 50 countries. Its greeting cards are printed in 16 languages.

American Greetings makes good use of its creative talent in the area of operations, with tight inventory management and better manufacturing techniques contributing to lower costs and rising margins. It's even in the process of reengineering its creative department by looking for ways to improve the creative work process. Rather than passing the idea and card development "down the line," a team approach speeds up originality and productivity.

American Greetings' focus on micromarketing to specific population groups targets the more diverse sectors that now comprise America. From college students needing to communicate with at-home family to Spanish-speaking consumers, American Greetings has the right card with the right message for them.

Financial statistics (figures in millions, except per-share amounts):

For fiscal year ended February 28	1991	1992	1993	1994
Revenues	$1,432	$1,573	$1,688	$1,781
Net income (loss)	82	97	112	131*
Earnings (loss)/share	1.30	1.40	1.55	1.77*
Dividend/share	.35	.38	.42	.46
Long-term debt	246	256	169	54
Stock price range/share:	1990	1991	1992	1993
High	$18\frac{3}{4}$	$20\frac{7}{8}$	$26\frac{1}{8}$	$34\frac{1}{4}$
Low	$13\frac{1}{4}$	$15\frac{1}{2}$	$18\frac{5}{8}$	$22\frac{1}{2}$

*Does not include accounting adjustment of $17.1 million or 23 cents per share.

Investment Assessment.   Even during a recession, American Greetings has kept earnings per share rising at double-digit rates (around 16 to 17 percent for the past three years). Market acceptance of the company's new CreataCard promises to revolutionize the industry. Each computer card–generated unit offers 1000 card designs tailored by the customer with specific languages and sayings. Even with the large rollout costs associated with it, CreataCard, is expected to be very profitable in fiscal 1995, with more than 10,000 units placed worldwide.

With the acquisition of Magnavision, the company also is the leader in the nonprescription eyeglass market, with outlets in the United States and 15 other countries.

Look for continued double-digit earnings growth, which should increase as the economy comes out of a recession. With American

Greetings poised to take market share from industry leader Hallmark and Gibson Greetings, it may become appropriate to send condolence cards to their managements.

☆ 9 McCORMICK & ☆ COMPANY, INC.

McCORMICK & COMPANY, INC.   Stock exchange: NASDAQ
18 Loveton Circle   Ticker symbol: MCCRK
Sparks, Maryland 21152   DRIP program: Yes
410-771-7301   Ownership:
                                                           Institutional: 53%
                                                           Insiders: 6%

Industry Review.   The food processing industry often has been shunned by investors for a variety of reasons, ranging from projected slow growth potential to the latest trauma, private label versus brand loyalty. The current session initially caused consumers to do some shifting from name-brand products to private labels in order to save money, but this trend appears to be reversing itself.

Industry niches, such as the seasonings and spices sectors, appear to be even more insulated from switches to private labels, since the retail prices of their individual products are relatively low, thereby eliminating the opportunity for large savings by brand-switching. In addition, consumer reluctance to try off-brand spices and seasonings stems from a real concern that the switch may cause a whole meal to "just not taste right."

Even with slowing domestic market growth, there are plenty of opportunities in foreign countries that can pick up the slack for companies who make the right geographic diversification moves.

Company Profile.   McCormick & Company, Inc. is the world's leading processor of spices and seasonings. The firm rounds out its product line with other specialty food products such as mayonnaise, salad dressing, cake decorations, and sauces.

Founded in 1889, McCormick has survived many economic cycles. The sharp drop in earnings in fiscal 1990 (ended November 30), in comparison to fiscal 1989, resulted from a large, extraordinary gain realized in fiscal 1989 on discontinuation of real estate operations. Income from operations has been moving upward since 1985, with recent years scoring double-digit jumps in the 13 to 15 percent range.

With in excess of $1.5 billion in sales, McCormick ranks near the midrange of the *Fortune* 500 listing. The company has paid cash dividends every year since 1925.

Management Talent. Until his unexpected death in mid-1994, Bailey A. Thomas Jr. served as the company's Chairman and Chief Executive Officer. McCormick employs a unique management structure, with 15 Multiple Management Boards that explore and encourage innovative ideas from employees around the world. This isn't one of those new management fads—McCormick's Multiple Management Board concept has been in place since 1932. H. Eugene Blattman, President & Chief Operating Officer, has taken Thomas's place as CEO.

Financial Status. The company enjoys a strong balance sheet, and ample cashflow to achieve its global expansion strategy. Cash dividends have increased 10 times in the past 5 years, and with a compounded rate of over 25 percent since 1987.

Cashflow has been increasing at the rate of nearly 20 percent annually over the past 5 years, and will exceed $2 per share in 1994. That's plenty of capital to keep expansion plans on track.

DRIP Details. McCormick's DRIP plan allows for additional cash purchases of common stock shares in the amounts of $100 to $3000 per quarter. There are limitations on purchases for some of the classes of stock. To obtain more DRIP details, contact the Shareholder Relations Office at 800-424-5885 or 410-771-7572.

Particular Strengths. The new global expansion push and strategic partnerships will be a boost to revenues and help to reduce costs, making McCormick an industry low-cost producer. A new multimillion-dollar research and development facility is geared up to introduce 200 new products into the market each year.

The company's "McCormick," "Schilling," and other trademarks are well recognized and respected around the world, and offer tremendous product-extension capabilities with their instant quality and brand recognition. McCormick's more than 40 percent share of the domestic retail market also lends itself to product extension.

Financial statistics (figures in millions, except per-share amounts):

For fiscal year ended November 30	1990	1991	1992	1993
Revenues	$1323	$1428	$1471	$1557
Net income (loss)	69	81	95	100
Earnings (loss)/share	.83	.98	1.16	1.22
Dividend/share	.23	.28	.38	.46
Long-term debt	211	208	201	346
Stock price range/share:				
High	13¼	26½	30¼	29¾
Low	9	12¼	20½	20

Investment Assessment. International expansion, such as McCormick's acquisition of Grupo Pesa in Mexico in early 1994 and the formation of a joint-venture, herb-and-spice business in Europe in September 1993, coupled with increased penetration of the U.S. market, will deliver double-digit earnings increases for the foreseeable future.

Cash dividend hikes will keep shareholders' income levels rising as well. Company management has an express policy of paying out 25 to 35 percent of net income in dividends.

☆ 10 PEPSICO, ☆ INCORPORATED

PEPSICO, INCORPORATED	Stock exchange: NYSE
PepsiCo World Headquarters	Ticker symbol: PEP
Purchase, New York 10577	DRIP program: Yes
914-253-2000	Ownership:
	Institutional: 56%
	Insiders: 1%

Industry Review. The cola wars rage on worldwide, with industry leader Coca-Cola Enterprises and second-ranked PepsiCo, Inc. vying for market share and entrance into new markets. Overseas consumption continues its upward trend (with a 7 to 10 percent growth rate) and the domestic market is now rebounding after a slowdown in the early nineties as the prolonged recession drifted along (domestic soft-drink sales growth promises to return to the pre-recession 3 to 4 percent growth-rate level).

New markets, some where sales have in fact been prohibited, include large population centers such as China, the former Soviet Union, the balance of Eastern Europe, and India. These areas and others around the world currently have soft-drink consumption far lower than that experienced in North America, making for gigantic expansion potential.

The industry also is being revolutionized by the appearance of "new-age" drinks such as bottled and canned flavored teas and water products. Both industry leaders have not let innovative competitors steal this growing market segment, countering with their own lines of teas and flavored waters.

The private-brand invasion represents another story, however. Private brands continue to increase in market share, now commanding some 9 percent of supermarket sales. Don't expect the industry giants to take this sitting down.

Company Profile.   PepsiCo, Incorporated ranks as the world's second-largest soft-drink producer. The company operates three business segments: soft drinks, snack food (Frito-Lay and PepsiCo Foods International), and restaurants (Pizza Hut, Inc., Taco Bell Corporation, and Kentucky Fried Chicken Corporation).

The firm maintains approximately 95 beverage concentrate and syrup plants and some 360 warehouses worldwide. Around 85 plants and 15 distribution operations are owned and managed by joint ventures between PepsiCo and others. Frito-Lay operates 40 food manufacturing and processing plants in the United States, while PepsiCo operates a number of food plants either solely or as joint ventures in 20-plus countries around the world.

PepsiCo subsidiary companies own over 3000 leases over 5700 restaurants and delivery/carryout units in the United States, and another 1300 outside of the country.

The company derives around 37 percent of its revenues from its restaurants segment, while only 28 percent comes from the snack food unit. However, the restructured snack food unit contributes the bulk of company-segment operating profits, with 38 percent compared to 25 percent for restaurants. The balance of revenues and operating profits derive from the beverages segment. Overall, 27 percent of annual revenues come from international operations, up from only 20 percent four years ago.

PepsiCo traditionally has outperformed the industry averages, with double-digit revenues and earnings growth. The company's five-year compounded revenue growth rate, for the period ended December 31, 1993, came in at 15.1 percent. Likewise, for the same period, PepsiCo's compounded net income from continuing operations jumped 15.8 percent.

Management Talent.   Chairman and Chief Executive Officer Wayne Calloway runs a first-class operation with a team of skilled industry managers. Top management such as Roger Enrico, Chairman and Chief Executive Officer of PepsiCo Worldwide Foods, and Robert G. Gettner, Executive Vice President and Chief Financial Officer, have come up through the ranks, and each possesses in excess of 20 years company experience.

Financial Status.   With PepsiCo's push into more international markets, long-term debt has grown from $5.6 billion in 1990 to over $7.4 billion in 1994. For example, management is committed to spend over $1 million in Portugal and Spain by 1999 to expand its penetration of those beverage and snack food markets. Despite the higher debt load, the amount is very manageable by a company with PepsiCo's revenues and cashflow.

Short-term investments totaling over $1.2 billion, and a cashflow of $4 per share, keeps plenty of capital in PepsiCo's treasury. Cash dividends have been increased every year for the past 21 years. Over the last 5 fiscal years, the cash dividend grew at a compounded rate of over 18 percent.

DRIP Details.   The company's dividend reinvestment program allows for additional purchases of company common stock in cash amounts ranging from $10 to $60,000 annually. There is no administrative cost to the shareholder. For information on the DRIP plan, contact: Chemical Bank, Dividend Reinvestment Department, P.O. Box 24850, Church Street Station, New York, New York 10242, or call 800-647-4273 or 212-613-7147.

Particular Strengths.   PepsiCo's three operating segments provide it with a balanced and less risky approach to tapping new markets, both at home and abroad. Complementary lines lead easily to product extension in existing and new markets.

Joint ventures, such as the one with Thomas J. Lipton Company (the number-one tea trademark in the United States), allow the company to gain market share with innovative non-soft-drink product introductions. On the research and development front, PepsiCo spends in excess of $100 million annually to keep ahead of the competition, with new-product introductions such as Bigfoot Pizza and Rotisserie Gold Chicken.

The strong emphasis on enlarging the international component of the firm's business will keep revenues and earnings growing at a fast pace. In addition to the big push in Spain and Portugal, PepsiCo has targeted other lucrative markets such as Mexico and South American countries. In 1994 the company announced plans for a distribution venture in Poland, with the aim of capturing half of that nation's soft-drink market by the end of the year.

A continual push toward restructuring and repositioning operations for more efficiency and lower costs keeps PepsiCo less dependent on price increases. New advertising and more aggressive marketing also adds to the success mix.

Financial statistics (figures in millions, except per-share amounts):

For fiscal year ended December xx	1990	1991	1992	1993
Revenues	$17,516	$19,292	$21,970	$25,021
Net income (loss)	1,077	1,080	374*	1,588
Earnings (loss)/share	1.35	1.35	.46*	1.96
Dividend/share	.38	.46	.51	.61
Long-term debt	5,900	7,806	7,965	7,443
Stock price range/share:				
High	$27\frac{7}{8}$	$35\frac{5}{8}$	$43\frac{3}{8}$	$43\frac{5}{8}$
Low	18	$23\frac{1}{2}$	$30\frac{1}{2}$	$34\frac{1}{2}$

*Includes the effects of accounting changes of $917 million or $1.15 per share.

Investment Assessment.   PepsiCo will be successful with its global strategy, delivering greater than 20 percent revenue and earnings gains from that sector of the business. Pepsi has been good to past shareholders. A $1000 investment in PepsiCo stock at year-end 1983 was worth $12,000 (assuming dividend reinvestment) on December 25, 1993, for a 28 percent compounded annual growth rate. The flat first-half-of-1994 earnings are only temporary. The future looks much brighter.

☆11 RUBBERMAID ☆ INCORPORATED

RUBBERMAID INCORPORATED	Stock exchange: NYSE
1147 Akron Road	Ticker symbol: RBD
Wooster, Ohio 44691	DRIP program: Yes
216-264-6464	Ownership:
	Institutional: 48%
	Insiders: 4%

Industry Review.   Rubbermaid serves the household products market segment, providing products that make life easier for consumers. While other industry companies have been plagued by some customer backlash against brand-name (higher-priced) goods, Rubbermaid's solid reputation for quality products at competitive prices has kept revenues and earnings on their upward trend. Putting aside the brand-name concerns, which appear to have been overblown, the industry enjoys consistent revenue growth, since consumers tend to purchase required household products and time- and energy-savers without regard for the condition of the economy.

Given that scenario, industry companies with aggressive and innovative research and development efforts and new-product introduction programs promise to outpace the rest of the industry.

Entry and expansion into key foreign markets will also come into play as a major growth impetus to well-positioned and globally-thinking household products firms. With the passage of NAFTA and the opening of new consumer markets in Mexico and, later, other Central and Latin American countries, Western Hemisphere sales of household products should rise sharply.

Likewise, with a return to a more vibrant international economy, both European and Far East markets will contribute to higher sales worldwide. Since consumers in other countries spend far less on household products than does the American consumer, revenue growth potential from foreign customers could far outstrip that achieved in the more mature U.S. and Canadian markets.

Household products companies that pay close attention to cost control and operating efficiencies will also fare better than their industry counterparts. Lower costs and higher productivity translate into more competitive pricing and better bottom-line profits.

Company Profile.   Rubbermaid Incorporated consistently ranks among America's most admired companies. In fact, after five years as the nation's second most admired company, the Wooster, Ohio household products firm took over first place in the Fortune magazine survey. For the previous seven years, Merck & Company, Incorporated owned the coveted top ranking (see Chap. 4, Scoring with Special Situations, for coverage of Merck). Rubbermaid's rise to the top is all the more impressive when you consider that the company was in management transition, with Wolfgang Schmitt taking the helm upon the unexpected resignation of Walter Williams after only 18 months on the job. Williams had stepped into the retiring Stanley Gault's big shoes, after his 11 years of leading Rubbermaid into an industry-prominent position.

One of Rubbermaid's major strength's lies in its broad product line. It manufactures and sells something for every part of the home, from kitchenware, to laundry and bath accessories, to patio furniture. The wide range of products include plastic toys, plastic laundry baskets, food and beverage containers, plastic gas cans, etc. You could say, "If you use it in your home, Rubbermaid makes it." The company sports in excess of 5000 products.

Its new product prowess keeps "copycat manufacturers" busy. Rubbermaid rolls out, on average, a new product for every day of the year.

Foreign operations account for some 15 percent of overall revenues. Company management recognized foreign market opportunities early, opening a Canadian operation in 1950 and entering the European market in 1965.

Rubbermaid also maintains an aggressive acquisition campaign, adding new products that fill gaps in its marketing strategy.

The company has achieved 42 consecutive years of rising revenues, 39 years of increased cash dividends, and over a decade of 17-plus percent average annual return on shareholder's equity.

Management Talent.   Chairman of the Board and Chief Executive Officer Wolfgang R. Schmitt's company experience stretches back to 1966, when he joined Rubbermaid's management training program. Well versed in all aspects of the business, from strategic planning to new-product development to customer partnerships (which he pioneered at Rubbermaid), Schmitt leads a talented management team with decades of industry and company experience.

Financial Status.   Rubbermaid's finances are strong. Long-term debt has decreased steadily since 1989, with less than $20 million (less than 40 percent of the 1989 debt load) currently on the books. With an operating margin in the 20 percent range, there's plenty of cash for key acquisitions, new equipment and facilities, and new-product introductions. Earnings per share have increased in excess of 46 percent since 1990.

Rubbermaid's cash coffers include some $194 million in cash, cash equivalents, and marketable securities. In addition, its cashflow per share has risen from less than $1.25 per share in 1989 to over $2.00 per share today. The company's healthy cashflow has allowed the Board to take good care of company shareholders, quintupling the cash dividend since 1983.

DRIP Details.   The company's dividend reinvestment program allows company shareholders to purchase between $10 to $3000 per quarter in additional company shares. There are no service or commission charges for these purchases. Information on the DRIP program may be obtained by writing to the Corporate Secretary, Rubbermaid Incorporated, 1147 Akron Road, Wooster, OH 44691-6000.

Particular Strengths. As mentioned earlier, Rubbermaid's broad product line and aggressive new-product introduction activities lie at the core of the company's success. The ability to seek out new acquisitions and integrate them into the Rubbermaid culture also gives the firm a decided edge over its competition.

Schmitt's European background fits well with Rubbermaid's targeted further penetration of this growing market. An acquisition in Mexico made Rubbermaid de Mexico the number one plastics housewares manufacturer in that country, and signaled the company's intent to serve that promising market. Other forays into new international markets include partnerships with Scott Paper in Mexico, Spain, and England, and a joint venture in Hungary. By the year 2000, Rubbermaid looks to have 25 percent of company revenues coming from outside the United States, versus approximately 15 percent today.

Rubbermaid not only reinvents its products so as to discover new uses, it also works hard at reinventing the company so as to squeeze out operating efficiencies. Over 600 employee teams search for ways to reinvent their jobs and the way they operate, to lower costs and improve quality.

Financial statistics (figures in millions, except per-share amounts):

For fiscal year ended December 31	1990	1991	1992	1993
Revenues	$1,534	$1,667	$1,805	$1,960
Net income (loss)	144	163	184*	211
Earnings (loss)/share	.90	1.02	1.15*	1.32
Dividend/share	.27	.31	.3525	.405
Long-term debt	39	28	20	20
Stock price range/share:				
High	22½	38¼	37⅜	37⅜
Low	15½	18½	27	27⅝

*Before effects of a $.13 one-time accounting change on post-retirement benefits.

Investment Assessment. Rubbermaid Incorporated is a premier household products company with an increasing international posture. The company and its stock have performed well over the years, despite a major management transition. (See Fig. 2-1, Rubbermaid Incorporated stock chart.) This financially strong company possesses the management talent, cash reserves, and product innovations to continue that trend. Thirty percent of company revenues derive from products not even in the company lineup five years ago. Look for significant earnings and dividend increases, and higher stock prices, in the years ahead.

RUBBERMAID NYSE-RBD

	RECENT PRICE	26	P/E RATIO	17.6 (Trailing: 19.1 Median: 22.0)	RELATIVE P/E RATIO	1.20	DIV'D YLD	1.7%	VALUE LINE	968

TIMELINESS **3** Average (Relative Price Perform- ance Next 12 Mos.)
SAFETY **2** Above Average (Scale: 1 Highest to 5 Lowest)
BETA 1.25 (1.00 = Market)

1997-99 PROJECTIONS

	Price	Gain	Ann'l Total Return
High	60	(+130%)	24%
Low	45	(+75%)	16%

Insider Decisions

	N D J F M A M J J
to Buy	0 1 0 0 0 0 0 0 0
Options	0 0 0 0 0 5 0 0 0
to Sell	0 2 0 0 0 1 0 0 0

Institutional Decisions

	4Q93	1Q94	2Q94
to Buy	95	106	107
to Sell	110	144	116
Hld's(000)	74170	75225	71925

Target Price Range 1997 | 1998 | 1999

(Relative Price Strength)

"5.5 x 'Cash Flow' p sh"

2-for-1 split / 2-for-1 split / 2-for-1 split / 2-for-1 split

Shaded areas indicate recessions

Options: PACE

	1978	1979	1980	1981	1982	1983	1984	1985	1986	1987	1988	1989	1990	1991	1992	1993	1994	1995	© VALUE LINE PUB., INC.	97-99
	2.09	2.48	2.72	2.89	3.04	3.52	4.19	4.63	5.43	6.91	8.12	9.12	9.59	10.41	11.27	12.22	13.15	14.65	Sales per sh	20.70
	.24	.24	.24	.33	.36	.43	.71	.60	.71	.90	1.00	1.22	1.24	1.41	1.58	1.82	2.00	2.20	"Cash Flow" per sh	3.55
	.15	.19	.12	.21	.22	.29	.35	.40	.48	.58	.68	.79	.90	1.02	1.15	1.32	1.45	1.65	Earnings per sh A	2.65
	.05	.05	.06	.07	.08	.09	.10	.11	.13	.16	.19	.23	.27	.31	.35	.41	.47	.55	Div'ds Decl'd per sh B	.75
	.17	.30	.28	.17	.13	.16	.34	.47	.47	.69	.57	.58	.65	.76	.84	.88	.90	.80	Cap'l Spending per sh	.85
	.94	1.07	1.12	1.25	1.39	1.59	1.77	2.08	2.45	2.97	3.48	4.06	4.80	5.53	6.16	7.05	7.65	8.45	Book Value per sh C	11.05
	123.74	123.07	123.21	123.58	123.83	124.03	135.29	144.95	146.50	146.86	147.00	147.33	159.99	160.19	160.24	160.36	160.00	155.00	Common Shs Outst'g D	145.00
	11.2	8.6	13.7	9.8	12.2	18.1	13.9	16.7	23.1	24.2	17.7	19.8	20.7	26.0	27.8	24.4	Bold figures are Value Line estimates		Avg Ann'l P/E Ratio	20.0
	1.53	1.24	1.82	1.19	1.34	1.53	1.29	1.36	1.57	1.62	1.47	1.50	1.54	1.66	1.69	1.44			Relative P/E Ratio	1.55
	2.6%	3.3%	3.8%	3.3%	2.9%	1.7%	2.0%	1.7%	1.2%	1.1%	1.6%	1.5%	1.4%	1.2%	1.1%	1.3%			Avg Ann'l Div'd Yield	1.4%

	1984	1985	1986	1987	1988	1989	1990	1991	1992	1993	1994	1995		97-99
	566.4	671.4	795.2	1015.0	1193.5	1343.9	1534.0	1667.3	1805.3	1960.2	2100	2300	Sales ($mill)	3000
	19.0%	21.0%	20.4%	18.3%	18.8%	18.9%	18.8%	19.2%	20.2%	21.8%	22.5%	23.0%	Operating Margin	26.5%
	21.1	30.3	33.3	47.5	47.4	62.7	55.4	62.7	69.9	80.9	90.0	100	Depreciation ($mill)	130
	46.9	57.1	70.1	99.3	116.4	143.5	162.7	184.0	211.4	230	260		Net Profit ($mill)	390
	45.6%	46.7%	42.9%	37.8%	38.9%	37.9%	38.1%	37.5%	38.2%	39.0%	39.0%		Income Tax Rate	39.0%
	8.3%	8.5%	8.8%	8.3%	8.3%	8.7%	9.4%	9.8%	10.2%	10.8%	11.0%	11.3%	Net Profit Margin	13.0%
	127.2	152.3	153.3	181.1	221.5	313.3	367.4	476.4	570.4	615	675		Working Cap'l ($mill)	950
	21.9	33.1	35.7	40.0	39.0	50.3	39.2	27.8	20.3	19.4	20.0	20.0	Long-Term Debt ($mill)	20.0
	239.0	301.7	359.4	435.9	511.4	598.4	768.2	885.7	987.6	1130.5	1225	1310	Net Worth ($mill)	1605
	18.3%	18.9%	18.1%	18.4%	18.3%	19.5%	18.2%	18.4%	18.6%	18.7%	18.5%	20.0%	% Earned Total Cap'l	24.0%
	19.6%	18.9%	19.5%	19.4%	19.4%	19.5%	18.7%	18.4%	18.6%	18.7%	18.5%	20.0%	% Earned Net Worth	24.5%
	14.3%	12.8%	14.0%	15.2%	14.0%	13.1%	12.8%	12.9%	12.9%	13.0%	12.5%	13.0%	% Retained to Comm Eq	17.5%
	27%	27%	34%	22%	26%	29%	30%	31%	31%	31%	33%	33%	% All Div'ds to Net Prof	28%

	Percent shares traded
1982	4.5 3.0 1.5

BUSINESS: Rubbermaid Inc. makes plastic and rubber products. Products include kitchenware, laundry & bath accessories, microwave ovenware, patio furniture, ready-to-assemble household furniture, products for home horticulture, office, food service, health care, and industrial maintenance. Acquired *Little Tikes* children's toys, '84; Microcomputer Accessories and Seco Inds. floor care products, '88. Eldon Industries (office supplies, soldering tools), '91. Foreign operations, former profit rate: 7.5%. Has about 11,978 employees, 22,508 shareholders. Chairman and Chief Executive Officer: Wolfgang R. Schmitt. Incorporated: Ohio. Address: 1147 Akron Road, Wooster, Ohio 44691. Telephone: 216-264-6464.

Figure 2-1. Rubbermaid, Inc. (*Copyright 1994 by Value Line Publishing Inc. Reprinted by permission; all rights reserved.*)

☆ 12 TOOTSIE ROLL ☆ INDUSTRIES, INC.

TOOTSIE ROLL INDUSTRIES, INC.   Stock exchange: NYSE
7401 South Cicero Avenue   Ticker symbol: TR
Chicago, Illinois 60629   DRIP program: No
312-838-3400   Ownership:
                                         Institutional: 20%
                                         Insiders: 72%

Industry Review.   Tootsie Roll Industries, Inc. operates in a specialty sector of the food industry, producing a variety of candies including, of course, Tootsie Rolls, Tootsie Pops, Mason Dots, and Charms. The candy industry continues to experience nearly 5.5 percent growth in revenues in the domestic market, around three times the growth rate for other food products. American market demographics promise to continue that growth pace for the foreseeable future.

The U.S. confectionery market is approaching $10 billion in annual sales. Tootsie Roll garners around a 2 to 3 percent market share, with plenty of room to grow through new-product introductions and strategic acquisitions in a consolidating industry.

Prices of sugar and other raw materials should remain firm, keeping pressure off industry pricing structures and cutthroat competition so as to maintain market share and profit levels.

International competition and overseas opportunities represent a staple for this industry. Companies with strong foreign presences will do better than less diversified firms. The inroads of Cadbury Schweppes PLC, into both Mexican and U.S. markets, illustrate the increasing trend in this direction.

Company Profile.   Tootsie Roll Industries has staying power. In a business where new candy ideas come and go with relative frequency, this Chicago-area firm has been in the candy business for nearly a century, its first product having hit the street back in 1896. The firm's old reliable Tootsie Roll candies are still being sold today and provide a solid revenue base, with some 37 million Tootsie Rolls flowing down the production lines of four U.S. factories and one Mexican factory daily.

The company also is adept at acquiring solid brand-name candies from other manufacturers. For example, during the past five years alone the popular Charms, Sugar Babies, Sugar Daddy, Pom Pom, and

Junior Mints brand names were brought into the Tootsie Roll fold, via straight company acquisitions and brand acquisitions.

Although Tootsie Roll currently derives 90 percent of its revenues from the domestic U.S. market, it operates Mexican manufacturing facilities and maintains sales offices in Canada, Hong Kong, and Mexico. The company is targeting larger candy exports to the Far East and Europe.

Revenues have risen consecutively for 17 straight years, and the firm has achieved record earnings for the past 12 years. It also has paid a cash dividend for the past 50 years, and boosted its dividend payout annually for over 30 years.

Management Talent.   Chairman and Chief Executive Officer Melvin J. Gordon and President and Chief Operating Officer Ellen R. Gordon have a vested interest in the operation and financial results of the company. Their combined 60-plus percent share of the voting power, as represented by 36 percent of the common shares and 72 percent of the Class B shares, firmly ties their personal wealth to the fortunes of the company. The Gordon family has been active in Tootsie Roll Industries ownership all the way back to the 1930s.

As evidence of management's talent in running a tight, profitable Good Ship Lollipop, the company produces 16 million lollipops daily. Tootsie Roll Industries earned recognition in a *Forbes* magazine listing as one of The 200 Best Small Companies in America for eight consecutive years, and numerous rankings in the *Forbes* Small Business Honor Roll.

Financial Status.   Until 1993, the company was virtually debt-free, with the exception of $7.5 million in industrial development bonds used as low-cost financing of the 115,000-square-foot expansion of existing company manufacturing facilities in Tennessee.

With the acquisition of the Warner Lambert manufacturing facilities and brand names, Tootsie Roll Industries took on $70 million of new debt. The acquisition will deliver some $60 million in new annual revenues and additional cashflow, to significantly pare down debt over the next few years.

Cash flows in at the rate of $4 per share, and should steadily increase to reach the $8 to $10 per share range before the turn of the century. Cash dividends have been increasing at around a 10 percent pace, with a 24 percent boost in 1993. In addition, the Board has been in the habit for the past 29 years of adding a sweetener, in the form of a 3 percent stock dividend each year.

Particular Strengths.   Upgrading and expansion of facilities in both Illinois and Tennessee stand to deliver lower production and distribution expenses. The company has been successful at bringing on popular brand-name candies and enhancing their contribution to the bottom line through aggressive marketing efforts. Strong cashflow and a rock-solid balance sheet make Tootsie Roll Industries one of the premier American candy companies.

Large market-share positions in key industry sectors will keep competitors at bay. For example, Tootsie Roll controls an estimated 50 percent of the lollipop and taffy markets.

The heavy insider ownership adds a major incentive for continued excellent performance, and bolsters expectations for revenues and earnings.

Financial statistics (figures in millions, except per-share amounts):

For fiscal year ended December 31	1990	1991	1992	1993
Revenues	$194	$208	$245	$260
Net income (loss)	23	27	32	35
Earnings (loss)/share	2.21	2.59	3.13	3.36
Dividend/share	.22*	.24*	.29*	.336*
Long-term debt	—	—	7	28
Stock price range/share:				
High	45⅞	70¾	82	83⅜
Low	28⅜	33⅝	58	64½

*Plus 3% stock dividend.

Investment Assessment.   Tootsie Roll Industries seeks to sustain its 15 percent annual earnings growth rate with new-product introductions, successful acquisitions, and ongoing improvements in operating productivity.

Listen to Elliott Schlang, Senior Vice President with Kidder, Peabody & Company Incorporated in Cleveland, Ohio, and publisher of *The Midwest Review*:

> We recommend holding Tootsie Roll shares as a core portfolio position for long-term investors seeking well-managed, high-quality, financially conservative companies. Tootsie Roll has strong brand name products, excellent balance sheet, and potential leverage from the Warner Lambert acquisition.

The real kicker in Tootsie Roll's future earnings possibilities and future stock price rests on how successfully it penetrates key overseas markets. But given the Gordons' track record and string of record years, Tootsie Roll should continue to be a sweet addition to any portfolio.

3

Top Service Stocks

The service sector of the nation's economy may be viewed in its two very different aspects: those companies that provide a service to the general public or retail customer, and those that provide vital services to other firms. This chapter covers two top performers from each of the service categories. Each company serves a well-defined, growing market niche with solid profit opportunities for those well-managed firms whose operations clearly are directed toward solving customers' needs and problems.

Designing products and services from the customer's perspective is a hallmark of forward-thinking, proactive management. The following companies have consistently put the customer first, and in the process achieved enviable operating and financial track records.

SERVICE STOCKS	INDUSTRY
Automatic Data Processing, Inc.	Computer & Financial Services
R. R. Donnelley & Sons Company	Commercial Printing
The Home Depot, Inc.	Building Supplies
Service Corporation International	Funeral Services

Innovative leaders in their respective industries, these service companies seek to gain market share at the expense of less aggressive and less financially sound competitors.

☆ 13 AUTOMATIC DATA ☆ PROCESSING, INCORPORATED

AUTOMATIC DATA	
PROCESSING, INCORPORATED	Stock exchange: NYSE
One ADP Boulevard	Ticker symbol: AUD
Roseland, New Jersey 07068	DRIP program: No
201-994-5000	Ownership:
	Institutional: 71%
	Insiders: 2%

Industry Review.   Automatic Data Processing (ADP) operates in two industry sectors, computer software and financial services, with a variety of product offerings. With both domestic and global competition heating up, firms are looking for ways to improve productivity and cut costs. One way to accomplish that goal is to look toward outside providers who specialize in certain office functions and systems. The outsourcing of such tasks as payroll preparation can often be performed more economically by these specialists, due to economies of scale and the prohibitive cost of maintaining staff and expensive equipment that may not be optimally utilized by just one company.

Management also may desire to concentrate its limited human and capital resources on what it does best, and let others perform essential tasks such as payroll that are not critical to the firm's main objectives.

The computer software and services industry has a track record of strong revenue growth and an attractive 20 percent operating margin. The financial services sector also has growth potential, due to industry consolidation and the rising cost of back-office operations for many of ADP's potential customers.

Company Profile.   ADP ranks as the nation's largest provider of payroll and tax filing services. In addition, its financial services segment provides computer workstations to brokerage firms for order taking, quotations, proxy services, and back-office record keeping. Adding a bit of industry and geographic diversification, the firm's Dealer Services segment supplies automated office systems to over 8000 automobile dealerships worldwide, while its Automotive Claims Service segment delivers computer-based, collision-repair-estimating capabilities and total loss valuation to automotive repair shops and auto insurance companies.

ADP has embarked on an active expansion campaign to broaden its service line and increase market share. Recent acquisitions include Quotron's back-office brokerage processing business and international equities quotation services; purchase of Hollander, with its nationwide network of automotive salvage yards and used-parts inventory; a merger of ADP Proxy Services with Independent Election Corporation; and international acquisitions of Autonom in Germany and MODEMS in the United Kingdom, both of which serve the auto dealer market.

With a variety of services, ADP helps over 300,000 clients worldwide to improve their businesses and bolster their bottom lines. The firm's dedication to its customers is clearly illustrated on the front of its 1993 annual report, which depicts its commitment to client loyalty and long-term client relationships via a handshake and a vow to deliver superior value. ADP's number-one growth strategy is firmly rooted in client retention through superior quality of service.

ADP's financial performance track record includes an enviable 44 consecutive years of growth in both revenues and earnings. Even more impressive is its *130* consecutive quarters of double-digit earnings per share growth, the best record of any publicly-held American company.

Management Talent.   Chairman and Chief Executive Officer Josh S. Weston has been at ADP since 1970, and he is backed by an administrative and operating management team well versed in the intricacies of their corporate functions or particular industry segments. Weston employs a hands-on management style. He personally visits every company location at least once a year, and requires all senior executives to follow his example.

Financial Status.   ADP is flush with cash, cash equivalents, and marketable securities in excess of $900 million, and working capital totaling more than $300 million. Given the company's substantial cash position, its long-term debt (around the $350 million range) is low, and the .23 to 1 debt-to-equity ratio is relatively paltry. There's plenty of capital available to finance future strategic acquisitions to improve market posture.

While other companies in the computer services industry have booked revenues when billed and paid for in advance, ADP conservatively does not record the revenue until the service has been performed. You won't find any negative earnings adjustments on Weston's watch.

Obviously, ADP's significant cash position stems from solid cashflow amounting to some $3.50 per share. Operating margins around the 25 percent level keep the company coffers full and cash dividends on the rise, most recently posting a 14 percent jump in 1993.

Particular Strengths.   ADP's solid client relationships allow its business to expand as its clients grow and request the office services firm to take on more administrative and back-office functions. In addition, with a number of successful acquisitions under its belt, ADP is poised to further penetrate its four market segments both here and abroad. The firm's ample treasury will allow it to take advantage of market opportunities.

Around 50 percent of ADP's payroll and tax-filing business is generated from clients with less than 100 employees, and more than 85 percent comes from clients with less than 1000 employees. Its large customer base adds stability to revenue and earnings growth. The firm's largest single customer accounts for less than 2 percent of annual revenues.

Financial statistics (figures in millions, except per-share amounts):

For fiscal year ended June 30	1990	1991	1992	1993
Revenues	$1,714	$1,772	$1,941	$2,223
Net income (loss)	212	228	256	294
Earnings (loss)/share	1.44	1.63	1.84	2.08
Dividend/share	.33	.38	.415	.475
Long-term debt	82	54	333	347
Stock price range/share:				
High	30⅛	46⅜	55½	56⅞
Low	22⅝	25	38⅞	46⅞

Investment Assessment.   An estimated 60 percent of firms still handle their payroll processing in-house. As the largest supplier of payroll and tax filing services, ADP stands to capture the lion's share of business converting to outside processors. This, plus the company's successful forays into related service lines in the brokerage, automative, and insurance industries, will keep earnings growing at a double-digit pace.

Throw in some more acquisitions for enhanced market share, and ADP should improve margins over and above the 25 percent it currently enjoys. For example, in April 1994, ADP purchased Peachtree Software Inc. and gained access to its customer base of more than 200,000.

In the last two fiscal years, ADP has spent an average of $120 million on systems development and programming, to improve efficiencies and upgrade product and service offerings. Its strict attention to providing value-added services will translate into add-on business and referrals.

ADP represents service with a $mile that its shareholders can take to the bank.

☆ 14 R. R. DONNELLEY ☆ & SONS COMPANY

R. R. DONNELLEY & SONS COMPANY
77 West Wacker Drive
Chicago, IL 60601
312-326-8000

Stock exchange: NYSE
Ticker symbol: DNY
DRIP program: Yes
Ownership:
   Institutional: 72%
   Insiders: 19%

Industry Review. While the overall publishing industry performance has been negatively impacted by intense competition, fluctuating ad revenues, and the economic slowdown, the commercial printing end of the publishing world has been moving full-steam-ahead. Strong demand for financial printing services, documentation services, and printing services for book publishers has kept this market segment growing at around 7 percent annually.

The proliferation of mutual funds, and now the entrance of banks into the mutual fund arena, promises to keep the financial printing presses humming. In addition, catalog printing remains a booming business, as more Americans opt to shop from the comfort of their own home via those direct-mail catalogs that now clog mailboxes from coast to coast.

Company Profile. Pick up *Time, Newsweek, TV Guide,* any of dozens of mail-order catalogs, or Sunday newspaper coupon inserts that arrive at your doorstep on a weekly basis, and you have in your hands the handiwork of R. R. Donnelley & Sons, the world's largest commercial printer. In a highly fragmented industry, the firm has more than doubled its domestic market share to 7 percent during the past two decades.

Donnelley generates its revenues from four market segments: book and magazine publishing and telecommunications services (44 percent), merchandising catalogs and metromail (37 percent), documentation services (11 percent), and financial printing and information services (8 percent). Besides being the dominant player in the U.S. market, Donnelley is a major supplier in the U.K. market.

Its growth plans include a mixture of internal growth, acquisitions, strategic partnerships, and additions of new lines of business. The documentation segment, for example, has doubled its contribution to company revenues since 1988 by taking on an international focus with the integration of Asian, North American, and European operations and the opening of new facilities in The Netherlands and Scotland.

Donnelley supports customers and picks up additional business by offering a full range of printing, documentation, and technological systems and services. Examples of its significant capabilities include coordination of global production for Microsoft's Windows; a computerized routing and mapping solution for the newspaper industry; and the printing and distribution of the largest financial printing contract ever, 2.5 million copies of two policyholder documents totaling 350 pages for Equitable Life Assurance Company, completed in only eight days!

The company operates approximately 60 owned and leased printing and mail production facilities in the United States, Barbados, England, Ireland, and Mexico. A nearly 40 percent equity position in Alpha Graphics, Inc. gives Donnelley a foothold in the quick-printing industry.

Management Talent.   John R. Walter, Chairman and Chief Executive Officer, heads this Chicago-based printing firm and has been a company officer since 1985. Donnelley's management team doesn't project a stodgy old printing company image, but rather is composed of key players in their forties to mid-fifties for the most part. It includes people thoroughly familiar with how to make the information age pay off for their customers and Donnelley's bottom line.

Financial Status.   One look at Donnelley's financial statements and you might think the company's presses were working overtime printing money rather than financial reports and catalogs. Working capital of around $500 million provides plenty of money for keeping technology state of the art and ahead of its competitors, none of whom can match Donnelley's financial resources.

Likewise, sufficient funds are available for key acquisitions and facility expansions to meet rising customer demand. Capital spending and acquisitions exceeded $400 million in 1993, a nearly 30 percent increase over year-earlier levels. The company also has two revolving credit arrangements totaling $550 million, ready for use as needed.

Long-term debt in the amount of $700 million consists mainly of debt taken on in late 1990 with the leveraged acquisition of the Meredith/Burda companies, with four printing plants and three pre-press centers, and subsequent smaller acquisitions.

Operating cashflow in excess of $400 million fuels Donnelley's acquisition program, facilities expansion, and modernization efforts. Cash dividends per share have grown at a better than 10 percent compounded rate for the past 10 years.

DRIP Details.   Donnelley's DRIP program permits company shareholders to purchase additional shares with dividends and cash, with no administration expenses or commissions charged to the shareholder on such purchases. Cash purchases of stock between $10 to $60,000 per year are permitted. For information, write or call the company's General Counsel and Secretary at 77 Wacker Drive, Chicago, IL 60601-1696, 312-326-8000.

Particular Strengths. The company's huge domestic position and increasing international presence will allow it to gain even more market share by putting to work its significant financial resources and technological know-how. For example, Donnelley invested $40 million in 1993 and early 1994 to expand the capacity of its Harrisonburg, Virginia, book manufacturing facility by 50 percent, to meet increased demand from trade and college book publishers.

Donnelley's financial strength and capital spending will make it a major beneficiary of the industry's ongoing consolidation. As smaller printers fail to invest in expensive new technology, larger and more modern full-service printers such as Donnelley will gain new business.

Each of the firm's four business segments commands a leading position in its respective market, allowing each to set rather than react to industry trends.

Like other successful companies, Donnelley has an excellent track record when it comes to seeking out and purchasing companies that provide synergistic operating and product-line synergies.

Financial statistics (figures in millions, except per-share amounts):

For fiscal year ended December 31	1990	1991	1992	1993
Revenues	$3,498	$3,915	$4,193	$4,388
Net income (loss)	226	205	235	109*
Earnings (loss)/share	1.45	1.32	1.51	.71*
Dividend/share	.48	.50	.51	.54
Long-term debt	647	528	523	700
Stock price range/share:				
High	30⅛	46⅜	33¾	32¾
Low	22⅝	25	23¾	26⅛

*Includes a one-time restructuring charge of $60.8 million or $.39 per share, net effects of accounting change of $69.5 million or $.45 per share, and a deferred income-tax charge of $6.2 million or $.04 per share.

Investment Assessment. R. R. Donnelley represents a turnaround situation among the top picks for the twenty-first century. It's a company that has experienced some tough times in the past few years.

First, there was the dilution caused by the large acquisition of Meredith/Burda. (The FTC has ordered Donnelley to divest itself of the Meredith/Burda plants. The company is appealing the ruling.) Next, plant expansion and high start-up costs hurt year-to-year earnings comparisons. Finally, the foreign currency impact of the strong dollar reduced the value of U.K. operations in consolidated results; the loss of Sears' catalog business forced the closing of Donnelley's Chicago plant, which produced the Sears catalogs and a $60.8 million charge against earnings in 1993; and the one-time impact of an accounting change for the handling of post-retirement benefits significantly cut into 1993 results.

With all of those negatives, Donnelley's stock treaded water through most of 1993—and therein lies the opportunity. The loss of Sears catalog business is now history, with most of the slack being picked up through increased business with other catalog distributors. The closing of the Chicago plant will actually work to the company's benefit in the long run. As the firm's oldest facility (1912), it was also the least efficient. The upgrading of other facilities that has occurred over the past few years will keep Donnelley the industry's low-cost, quality producer.

Along similar lines, the Meredith/Burda acquisition has now been fully absorbed, and will work to enhance the company's overall capabilities and operating efficiency.

In addition, Donnelley has worked hard at reducing its dependence on large customers. Since 1982, sales to its 10 largest customers have been reduced from 38 to under 24 percent today.

Donnelley's financial strength, healthy cashflow, and dominant market position will make it a winner in the industry consolidation now in progress. It can afford to pick and choose the choice acquisitions at the opportune moment.

The company's technological expertise is its ace in the hole. With the growing importance of global trade, Donnelley's extensive global telecommunications, distribution, and printing capabilities will lure business away from less qualified competitors.

All in all, the company is stronger and in a better position than ever before to take advantage of domestic and global market opportunities. As the company makes progress on these fronts and higher margins and earnings ensue, higher stock prices will follow. A September 1992 2-for-1 stock split brought the firm's stock price into a more attractive range for individual investors. (See Fig. 3-1, R. R. Donnelley & Sons company stock.) Look for Donnelley to be one of the top turnaround stocks of the twenty-first century.

DONNELLEY (R.R.) NYSE-DNY	RECENT PRICE 29	P/E RATIO 16.1 (Trailing: 17.9 Median: 16.0)	RELATIVE P/E RATIO 1.05	DIV'D YLD 2.2%	VALUE LINE 1792

TIMELINESS (Relative Price Performance Next 12 Mos.) 3 Average
SAFETY 1 Highest
(Scale: 1 Highest to 5 Lowest)
BETA 1.05 (1.00 = Market)

1997-99 PROJECTIONS

	Price	Gain	Ann'l Total Return
High	55	(+90%)	19%
Low	45	(+55%)	14%

Insider Decisions

	O	N	D	J	F	M	A	M	J
to Buy	0	0	0	0	0	0	1	0	1
Options	1	0	1	0	0	1	0	1	0
to Sell	1	1	3	1	1	1	0	0	2

Institutional Decisions

	3Q'93	4Q'93	1Q'94
to Buy	77	79	78
to Sell	118	112	124
Hld's(000)	108346	108770	110538

	1983	1984	1985	1986	1987	1988	1989	1990	1991	1992	1993	1994
High:	12.0	12.3	16.1	20.0	22.7	19.4	25.6	26.3	25.6	33.8	32.8	31.8
Low:	7.3	8.0	11.5	14.7	12.8	14.9	17.1	17.1	19.4	23.8	26.1	26.9

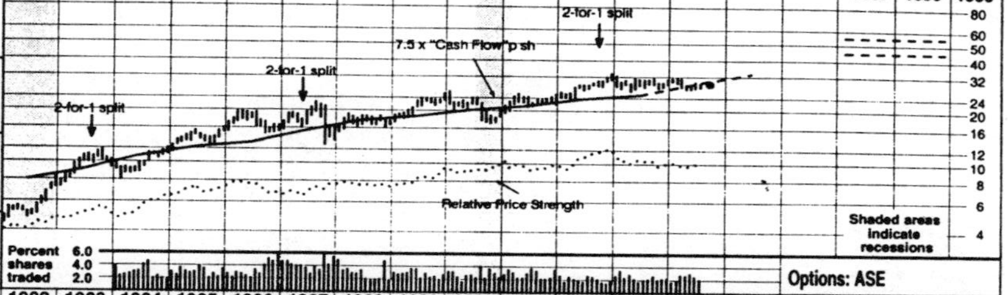

Options: ASE

1978	1979	1980	1981	1982	1983	1984	1985	1986	1987	1988	1989	1990	1991	1992	1993	1994	1995	© VALUE LINE PUB., INC.	97-99
5.29	6.47	7.44	8.24	9.23	10.14	11.86	13.35	14.08	16.02	18.53	20.04	22.58	25.20	27.05	28.46	31.50	34.40	Sales per sh	44.50
.60	.67	.75	.87	1.07	1.22	1.46	1.65	1.75	2.06	2.36	2.49	2.71	2.87	3.18	3.34	3.90	4.45	"Cash Flow" per sh	6.00
.37	.43	.46	.53	.60	.75	.88	.97	1.01	1.15	1.32	1.43	1.46	1.32	1.51	1.55	1.80	2.05	Earnings per sh [A]	3.00
.11	.13	.14	.16	.18	.21	.25	.29	.32	.35	.39	.44	.48	.50	.51	.54	.60	.68	Div'ds Decl'd per sh [B]■	1.00
.54	.97	.92	.71	.57	1.13	1.15	1.07	1.61	1.36	1.21	1.53	1.67	1.85	1.47	1.99	2.25	2.25	Cap'l Spending per sh	2.75
2.72	3.02	3.34	3.71	4.11	4.63	5.22	5.87	6.34	7.45	8.34	9.28	10.30	11.14	11.93	11.96	13.20	14.60	Book Value per sh [C]	20.00
147.59	148.04	149.36	151.03	152.20	152.44	153.01	152.72	158.61	154.98	155.37	155.81	154.93	155.35	155.03	154.16	154.00	154.00	Common Shs Outst'g [D]	154.00
9.2	8.2	8.4	8.9	9.7	13.1	11.6	14.3	16.9	15.8	13.1	15.0	14.6	17.2	18.5	19.0	Bold figures are	Value Line	Avg Ann'l P/E Ratio	16.0
1.25	1.19	1.12	1.08	1.07	1.11	1.08	1.16	1.15	1.06	1.09	1.14	1.08	1.10	1.12	1.12	estimates		Relative P/E Ratio	1.25
3.2%	3.6%	3.7%	3.4%	3.1%	2.1%	2.5%	2.1%	1.9%	1.9%	2.2%	2.1%	2.3%	2.2%	1.8%	1.8%			Avg Ann'l Div'd Yield	2.1%
						1814.5	2038.4	2233.5	2482.9	2878.4	3122.3	3497.9	3914.8	4193.1	4387.8	4850	5300	Sales ($mill)	6850
						16.3%	16.7%	16.6%	16.9%	16.5%	16.0%	15.9%	15.4%	15.8%	15.7%	16.0%	16.5%	Operating Margin	17.0%
						90.3	103.7	119.1	140.3	160.6	165.8	194.3	241.2	258.2	274.8	320	365	Depreciation ($mill)	450
						133.9	148.4	158.3	178.3	205.3	221.9	225.9	204.9	234.7	239.7	280	320	Net Profit ($mill)	465
						42.0%	42.0%	40.6%	38.8%	35.2%	37.0%	37.3%	36.0%	35.0%	34.6%	32.0%	32.0%	Income Tax Rate	32.0%
						7.4%	7.3%	7.1%	7.2%	7.1%	7.1%	6.5%	5.2%	5.6%	5.5%	5.8%	6.0%	Net Profit Margin	6.8%
						222.4	297.0	296.7	288.7	316.8	314.4	504.1	437.0	409.9	424.5	475	575	Working Cap'l ($mill)	1150
						14.3	15.0	18.4	193.8	121.0	62.6	647.1	527.5	522.6	673.4	650	650	Long-Term Debt ($mill)	650
						798.5	895.9	1005.0	1155.1	1296.4	1445.8	1595.6	1730.4	1849.0	1844.0	2030	2245	Net Worth ($mill)	3075
						16.6%	16.3%	15.5%	13.6%	14.9%	15.0%	10.6%	10.1%	10.6%	10.3%	11.5%	12.0%	% Earned Total Cap'l	13.0%
						16.8%	16.6%	15.7%	15.4%	15.8%	15.3%	14.2%	11.8%	12.7%	13.0%	14.0%	14.5%	% Earned Net Worth	15.0%
						12.0%	11.6%	10.9%	10.7%	11.2%	10.6%	9.5%	7.4%	8.4%	8.5%	9.0%	9.5%	% Retained to Comm Eq	10.0%
						29%	30%	31%	31%	30%	31%	33%	38%	34%	35%	33%	33%	% All Div'ds to Net Prof	33%

BUSINESS: R.R. Donnelley & Sons Co. is the world's largest commercial printer (has about 7% of the domestic market). Prints and binds a major share of national pubs. (including Time, Newsweek, TV Guide), telephone directories, encyclopedias, and school & religious books. Ben Johnson is UK sub. The ten largest customers account for 22% of sales. Sales breakdown: catalogs, 32%; magazines, 18%; directories, 14%; books, 13%; Documentation Serv., 12%; financial 6%; other, 5%. Acqu. Meredith/Burda 9/90. Has 34,000 empls., 10,400 stkhldrs. 1993 deprec. rate: 8.2%. R.R. Donnelley descendants own about 22% of stk. (2/94 proxy). Chairman & C.E.O.: John R. Walter. Inc.: Delaware. Address: 77 West Wacker Drive, Chicago, Illinois 60601-8375. Telephone: 312-326-8000.

Figure 3-1. R. R. Donnelley & Sons Company stock report. (*Copyright 1994 by Value Line Publishing Inc. Reprinted by permission; all rights reserved.*)

☆15 THE HOME ☆ DEPOT, INC.

THE HOME DEPOT, INC.   Stock exchange: NYSE
2727 Paces Ferry Road   Ticker symbol: HD
Atlanta, Georgia 30339   DRIP program: Yes
404-433-8211   Ownership:
                                 Institutional: 54%
                                 Insiders: 8%

Industry Review.   The retail building-supply industry in which The Home Depot, Inc. operates has been undergoing a number of changes over the past two decades. Store size has grown substantially, from the traditional 20,000-square-foot lumber yard/hardware store concept of the seventies to the 100,000- to 120,000-square-foot superstores taking over market share today.

In addition to opening larger stores, industry giants also are embarking on an unprecedented foray into new markets, forcing industry consolidation as smaller and less efficient competitors fall by the wayside. For example, Home Depot has made moves to enter the Mexican market; recently purchased a 75 percent stake in Molson's Aikenhead's Home Improvement Warehouse retail chain serving the Canadian market; and announced plans to open 23 stores in the Chicago market as part of its Midwest expansion strategy.

The trend toward serve-yourself, one-stop warehouse shopping as exhibited in the superstore concept has attracted major business away from the smaller, independent chains, and the pace is accelerating. Broader product lines, higher volume, and more frequent inventory turns (6.4 inventory turns in 1991, compared to over 7 in 1994) spell lower operating costs and higher margins—an attractive combination for future industry earnings.

The industry leader, Home Depot, has expanded beyond the do-it-yourself market and now caters to a wide variety of customers ranging from do-it-yourselfers to home building and remodeling contractors. Its superstores not only offer how-to-do-it advice but now also provide professional installation of purchased building-supply items.

Industry gross margins average around 27 percent, and revenue growth has been accelerating, climbing to an estimated 17.5 percent for

1994. Even more important, the industry net-profit margin has been moving ahead, improving from under 3 percent in 1990 to over 4 percent in 1994.

Company Profile. The Home Depot, Inc. leads the retail building-supply market in innovation and aggressive expansion, and ranks as one of the nation's fastest-growing retailers.

Home Depot is indisputably the industry leader, since it has single-handedly initiated most of the innovations (superstore warehouses, professional installation, etc.) now transforming the industry. As a result, the company's growth has been nothing short of phenomenal, going from less than 20 to over 260 building-supply stores in less than a decade.

While other industry companies have sought to copy Home Depot's growth strategy, they haven't been able to duplicate its overall success. The company leads the industry in most performance measures such as revenues per square foot of store space and growth in the average amount of sale per transaction.

Moving beyond the boundaries of its original Georgia market, Home Depot now operates retail building-supply stores in 23 states stretching from Connecticut to Texas to Arizona. As mentioned earlier, plans to enter new markets will boost that number substantially and add other countries to the Home Depot's roster. Currently, the company ranks among the nation's 30 largest retailers, with over $9.2 billion in annual revenues.

Over the past five years, revenue growth has exceeded 35 percent, and given expansion plans now in the works, it looks to grow even faster in the future. Home Depot's earnings haven't taken a hit in the wake of aggressive growth, either. The company recorded eight years of consecutive record earnings, posting a 26.1 percent increase in fiscal 1993. For the past 10 years, Home Depot has increased its net earnings per share at a compounded rate in excess of 38 percent.

Management Talent. Chairman and Chief Executive Officer Bernard Marcus has held those positions since the company's inception in 1978, and along with President and Chief Operating Officer Arthur M. Blank is a cofounder of the company. Company executive vice presidents and vice presidents possess extensive company and industry experience. Their track record of leading the industry in growth and innovations speaks for itself.

Financial Status. From a balance-sheet standpoint, over $1.1 billion in cash, cash equivalents, and marketable securities makes the company treasury look like Fort Knox. And with a five-year annual compounded stockholder's equity growth rate exceeding 42 percent, the future looks even brighter. Long-term debt is a manageable $845 million, with the majority of it consisting of low-cost $4\frac{1}{2}$ percent convertible notes issued in February 1992.

Working capital stands at an impressive $1.1 billion, and cashflow amounting to some $1.50 per share will bolster cash reserves. Existing credit lines and operating cashflow will provide ample capital for new store openings and planned acquisitions.

DRIP Details.   The company DRIP program allows for additional cash purchase of company stock in amounts from $10 to $4000 per month. Information on the program may be obtained by writing to Wachovia Bank of North Carolina, N.A., Dividend Reinvestment Section, P.O. Box 3001, Winston-Salem, North Carolina 27102, or by calling Mr. Larry Watkins at the toll-free telephone number 1-800-633-4236.

Particular Strengths.   Home Depot's tried-and-true strategy of penetrating markets will serve it well as it enters new markets in Chicago, Detroit, Canada, and other countries. State-of-the-art accounting and inventorying systems such as computerized point-of-purchase sales registers and electronic bar-coding keeps costs down and helps to eliminate stockouts.

As indicated earlier, the company's solid financial posture allows it to attack new markets head-on, but the company isn't forsaking old customers in its thrust to enter new territories. It is committed to spending to increase business in existing markets by opening larger, more convenient stores near current operations. This "cannibalization" strategy keeps its customer base intact and draws new customers.

But perhaps one of the company's greatest strengths lies in its work force, and the firm's approach to dealing fairly with employees. A "share the wealth" ethic permeates top management. As opposed to the situation one finds at many other retail operations, no one at Home Depot works for minimum wage. In fact, nearly 95 percent of all employees work full-time and are eligible for the company's medical and life insurance plans. In addition, all company employees may take ownership in the company through an Employee Stock Ownership Plan (ESOP), Employee Stock Purchase Plan, or Omnibus Stock Option Plan.

Financial statistics (figures in millions, except per-share amounts):

For fiscal year ended January xx	1991	1992	1993	1994
Revenues	$3,815	$5,136	$7,148	$9,239
Net income (loss)	163	249	362	457
Earnings (loss)/share	.45	.60	.82	1.01
Dividend/share	.04	.055	.0825	.113
Long-term debt	531	271	844	845
Stock price range/share:	1990	1991	1992	1993
High	14½	35⅛	51½	50⅞
Low	7¾	11½	29¾	35

Investment Assessment.   As they say, "The past is prologue." Home Depot's aggressive move into new domestic and foreign markets promises to make its impressive past growth record look like it was taking it easy. To be sure, mistakes will be made but they won't keep this company and its astute management from reaching its long-term goals.

The foundations are already firmly in place: solid cashflow and financials, excellent gross and net margins, a well-run operation, dedicated work force, and marketing and expansion plans in full swing.

Home Depot has spent the past few years market-testing new concepts that will help to propel growth in the future and to cut operating costs. Among these are nighttime receiving and restocking to ensure that there will be no stockouts the next day and to allow store employees to concentrate on serving customers rather than chasing down stock; an enlarged garden center with year-round sales opportunities; and a streamlined lumber and building materials checkout and loading procedure, to get professional customers on their way faster—for these folks, time is money.

The company's strategy of offering professional installation service for purchased items is another homegrown brainstorm. By delivering the same high-quality installation as it offers in its in-store products and service, Home Depot stands to gain more sales and new customers. The company anticipates that installation services for most of its products will be in all of its stores by the end of 1995.

Home Depot looks to more than triple its number of stores by the end of 1998, to nearly 825 outlets in the United States and beyond. Don't be surprised if earnings and the company's stock price follow suit. (See Fig. 3-2, The Home Depot, Inc. stock chart.) Home Depot represents a solid, long-term core investment upon which you may build your portfolio.

Figure 3-2. The Home Depot, Inc. stock chart. (Copyright 1994 by Value Line Publishing Inc. Reprinted by permission; all rights reserved.)

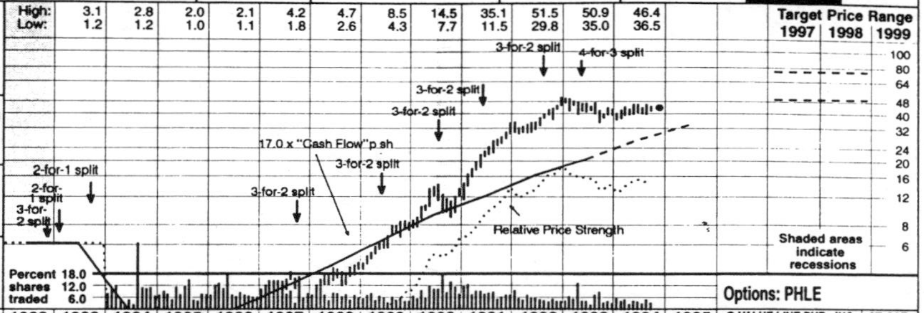

☆16 SERVICE☆ CORPORATION INTERNATIONAL

SERVICE
  CORPORATION INTERNATIONAL
1929 Allen Parkway
Houston, Texas 77019
713-522-5141

Stock exchange: NYSE
Ticker symbol: SRV
DRIP program: No
Ownership:
  Institutional: 72%
  Insider: 3%

Industry Review.   Service Corporation International serves a *dying* industry—but that's good for business. The "death care" industry provides extremely consistent growth combined with high margins and healthy cashflows. Originally a highly fragmented industry, in recent years consolidation has taken place, with industry giants such as Service Corporation International (SCI) and The Loewen Group leading the acquisition pace.

As the industry consolidates, economies of scale come into play. New efficiencies will help to lower costs, and further enhance the already attractive margins. Industry operating margins range from 25 to 30 percent for cemetery operations and between 27 to 32 percent for funeral business. Given the aging North American population, demographic trends are favorable for continued stable growth.

Company Profile.   Service Corporation International is the largest provider of funeral services in North America, and as its name implies, it takes an international approach to the market, with operations in both Australia and Canada.

SCI owns and operates nearly 800 funeral homes and 192 cemeteries in 39 states, the District of Columbia, four Canadian provinces, and five Australian territories. The Canadian operations are carried out by a public company that is approximately 70 percent owned by SCI.

Management uses a cluster strategy in its acquisition program, penetrating certain geographic areas with several funeral home facilities located in groups, to derive the benefit of lower costs from centralized transportation, labor, advertising, and other business functions. This streamlined operating structure lowers cost significantly and improves SCI's competitive posture in the market.

With approximately 10 percent of the U.S. funeral business, SCI has started expansion abroad with the $69 million, late-August-1993 acquisition of the Pine Grove Funeral Group in Australia. The move added 58 funeral homes and 8 cemetery/crematorium facilities to company operations, and is estimated to add $32 million to SCI annual revenues. Management also is considering enlarging its international presence, with potential expansion moves into other countries such as the United Kingdom, France, Hong Kong, Mexico, and Taiwan.

Product extension in the form of prearranged funerals and preneed cemetery sales is also adding to future revenues and the bottom line. An estimated $159 million in future business has been produced in 1993 through the prearranged funerals program. Putting that into perspective, SCI earned revenues in 1993 of around $900 million. The company operates 45 flower shops, which serve as another product extension and revenue-generator.

In addition to the funeral and cemetery businesses, SCI also provides financing to independent funeral homes and cemeteries through its wholly-owned subsidiary, Provident Services, Inc.

In an effort to move decision making down to the operating levels, the company reorganized in 1993 and decentralized the company, with the introduction of company presidents running each of the firm's six regions.

Since 1989, SCI has earned a compounded annual revenues growth rate of 14 percent, and an annual compounded earnings per share growth rate of 20 percent.

Management Talent.   Chairman and Chief Executive Officer Robert L. Waltrip has been a company officer since 1962, and is the founder of the company. President and Chief Operating Officer L. William Heiligbrodt has previously served in various SCI corporate top management positions, and was Vice Chairman and Chief Executive Officer of a multi-industry holding company prior to joining SCI.

Senior Vice President Glenn McMillen, an industry-seasoned veteran, has been chosen to head the newly acquired Australian Pine Grove Funeral Group, which is the largest death care service provider in that country. SCI's new management structure should prove more efficient and profitable in the long run.

Financial Status.   SCI has around $21 million in cash, and working capital in excess of $250 million, with which to pursue its aggressive acquisition strategy. Long-term debt stands a bit over $1 billion. The company has revolving credit agreements with a group of banks totaling $250 million, and an additional bank line of credit for $75 million as needed for operations.

High gross margins contribute to a cashflow around $2 per share. Prearranged funeral contracts in excess of $1.1 billion add a great deal of stability and predictability to future revenues and cashflow streams.

Particular Strengths.   As the world's largest provider of funeral services, SCI purchases more caskets, vehicles, cremation urns, grave markers, and other related products than any other company. This translates into purchasing power and substantial price discounts.

It also allows SCI to work closely with product suppliers to develop new industry products and to improve the quality and pricing of existing product lines.

Management has been adept at successfully fulfilling its cluster market strategy and penetrating key major metropolitan markets. This approach should permit SCI to capture even more domestic market share in the years ahead, as its lower costs and dedication to superior service attract new customers.

The expansion into markets outside of North America opens up new opportunities and new risks. The company has faltered once before, in the late 1980s, as it tried to integrate vertically and finally had to restructure. This time, management is taking a more conservative, step-by-step approach, and sticking to what it does best.

Financial statistics (figures in millions, except per-share amounts):

For fiscal year ended December 31	1990	1991	1992	1993
Revenues	$563	$643	$772	$899
Net income (loss)	60	73	87	103*
Earnings (loss)/share	.85	1.03	1.13	1.21*
Dividend/share	.37	.37	.39	.40
Long-term debt	577	787	980	1,062
Stock price range/share:				
High	16	18⅜	18¾	26⅜
Low	8¾	13½	15⅝	17⅞

*Excludes charge of $2 million or $.03 cents per share to absorb effects of accounting change.

Investment Assessment.   Long-term earnings growth in the 15 to 20 percent range; expanding market share; and an international expansion program under way. All these point to higher earnings per share for Service Corporation International.

SCI stands to come out a clear winner, as industry consolidation continues both in North America and abroad. The company has proven that its cluster strategy works, and has successfully folded in a number of acquisitions in the past three years. SCI generally keeps on the existing, usually family-run, funeral home management. This maintains continuity in the local community and allows the funeral home operator to tailor services to local customs and traditions.

Look for SCI to continue its five-year track record of higher stock prices, as earnings improve into the next decade. (See Fig. 3-3, Service Corporation International stock price chart.)

SERVICE CP. INT'L NYSE-SRV

RECENT PRICE	**27**	
P/E RATIO	**18.6**	(Trailing: 19.7, Median: 17.0)
RELATIVE P/E RATIO	**1.25**	
DIV'D YLD	**1.6%**	
VALUE LINE	**1392**	

TIMELINESS 3 (Relative Price Perform- ance Next 12 Mos.) — Average
SAFETY 3 (Scale: 1 Highest to 5 Lowest) — Average
BETA .95 (1.00 = Market)

High	10.5	9.6
Low	5.9	6.0

1997-99 PROJECTIONS

	Price	Gain	Ann'l Total Return
High	55	(+105%)	21%
Low	40	(+50%)	12%

Insider Decisions

	O	N	D	J	F	M	A	M	J
to Buy	0	0	0	1	0	0	0	0	0
Options	0	0	0	1	0	0	0	0	0
to Sell	0	0	0	2	0	0	0	1	0

Institutional Decisions

	3Q'93	4Q'93	1Q'94
to Buy	75	74	71
to Sell	71	74	84
Hld's(000)	59763	62215	63501

Percent shares traded: 9.0 / 6.0 / 3.0

Legend: 12.0 x "Cash Flow" p'sh · 3-for-2 split · Relative Price Strength · Shaded areas indicate recessions

Target Price Range 1997 1998 1999 — price scale: 50, 40, 32, 24, 20, 16, 12, 10, 8, 6, 4, 3

Options: PHLE

Capital structure / statistical array ($ mill, years 1984–1995, bold = Value Line estimates)

	1984	1985	1986	1987	1988F	1989	1990	1991	1992	1993	1994	1995	© VALUE LINE PUB., INC. 97-99
Sales per sh (A)	4.19	4.57	5.68	7.50	6.39	7.15	8.19	8.47	10.04	10.60	12.20	13.65	19.45
"Cash Flow" per sh (B)													3.95
Earnings per sh (B)													2.80
Div'ds Decl'd per sh (C)													.60
Cap'l Spending per sh													1.30
Book Value per sh (D)													19.65
Common Shs Outst'g (E)								75.98	76.91	84.86	86.00	88.00	95.00
Avg Ann'l P/E Ratio													17.0
Relative P/E Ratio													1.30
Avg Ann'l Div'd Yield													1.3%
Sales ($mill)(A)	234.2	264.0	366.6	540.0	462.6	518.8	563.2	643.3	772.5	899.2	1050	1200	1850
Operating Margin	23.7%	23.6%	20.7%	21.0%	24.8%	26.5%	27.7%	29.9%	31.0%	30.9%	31.0%	31.0%	32.0%
Depreciation ($mill)	10.1	11.7	17.1	29.9	31.1	24.2	27.2	35.0	47.4	58.2	70.0	80.0	115
Net Profit ($mill)	34.9	41.0	51.6	63.5	d11.9	50.7	63.5	73.4	86.5	103.1	123	148	260
Income Tax Rate	36.4%	36.5%	40.0%	36.0%	NMF	36.9%	36.1%	32.6%	37.9%	40.6%	40.0%	40.0%	40.0%
Net Profit Margin	14.9%	15.5%	13.3%	11.8%	NMF	9.8%	11.3%	11.4%	11.2%	11.5%	11.7%	12.3%	14.1%
Working Cap'l ($mill)	61.4	155.0	109.9	138.1	194.7	120.7	113.4	156.4	151.5	171.9	200	195	350
Long-Term Debt ($mill)	58.2	164.9	223.9	354.6	454.9	485.7	577.4	786.7	980.0	1062.2	1110	1100	1100
Net Worth ($mill)	255.5	299.0	478.6	568.7	516.4	557.8	434.3	615.8	683.1	884.5	1020	1180	1865
% Earned Total Cap'l	11.8%	9.4%	8.3%	8.1%	8%	6.4%	8.0%	6.7%	6.8%	6.8%	7.0%	8.0%	10.0%
% Earned Net Worth	13.7%	13.7%	10.8%	11.2%	NMF	9.1%	14.6%	11.9%	12.7%	11.7%	12.0%	12.5%	14.0%
% Retained to Comm Eq	11.2%	11.0%	8.1%	7.9%	NMF	7.7%	7.7%	8.3%	8.3%	7.9%	8.5%	9.0%	11.0%
% All Div'ds to Net Prof	18%	20%	25%	29%	NMF	62%	47%	36%	34%	32%	29%	27%	22%

BUSINESS: Service Corp. International is the largest funeral service and cemetery operator in North America. Owns and operates 873 funeral homes and 204 cemeteries in 40 states, the District of Columbia, Canada, and Australia. Also owns and operates flower shops, limousine services, burial vaults, and 82 crematory facilities. Provides capital financing to other funeral home/cemetery operators through Provident Services subsidiary. '93 depreciation rate: 4.9%. Estimated plant age: 5 years. Has 12,716 employees, 8,700 shareholders. J.P. Morgan & Co. owns 7.6% of stock; FMR Corp., Inc. 6.3%; Insiders 3.7% (4/94 proxy). Chairman & Chief Executive Officer: R.L. Waltrip. Incorporated: Texas. Address: 1929 Allen Parkway, Houston, Texas 77019. Tel: 713-522-5141.

Figure 3-3. Service Corporation International stock chart. (Copyright 1994 by Value Line Publishing Inc. Reprinted by permission; all rights reserved.)

4

Traveling Abroad with American Depositary Receipts

To the detriment of substandard portfolio performance, the average American investor invests only between 4 to 5 percent in overseas investments. True, in the past the complexities of dealing on foreign exchanges often discouraged many U.S. investors from venturing out beyond our nation's shores. Likewise, the number of foreign stocks meeting U.S. stock exchange trading requirements and actually trading on U.S. exchanges was limited, to say the least.

Today, however, all that has changed. Within the past few years, interest in foreign securities has skyrocketed, and as a result more and more foreign companies have made the effort to get listed on U.S. exchanges and trade in the American market.

According to Morgan Stanley Capital International, emerging market equities returned, from 1945 through 1992, an inflation-adjusted 11.5 percent annual rate of return. Likewise, for the same time frame, Japanese stocks earned 11.4 percent and the Europe/Asia Stock Index earned a return of 8.2 percent. In comparison, the S&P 500 index gained only 7.2 percent.

For those seeking to take advantage of the higher growth rates and larger returns available in foreign economies, professional investment managers recommend a portfolio mix containing between 20 to 30 percent foreign securities.

A number of ways exist to tap into the various foreign market investment alternatives, including mutual funds, closed-end country funds, and American Depositary Receipts (ADRs). In this chapter we will discuss what ADRs are and how they work, as well as pick those ADRs that promise to outperform the market on into the twenty-first century. For a discussion of global, international, and country mutual and closed-end funds, refer to Chap. 7, Funding Your Portfolio with Mutuals.

In essence, ADRs represent proxies for foreign stocks. You can purchase ADRs on U.S. exchanges, just as you would shares of stock in any American or Canadian corporation. It's no more complicated than that. Depending on where you live, you may run into some Blue Sky Laws that prohibit you from buying a specific foreign company's ADRs in a particular state, but those barriers are coming down daily.

According to the Bank of New York, which brings the majority of new ADR issues to the American market annually, record levels in the ADR market were achieved in 1993 for trading volume, capital raised, and the number of new ADR programs established.

Newly sponsored programs increased 32 percent, with 124 publicly traded ADRs. ADR issues came from nearly 30 different countries; some, like The People's Republic of China, Thailand, and Turkey, for the first time. (See Fig. 4-1, showing the percentage of Total Depositary Receipt programs by country.)

During 1993, foreign companies raised around $10 billion via ADR offerings in the United States, compared to only $5.3 billion a year earlier. Trading volume in 1993 rose to 6.3 billion ADRs, up 46.5 percent from 1992 levels. Even more impressive, ADR dollar volume jumped 60 percent, to a whopping $200 billion, for ADRs traded on the New York Stock Exchange, American Stock Exchange, and NASDAQ. (See Fig. 4-2, showing the annual dollar volume in ADR trading.)

"Nineteen ninety-three brought an unprecedented level of interest in international equity markets by U.S. investors," says Joseph M. Velli, Executive Vice President for the Bank of New York's ADR Department. "U.S. investors like ADRs due to their cost advantage, convenience, and enhanced liquidity compared to purchasing shares directly in a foreign market."

More ADR opportunities will open up in the coming years with the continued global trend privatization, and as companies in emerging markets seek capital to expand.

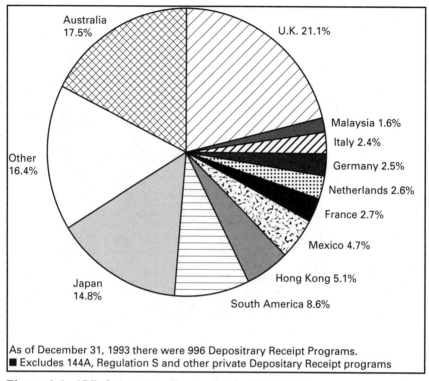

Figure 4-1. ADRs by country. *(Source: Bank of New York.)*

To be sure, investing in foreign companies requires just as much, and probably more, analysis on the investor's part. And investing overseas involves additional risks: currency risk, regional economic risk, political risk, etc.

Of course, as more and more investors seek out foreign investments, additional information will become available. Value Line already covers a number of large ADR companies. Likewise, Morningstar started coverage of ADRs with the launching of "Morningstar American Depositary Receipts" in May 1994. A trial three-month subscription costs $35, and includes one-page reports on 700 foreign stocks traded on U.S. exchanges as ADRs. For information, call 800-876-5005.

Today more than 1400 ADRs, representing shares in foreign companies, are available in the United States. Reflecting an indication of ADR performance, Merrill Lynch compiled an index of 199 ADRs traded on U.S. stock exchanges. The index reflected a significant gain in 1993, moving upward nearly 30 percent versus only 7 percent recorded for the S&P 500.

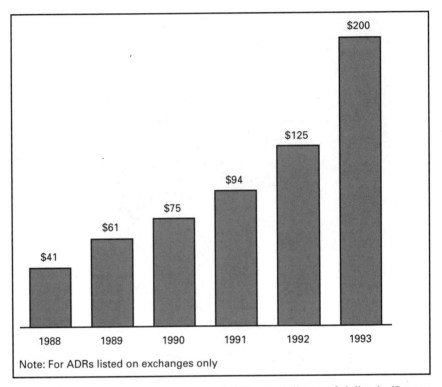

Figure 4-2. Annual trading volume of ADRs (in billions of dollars). *(Source: Bank of New York.)*

While Merrill Lynch mainly tracks the "blue chip" ADR companies, there are plenty of other solid foreign firms, with excellent revenue and earnings prospects with which to push up their market prices.

For example, Servicios Financieros Quadrum, SA, a Mexican asset-based financing company, was one of the top ADR performers in 1993, with a nearly 170 percent jump in its ADR price. (Discussion of Servicios Financieros and other foreign companies with bright futures follows.)

Each section of this chapter covers a specific area of the world, with a discussion as to why that economy (and specific company) is seen to be fertile investment ground in our increasingly global economy. Grab a comfortable chair and let this book take you to exciting foreign places, places you can later visit after you make your fortune investing in ADRs.

ADR COMPANY	COUNTRY	INDUSTRY
Coca-Cola FEMSA, S.A. de C.V.	Mexico	Soft Drink
Grupo Tribasa, S.A. de C.V.	Mexico	Construction
Servicios Financieros Quadrum, S.A.	Mexico	Financing
Sol Petroleo S.A.	Argentina	Petroleum
MADECO S.A.	Chile	Copper/Aluminum
Mavesa, S.A.	Venezuela	Food Processing
Danka Business Systems PLC	U.K.	Office Equipment
Amoy Properties Limited	Hong Kong	Real Estate Inv.
Shanghai Erfangji Company, Ltd.	China	Textile Machinery
Hai Sun Hup Group Ltd.	Singapore	Transportation
Teva Pharmaceutical Industries Ltd.	Israel	Pharmaceutical

As evidenced by the preceding list, there's plenty of room to diversify, both geographically and by industry, in the ADR market. In the wake of the North American Free Trade Agreement (NAFTA), Mexican companies with unique markets stand to benefit from expanded trade opportunities with the United States and Canada. On top of that, as the Mexican economy expands and that country's own citizens scale the economic ladder, they will have more disposable income with which to purchase more consumer goods and services.

Expanded trade also works to keep inflation and interest rates down, while opening up new areas for development and investment as capital and technological and management expertise flow from more industrialized nations to less developed but promising areas of the world.

While the Mexican economy began to slow down in 1991, the passage of NAFTA is expected to have an immediate stimulative effect, adding at least a percentage point to Mexican economic expansion in 1994 alone. More importantly, the passage of NAFTA signals the move toward more free-market trading in the world economic system—a good omen for international investing and worldwide development.

Given that scenario, the ADRs of the companies just listed (now to be looked at one by one) represent one way in which American investors can participate in the substantial growth opportunities to be found in foreign markets.

In 1993, the Mexican market enjoyed a 47 percent rise in U.S. dollars, as compared to a 7 percent rise for the U.S. market. The Mexican Bolsa (stock exchange) carries a market capitalization of around $170 billion. A new commitment to fiscal responsibility and sound monetary policies by the Mexican government has contributed to a dramatic improvement in the country's inflation rate. From a rate of around 160 percent in 1987, inflation dropped to around 30 percent in 1990 and 5 percent in 1993. With the passage of NAFTA, increasing corporate earnings, and low inflation, the Mexican economy and Mexican Bolsa promise to perform well in the years ahead.

☆17 COCA-COLA FEMSA,☆ S.A. DE C.V.

COCA-COLA FEMSA, S.A. DE C.V. Country: Mexico Industry: Soft-drink beverage	Stock exchange: NYSE Ticker symbol: KOF Ratio (ADR:ORD): 1:10 Series shares

ADR Trading Information.   Coca-Cola FEMSA ADRs came to market at $20.50 in September 1993, and rose to a 1993 high of $33¾ per ADR. The ADRs hit the $36¾ price level in early 1994, before pulling back a bit.

Company Market.   Coca-Cola FEMSA, S.A. de C.V. serves the Mexican soft-drink market, which exhibits a high degree of soft-drink acceptance and favorable demographics. In fact, Mexican consumption of soft drinks trails only that of the United States, and totals nearly 2.1 billion unit cases annually, with nearly 1.3 billion consisting of cola unit cases.

Currently, fragmented distribution systems and disparity in regional economic conditions are hampering additional sales. As the nation's infrastructure and economic conditions improve, sales of soft drinks should rise dramatically.

Mexican soft-drink consumption has grown at an estimated 7.4 percent rate since 1988. With 38 percent of the population under age 15, the prime soft-drink consumption age, there's plenty of room for growth.

The two major cola brands in Mexico are Coca-Cola and Pepsi, with a combined 99.5 percent market share. In the Valley of Mexico territory, in 1992, Coca-Cola captured 32.7 percent of all soft-drink sales versus 27.8 percent for Pepsi.

Company Profile.   Coca-Cola FEMSA, S.A. de C.V. produces and distributes soft drinks in Mexico City (Valley of Mexico territory) and in Southeastern Mexico. The company possesses the exclusive license to produce and market Coca-Cola, Diet Coke, Sprite, Diet Sprite, and

Fanta in these markets. The Valley of Mexico territory, with a population of around 16 million, ranks as the world's largest Coca-Cola bottling operation in terms of population for a single market. Coca-Cola FEMSA's two markets comprise approximately 29 percent of the Mexican population.

Coca-Cola FEMSA operates eight bottling plants in the Valley of Mexico territory, with an annual capacity of nearly 190 million unit cases, plus another five bottling facilities in the Southeast with an annual capacity of over 76 million unit cases. The company moves its soft drinks to market via 42 strategically located distribution centers and a fleet of over 1800 trucks to more than 146,000 retailers in both markets.

Coca-Cola FEMSA's major shareholder, FEMSA, has long been a force in the Mexican beverage market. Its history may be traced back to 1890 with the founding of Mexico's first brewery. FEMSA is the largest food, beverage, and tobacco company listed on the Mexican Bolsa.

Management Talent. Chief Executive Officer Alfredo Martinez Urdal recently took over that position in 1993, with previous experience as General Director for Grupo Chihuahua. The balance of his management team has extensive company and industry experience with the company's predecessors or affiliate companies.

Financial Status. Company revenues are increasing at a 9 percent pace. Unit case sales have jumped in excess of 16 percent since 1990. Cashflow is ample for anticipated capital expenditures. The company's balance sheet is strong. All long-term debt was eliminated in 1993 with the proceeds of an investment by Impulsora de Mercados in exchange for Series A shares.

Particular Strengths. Coca-Cola FEMSA has major market share in a vibrant and growing Mexican economy. The company's share of total soft-drink sales, relative to major competitor PepsiCo., amounted to over 52 percent in the Valley of Mexico and over 70 percent in Southeast Mexico. Getting a stronger lock on the market in May 1993, Coca-Cola FEMSA began to supply post-mix to McDonalds restaurants in the Valley of Mexico on an exclusive basis. The company estimates that McDonalds uses in excess of 1.3 million unit cases of post-mix annually. Increasing unit case sales will keep cash flowing and lower operating costs through economies of scale.

The retooling of one bottling plant and the construction of a large new bottling facility in the Valley of Mexico will boost annual capacity, enhance the company's ability to produce different products, and streamline operating efficiencies.

Financial statistics (figures in millions of New Pesos, except per-share amounts):

For fiscal year ended December 31	1991	1992	1993
Revenues	NP1,526	NP1,664	NP1,903
Net income (loss)	158	112	162
Earnings per share	.66	.34	.44
ADR price range/ADR:			
High			33¼
Low			20½

Investment Assessment.   The net income reduction in 1992 resulted from several nonrecurring items such as an adjustment for past service costs of the company's pension plan, and interest expense and foreign exchange losses related to indebtedness owed to FEMSA.

In 1993, revenues, operating income, and margins all improved, to raise net income some 20 percent. Of course, the elimination of the debt to FEMSA in June 1993 contributed to lower interest expense for the year and to the improved net income.

The bottom line? Coca-Cola FEMSA has a solid market position, upon which it can continue to increase revenues and earnings.

☆ 18 GRUPO TRIBASA, ☆ S.A. DE C.V.

GRUPO TRIBASA, S.A. DE C.V.	Stock exchange: NYSE
Country: Mexico	Ticker symbol: GTR
Industry: Construction	Ratio (ADR:ORD): 1:2

ADR Trading Information.   Grupo Tribasa, S.A. de C.V. ADRs initially traded in September 1993 at $15.50 per ADR. They hit a high of $37 in 1993, moved on to post a high of $40¼ per ADR in 1994, before dropping back to the $28-per-ADR level.

Company Market.   Mexico's construction industry is sure to benefit from the enactment of NAFTA, as greater emphasis than ever before is placed on improving the nation's infrastructure.

Construction projects under *any* new administration may require more time to gain approval, as the new government leaders set their own policy priorities and get their feet wet running the country. But in the long run, development of Mexico's infrastructure will certainly be in the country's best interest.

In Mexico the government operates a concession program, through which contractors are required to arrange financing commitments sufficient to cover a substantial portion of highway construction costs. This program offers both opportunities and risks. On the upside, a concession company, as a contractor and owner of a highway project, can not only earn revenues and profits as a contractor but also earn money as a capital investor. The downside risk includes lower than anticipated cashflows from highway tolls to support the project financing, thereby creating a default situation during which the government can terminate the highway concession without compensation before the concession term has expired.

The move to private-sector financing has spurred Mexican highway construction activity in recent years. In addition, other infrastructure programs are coming up for review for financing under the concession program framework. The Mexican trend toward privately financed public-works projects decreases Mexican construction companies' dependence on public-sector financing.

Company Profile.   Grupo Tribasa, S.A. de C.V. operates in the Mexican construction market. The nation's second-largest construction company segregates its operations into three segments: construction, highway and other project concessions, and sales of construction materials.

Since 1989, Grupo Tribasa has concentrated on the highway concession market, which now contributes in excess of 90 percent of company revenues from concession-related construction. It plans to transfer its expertise and success in the highway concession program to other infrastructure concessions as the government expands its private financing of public projects to other types of construction such as water systems, light rail, and maritime port projects.

Management Talent.   Husband-and-wife team David Penaloza Sandoval and Adrianna Alanis de Penaloza serve as President and Executive Vice President, respectively, and over the past quarter of a century have successfully grown the company into the nation's second-largest construction firm.

Financial Status. The bulk of the company's $560 million in long-term debt has been incurred to finance various highway concession projects. Other long-term debt has arisen from the purchase of machinery and equipment under capital leases. The company is exploring sale-leaseback financing of a substantial portion of its equipment fleet, which would permit it to obtain long-term, off-balance-sheet financing. Grupo Tribasa has nearly $300 million in cash, cash equivalents, and short-term investments.

Particular Strengths. As one of Mexico's two largest construction firms, Grupo Tribasa possesses the management and operating talent to tackle virtually any major Mexican construction project. Its ties to Grupo Financiero Interacciones, S.A. de C.V. (Grupo Tribasa owns 3.84 percent of its shares) help to create a strong financing relationship for the concession projects the company undertakes.

In a move to enhance its construction expertise and opportunities, in May 1993 Grupo Tribasa merged with Gimsa, a company specializing in industrial construction, and Ciesa, a specialist in bridge construction. Gimsa has performed numerous industrial projects for Pemex, the Mexican oil company.

In the aftermath of NAFTA, more foreign construction companies are expected to bid for projects in Mexico. While that may create additional competition for some projects, Grupo Tribasa stands to benefit from potential joint-venture arrangements with major U.S. and other countries' large engineering and construction firms.

Tribasa works hard at securitizing its toll revenues after the initial operating period following construction completion. This allows the company to accelerate the payout on its equity interest in the concession and, after repayment of the securitized financing, to still maintain a residual interest in toll revenues over the remaining life of the concession.

Extensive experience in road, drainage, airport runway, port, tunnel, dam, and building construction projects makes Grupo Tribasa a major player in the Mexican infrastructure market.

Financial statistics (figures in millions of constant Pesos, except per-share amounts):

For fiscal year ended December 31	1991	1992	Nine Months 1993
Revenues	N1,470	N1,874	N1,612
Net income (loss)	113	311	242
Earnings per share	.98	3.11	1.84
ADR price range/ADR:			
High			37
Low			15½

Investment Assessment. Grupo Tribasa's ADRs were one of the market's hot spots in 1993. The Company's ADR price rose more than 120 percent, based on expectations of NAFTA's impact on future Mexican infrastructure construction activity.

Grupo Tribasa has proved itself adept at innovative project financing and securitized refinancings after construction completion. The company's expansion into industrial construction gives it an entrée to other major infrastructure projects to come down the pike, as Mexico strives to improve its infrastructure and become a global competitor.

Recent moves to improve the firm's balance sheet will prove beneficial in cutting interest expenses, enhancing cashflow, and giving the firm more flexibility to obtain new concession work.

In 1993, operating earnings showed an impressive improvement, and the company was awarded several major road construction projects and concessions. In addition, Tribasa and other members of a construction consortium won the concession award to build an N$2.4 billion water-treatment system and operate it for 15 years. The construction project, of which Tribasa will perform 50 percent, begins in 1994 and continues for 30 months. Tribasa will own 45 percent of the water-treatment-facility concession. The company's construction backlog has increased by around 25 percent since the end of 1992, given an improved mix of concessioned highways (41 percent), water-treatment and other non-highway concessions (31 percent), and other highway and nonconcessioned work (28 percent).

The price of Grupo Tribasa ADRs should rebound dramatically, with improving earnings and increased cash and income flow from operating concessions.

☆ 19 SERVICIOS ☆ FINANCIEROS QUADRUM, S.A.

SERVICIOS FINANCIEROS		
QUADRUM, S.A.	Stock exchange:	NASDAQ
Country: Mexico	Ticker symbol:	QDRMY
Industry: Asset-Based Financing	Ratio (ADR:ORD):	1:10

ADR Trading Information. One of the best-performing ADRs in 1993, the Servicios Financieros Quadrum, S.A., ADR price rose from an initial offering price of $11 per ADR to hit a high of $32⅜ in 1993 and an all-time high of $32⅝ in early 1994. Since then, the shares have dropped dramatically to the $16 level.

Company Market. Asset-based financing takes several forms, from factoring to equipment, machinery, and commercial and industrial real-estate-leasing operations. In contrast to the U.S. factoring business, which purchases accounts receivable on a non-recourse basis, Mexican factoring involves the purchase of accounts receivable with the right to sell back to the client, at full face value, accounts not paid by the specified due date. The seller's repurchase obligations may be secured by security interests in other collateral.

With the improving Mexican economy and business growth opportunities, many Mexican businesses have turned to factoring to provide needed cashflow and funds for expansion.

In January 1991 the Mexican government instituted regulation of the factoring industry, with minimal capital and other regulatory requirements. As a result, the factoring industry experienced a significant falling-out of the less financially stable factoring companies and, therefore, far less competition for factoring business.

Asset-based leasing in Mexico is provided from several sources: bank affiliates, financial groups, and independent leasing companies such as Servicios Financieros Quadrum. Leases typically take the form either of finance leases or of operating leases providing for a down payment and monthly payments through the lease term.

Company Profile. As an independent finance company, Servicios Financieros Quadrum has had to be innovative with regard to its products and services in order to gain market share. The company ranks as the second-largest independent leasing company in Mexico, in terms both of the size of its leasing portfolio and of net worth. Leasing activities consist of approximately $85 million for over 1000 clients, and include transportation equipment, industrial machinery, office equipment, and industrial and commercial real estate.

The factoring segment provides asset-based financing to small to mid size Mexican companies and individuals. Its factoring portfolio totals around $135 million to more than 450 clients. Servicios Financieros is the largest factoring company in Mexico in terms of outstanding loans and net worth.

Management Talent. Chairman Ernesto Warnholtz has held that post since 1990, and he has many years of experience as an investor in and executive of several Mexican industrial companies. Warnholtz heads a young (average age, mid-thirties) and aggressive management team culled from various other financial service companies.

Financial Status. Servicios Financieros has an impressive string of consecutive years of increased net income, stretching back into the eighties. Both the company's factoring and leasing portfolios have increased dramatically during 1993. Another indication of improved performance is the reduction of the firm's past-due portfolio to less than 4.5 from 4.7 percent.

Particular Strengths. The company's already large positions in the Mexican factoring and leasing industries will be further enhanced by the national Mexican banking charter that Servicios Financieros obtained recently. It was one of only four banking charters to be issued in the last 20 years. Currently there are fewer than 25 commercial banks operating in Mexico.

The company's new banking entity will begin operations in 1994, targeting specialized market segments tied to its asset-based financing activities. As such, it will not compete head-on with the major portion of the Mexican banking industry.

Financial statistics (figures in thousands of nominal new Pesos, except per-share amounts):

For fiscal year ended December 31	1991	1992	1993
Revenues	NP 240	NP 291	
Net income (loss)	17	(13)	
Earnings (loss) per share	1.66	(1.20)	
ADR price range/ADR:			
High			32⅜
Low			11

Investment Assessment. With more attention being paid to asset quality as Servicios Financieros expands its factoring and leasing portfolios, look for margins to improve. Coupled with expanded opportunities via the new banking operation, the financing company should rebound from the loss incurred by its telecommunications sector in 1992.

☆20 SOL PETROLEO S.A.☆

SOL PETROLEO S.A.	Stock exchange: OTC
Country: Argentina	Ticker symbol: SOLPY
Industry: Petroleum	Ratio (ADR:ORD): 1:1

ADR Trading Information.   No stranger to the financial markets, the company's shares have been traded on the Buenos Aires Stock Exchange continuously since 1925. Keeping an upward pressure on oil company prices, the Argentine market experienced tremendous demand in mid-1993 for shares of the previously state-owned oil company, Yacimientos Petroliferos Fiscales (YPF). The Argentine market gained 58 percent in $US in 1993.

Company Market.   Sol Petroleo is an integrated petroleum company involved in exploration, production, refining, and distribution in Latin America and overseas. Argentina's is one of Latin America's fastest-growing economies. The government has made moves to encourage trade, including stabilization of exchange rates, reduction of import barriers, and the privatization of most state industries.

The proliferation of free-market economies in Latin America is opening up new markets for petroleum industry companies. In Argentina, gasoline consumption is expected to grow at a rate of somewhere between 15 and 20 percent.

Company Profile.   Sol Petroleo's operations in both Bolivia and Argentina are benefiting from improved economies and the removal of government restrictions. The company's shares are 67 percent owned by Phoebus Energy, Ltd., a corporation in turn owned 50 percent by a subsidiary of the U.S. petroleum-refining and marketing firm, Diamond Shamrock, Inc., with in excess of $2.6 billion in annual revenues.

The company delivers feedstock-refined petroleum products to industrial companies in the chemical, tire, paint, and food industries. In addition, it is expanding its network of service stations with the help of Diamond Shamrock.

Management Talent.   Management draws heavily on its active Board of Directors, which include personnel from international petroleum companies such as Diamond Shamrock and Austrofueguina S.A., both of which have a financial interest in Sol Petroleo.

Financial Status.   The company carries a net worth of $29 million, and has made inroads into new markets in fiscal 1993 (ended June 30). With increased revenues as the economy and new markets expand, Sol Petroleo should switch from a loss to a profit position.

Particular Strengths.   The company's reserves in Bolivia position it to be an active player, as Bolivia becomes the geographic production and distribution center for Latin American customers in Argentina, Brazil, Chile, Paraguay, Peru, and Uruguay.

Over 50 percent of the company's refined products are exported to global markets, giving the company a broad customer base. Completion of new natural-gas pipelines to South American markets will also serve to extend its markets.

With the deregulation of the retail market, Sol Petroleo has opened more than 20 service stations in the $2 billion Buenos Aires area in the past two years.

Financial statistics (figures in millions of Pesos, except per-share amounts):

For fiscal year ended June 30	1991	1992	1993
Revenues	73	19	52
Net income (loss)	(14)	(3)	(1)

Investment Assessment.   Expanding markets, new-product capability, new pipelines coming on-stream, entrance into the retail service station market, and added capacity—all of these point to better years ahead for Sol Petroleo S.A. Deregulation of the hydrocarbon sector in 1991 prohibited the company from exporting until September 1991, sharply reducing both fiscal 1991 and fiscal 1992 operating and financial results. The company is now back on track, regaining export business lost during the restrictive period.

Sol Petroleo, though a small player, is uniquely positioned to benefit from changing government policies and enlarging markets. For adventuresome investors.

☆ 21 MADECO S.A. ☆

MADECO S.A.
Country: Chile
Industry: Copper/aluminum products

Stock exchange: NYSE
Ticker symbol: MAD
Ratio (ADR:ORD): 1:10E

ADR Trading Information.   The initial offering of MADECO S.A. ADRs hit the street in mid-1993 at a price of $15 per ADR. Since then the ADRs have surged to a 1993 peak of $29¼ per ADR, before topping out at $41¼ per ADR in early 1994 and declining to the $30 range.

Company Market.   MADECO S.A. produces a variety of products made of copper and aluminum, for four specific markets: telecommunications (25 percent); construction (33 percent); consumer products packaging (14 percent); and mining, energy, and related industrial products (28 percent).

Substantial demand exists for telephone lines in both Argentina and Chile, and anticipated growth in both economies will boost demand for commercial and residential telecommunications cable and line installation services.

There has been a strong demand for construction materials in recent years, as the Chilean economy has rebounded due to the liberal government investment and trade policies instituted beginning in 1990. Gross domestic product increased from 2.1 percent in 1990 to over 10.4 percent in 1992, while the inflation rate was cut from over 27 percent to a four-year low of 12.7 percent in 1992.

Anticipated new mining projects promise to increase sales to this market segment over the next half-decade, but a decrease in the number of energy projects will partially offset the higher mining-product revenues. Continued growth in the Chilean food industry signals a greater demand for consumer-product packaging.

Company Profile.   MADECO S.A. is Chile's leading manufacturer of copper and aluminum products, its largest manufacturer of copper building wire, its largest flexible-packaging-product manufacturer, and the producer of a variety of mining, energy, and other products ranging from transmission cable to aluminum sheets for appliances, and from coin blanks and minted coins to solar heating equipment.

Of its $270 million in revenues, nearly 68 percent is derived from sales within Chile, over 9 percent from neighboring Argentina, and around 23 percent from exports to other countries around the globe.

The company is the only domestic supplier of telecommunications cable to four of the five line installers. The number of lines installed has increased dramatically over the past few years, nearly tripling. Nonetheless, the Chilean Ministry of Transportation and Telecommunications estimated in 1990 that there were only 10 lines per 100 inhabitants in Chile, versus 30 per 100 in Spain and 50 per 100 in the United States.

The company dominates the domestic market for copper tubes, aluminum profiles, and building wire. In addition, it exports to more than

30 countries. MADECO's consumer-packaging products meet the stringent standards of world-class food producers such as Nestlé Chile S.A. In fact, Nestlé is one of MADECO's five largest customers.

The company's Alusa subsidiary is the nation's largest producer of printed flexible plastic, aluminum foil, and laminated packaging products, with an overall 40 percent market share.

Management Talent. Principal shareholders with nearly 66 percent of outstanding shares, the Luksic family also plays an active role on the Board of Directors. The Luksics control more than 50 companies in Argentina and Chile, with combined revenues in excess of $1 billion. Most members of the MADECO management team, led by Carlos Vicuna Fuentes, sport over 20 years of experience with the company.

Financial Status. MADECO has steadily increased revenues and net income in recent years. Improving earnings provide plenty of cashflow and capital for expansion, facility renovations, and acquisitions. Unlike a lot of other Latin American ADRs, the company pays a cash dividend. Since 1986, MADECO has paid cash dividends equivalent to at least 50 percent of annual net income. The most recent cash dividend totaled 10.62 cents per ADR paid in February 1994.

Particular Strengths. Major market positions in the majority of its product lines gives MADECO plenty of operating flexibility. As the Chilean and Argentinean economies continue to expand, MADECO should be one of the major beneficiaries. Its diverse operations help to protect revenues and earnings against a downturn in any one industry sector, and its strong position in the food-packaging market will allow it to piggyback growth in the expanding food industry.

Financial statistics (figures in millions of Chilean Pesos, except per-share amounts):

For fiscal year ended December 31	1991	1992	1993
Revenues	108	121	128
Net income (loss)	11	11	13
Earnings per share	36.09	37.31	46.54
ADR price range/ADR:			
High			29¼
Low			15

Investment Assessment. With a rebound in the Latin American and world economies, MADECO is positioned to post steady revenue and earnings gains. The company is well managed, and possesses strategic major-market positions in the industries it serves.

☆ 22 MAVESA, S.A. ☆

MAVESA, S.A.
Country: Venezuela
Industry: Food processing/
    consumer products

Stock exchange: OTC
Ticker symbol: MVSAY

Ratio (ADR:ORD): 1:20

ADR Trading Information. Mavesa, S.A. ADRs came to market at an initial price of $8.16 per ADR in mid-1993.

Company Market. Mavesa, S.A. operates in the Venezuelan food processing and consumer products industries. As in the United States, brand recognition and an efficient distribution system are key determinants for success in the competitive consumer products and food industries.

Company Profile. Mavesa, S.A. is one of Venezuela's largest food processors, and enjoys major market shares in a number of products including margarine (89 percent), vinegar (67 percent), cheese products (48 percent), mayonnaises (40 percent), and vegetable oils (40 percent). In addition, the company dominates the laundry soap segment, with a 78 percent market share. Its brand names are well known. Besides dominating the domestic market, Mavesa also exports internationally.

The firm operates six modern production facilities, and has in place an established product-distribution system that has been in development since the company's founding in 1949.

Management Talent. Executive President and Director Juan Fernando Roche has been employed at Mavesa since 1982, and holds a Master of Business Administration degree from the University of Wisconsin. Management team members have industry experience with international food and consumer-product giants such as Gillette and Pillsbury.

Financial Status. The company has over $100 million in short-term investments and less than $20 million in long-term debt. The company's strong balance sheet and good cashflow provide ample capital for expansion, modernization, key acquisitions, and new product introductions.

Particular Strengths. Mavesa is using its strong market position and brand recognition to extend its product lines and fend off heightened competition from lower-priced competitor products. The company's efficient distribution system and high-tech manufacturing facilities give it an edge over less-well-positioned competitors. Mavesa's sales and distribution system services nearly 55,000 stores throughout Venezuela, representing 90 percent of all stores that sell food and consumer products. Rising market share in most of the firm's product lines delivers increased economies of scale and lower costs.

Financial statistics (figures in millions of U.S. dollars, except per-share amounts):

For fiscal year ended Oct. 31	1992	1993
Revenues	$242	$196
Net income (loss)	13.5	7.5
Earnings per share	.34	.19

Investment Assessment. Feeling the pressure from low-priced competition, Mavesa experienced reduced revenues in 1993. Yet the company's financial prowess, introduction of new products specifically designed to meet the competition head-on, and superior market position and distribution system will allow it to regain market share.

The ADR price should respond favorably as Mavesa returns to its track record of earnings increases. The one factor that could dampen enthusiasm for Mavesa's shares and ADRs is the ability of Venezuela to maintain an orderly political and economic environment in the years ahead, as evidenced by the government's move in June 1994 to set price controls. There are some good possibilities but with Mavesa not for the risk-averse investor.

☆ 23 DANKA BUSINESS ☆ SYSTEMS PLC

DANKA BUSINESS SYSTEMS PLC
Country: United Kingdom
Industry: Office equipment/supplies

Stock exchange: NASDAQ
Ticker symbol: DANKY
Ratio (ADR:ORD): 1:2

ADR Trading Information. Danka Business Systems' ADRs first traded in the United States in late 1992, with an initial issue price of 4% per ADR. They hit a high of 5% per ADR in 1992, rose to $20 per ADR in 1993, and peaked at 23% per ADR in early 1994 before drifting back to the $18-per-ADR level. Danka's ADRs ranked as the top-performing of all ADRs in 1993, with a better than 295 percent rise.

Company Market. Although headquartered in the United Kingdom, Danka Business Systems generates over 90 percent of its annual revenues from the United States, and is currently expanding its U.S. network of stores featuring copiers, fax machines, and other automated office equipment and supplies.

Traditionally a fragmented industry with a proliferation of local mom-and-pop operators, the U.S. office equipment and supplies market is rapidly consolidating through acquisitions and aggressive expansion plans by major industry players.

Company Profile. Danka Business Systems PLC is the second-largest independent distributor of office equipment and supplies in the United States, with over 130 outlets in 25 states. It dominates the Southeastern U.S. market, and maintains a strong position in the Midwestern and Northeastern markets. It serves the office needs of industrial, commercial, and institutional customers.

The company is actively expanding its U.S. retail outlets, with nine acquisitions in 1993 alone. In a major move to expand national service coverage, Danka purchased a wholesale warehouse and 18 retail outlets in 14 states, many of which had not been heavily covered by Danka previously.

The firm is the leading distributor for Konica, Minolta, and Copystar copiers in the United States, and is one of the largest suppliers of Canon copiers.

Management Talent. Director and Chairman Mark A. Vaughan-Lee has held those corporate capacities since 1986. His previous experience includes the directorship of an investment banking firm. Chief Executive Dan M. Doyle founded Danka Industries, Inc., which had been acquired by Danka Business Systems PLC in late 1986. Vaughan-Lee, Doyle, and several other officers own substantial company shares.

Financial Status. The company generates significant cashflow for use in ongoing operations and acquisitions. Long-term debt stands at a minimal $19 million.

Particular Strengths. In 1993, inventory turnover increased by 63 percent, and earnings per share jumped by 58 percent. A solid focus on customer service, and the breadth of its product line, are making Danka the dealer of choice. Danka retains over 90 percent of its service-and-supplies customers from one year to the next, compared to the industry average of 60 to 70 percent. On top of that, 70 percent of equipment sales come from existing customers looking to upgrade.

Its financial stability and successful acquisition track record will keep it a major player as industry consolidation continues. There's plenty of room to grow: Despite its position as the second-largest independent distributor, Danka controls only an estimated 1 percent of the market.

Financial statistics (figures in millions of US$, except per-ADR amounts):

For fiscal year ended March 31	1992	1993	1994
Revenues	$236	$353	$531
Net income (loss)	5	21	27
Earnings per ADR	.11	.51	.585
ADR Price Range/ADR:			
High	10¼	40	
Low	8¾	10⅛	

Investment Assessment. The addition of Dex Business Systems to Danka's operations not only provides a number of operational synergies but expands its customer base and geographical scope.

Danka sports a growing customer base, which in turn seeks more sophisticated equipment with higher margins. The company is continuing its winning ways in fiscal 1994, with increased revenues, faster inventory turns, and higher earnings per ADR.

Look for Danka to carve out even more market share in the years ahead, plus maintain its ability to generate higher earnings and stock prices.

☆24 AMOY☆
PROPERTIES LIMITED

AMOY PROPERTIES LIMITED   Stock exchange: OTC
Country: Hong Kong   Ticker symbol: APL
Industry: Real Estate Investment   Ratio (ADR:ORD): 1:5

ADR Trading Information. Amoy Properties Limited ADRs came to market in the United States in early 1993, and have traded in a range between $10\frac{1}{8}$ per ADR and $6\frac{1}{4}$ per ADR.

Company Market. Amoy invests in office and commercial real estate properties in Hong Kong. Southeast Asia represents one of the fastest-growing economies in the world, paced by expanding Chinese trade. While there is some concern about the Chinese takeover of Hong Kong in 1997, the long-term future for investment in Hong Kong looks bright.

In fact, interest in the Hong Kong stock market, on the part of many companies that do business in China, pushed the Hong Kong Exchange up 97 percent in $US during 1993.

Amoy intends to eventually expand its operations into China's key real estate markets such as Shanghai, Beijing, and Guangzhou, using the same strategies that have worked so well in Hong Kong.

Company Profile. Amoy Properties Limited is one of the largest property investment companies in Hong Kong. Its strategy consists of purchasing properties along key transportation routes. It specializes in adding value to its property portfolio via refurbishment, redevelopment, and an improved tenant mix.

As one of the largest and financially strongest players in the Hong Kong commercial and office real estate market, Amoy encounters less competition for major properties. The company typically purchases over HK$2 billion in properties on an annual basis. Holdings include industrial buildings, galleria shopping developments, office complexes, and restaurants.

Management Talent. Amoy Properties Limited is a subsidiary of Hang Lung Development Company, Limited, which also owns Grand Hotel Holdings, Limited. Amoy and Hang Lung complement each other, since Amoy specializes in office and commercial properties while Hang Lung specializes in residential properties. Ronnie Chichung Chan serves as Amoy Chairman.

Financial Status. To take advantage of real estate opportunities, Amoy raised HK$2.3 billion through a rights issue of 3 new shares for each existing 10 shares in April 1992.

Particular Strengths. Amoy's status as one of the largest office and commercial real estate investors in Hong Kong gives the company the clout to make big deals work in its favor. With its long-term investment perspective, it has successfully managed and redeveloped properties.

Amoy maintains a well-balanced portfolio, with 50 percent in commercial properties, 36 percent in office properties, and 14 percent in residential and industrial properties. It strategically acquires properties along high-transportation routes and in expanding areas.

Financial statistics (figures in millions of US$, except per-ADR amounts):

For fiscal year ended June 31	1991	1992	1993
Revenues	$183	$228	$251
Net income (loss)	118	157	176
Earnings per ADR	.31	.35	.39
ADR price range/ADR:			
High			8½
Low			6⅜

Investment Assessment. Amoy Properties Limited's strategy of improving tenant mix and upgrading acquired properties works well in Hong Kong, and promises to transfer easily to mainland China as that country opens up more to outside investment.

Enhanced properties lead to higher rents and a fatter bottom line. Amoy's impressive track record of sharply rising earnings should continue unabated.

☆ 25 SHANGHAI ☆ ERFANGJI COMPANY, LIMITED

SHANGHAI ERFANGJI
   COMPANY, LIMITED
Country: People's Republic of China
Industry: Industrial
   Machinery/Textile

Stock exchange: OTC
Ticker symbol: SHFGY

Ratio (ADR:ORD): 1:10

ADR Trading Information. Shanghai Erfangji Company, Limited became the first People's Republic of China firm to be traded in the United States, with the establishment of its ADRs in late 1993. The ADRs have traded in a wide range, with a high of $49\frac{3}{8}$ per ADR and a low of $7\frac{1}{4}$ per ADR.

Company Market. China's economy has been expanding at a better than 13 percent chip (compared to 2 to 4 percent growth for the United States and Western Europe), ranking the country at the head of the world's five strongest economies in terms of real gross national product growth.

Assuming no major political or economic disruptions, China's emergence as a world-class trading partner will remain on track. With over 1.2 billion people, China represents a huge untapped consumer market with rising levels of financial independence. President Clinton's renewal of China's most-favored-nation status in May 1994 promises to keep China's growth prospects intact. China's gross domestic product is expected to grow at a rate of around 10 percent in 1994.

Due to China's low-cost labor (around one-fourth of Mexico's labor cost), labor-intensive manufacturing plants, such as textiles, will be attracted to China. A number of textile firms already operate in special economic zones established by China to attract foreign investment.

Company Profile. Founded in 1923, Shanghai Erfangji Company, Limited is one of the largest Chinese manufacturers of textile machinery. In 1988 the company became the first Chinese state-owned, textile-machinery enterprise to gain autonomy in its import and expert activities, and in 1991 became a joint-stock company.

Shanghai Erfangji is a leading Chinese producer of natural and synthetic fiber-spinning machinery. Annual production capacity entails 2400 natural-fiber-spinning machinery units and 30 sets of synthetic-spinning machinery.

The company also is test-marketing designs of additional lines of spinning machinery, to be used in conjunction with its existing products. A technology-transfer and joint-manufacture contract with a German producer targets increased production of a new generation of spinning equipment, such as the automatic cone-winder introduced in 1993. Another advance in high-tech operations was made when Shanghai Erfangji invested in a Computer Integrated Manufacturing System (CIMS) in the early 1990s.

Management Talent.   Making the move from a state-owned company to a competitive one operating in a more-or-less free-market economy is never easy. Yet under Chairman Zheng Kequin, the company has established quality-control standards and restructured its operations so as to improve production efficiency.

Financial Status.   While still a fledgling enterprise in the competitive realm, Shanghai Erfangji has made good progress in improving revenue and earnings. The proceeds from stock and ADR issues have bolstered the balance sheet and provided capital for plant and equipment modernization.

Particular Strengths.   As one of China's 500 largest enterprises, and one that has been in business since 1923, Shanghai Erfangji knows the ins and outs of the Chinese spinning machinery market. It has long-standing relationships with many of its customers, which may need to upgrade their machinery as they strive to remain competitive in an environment of international trade. In addition, China's attractiveness as a low-cost location for textile manufacturing will lure new customers to Shanghai Erfangji.

Financial statistics (figures in millions of US$, except per-ADR amounts):

For year ended December 31	1991	1992	1993
Revenues	84	115	146
Net income (loss)	5	26	25
Earnings per ADR	.38	.78	.59
ADR price range/ADR:			
High			$49\frac{3}{8}$
Low			$18\frac{3}{8}$

Investment Assessment. Shanghai Erfangji targets becoming a major textile-machinery manufacturer in the international market, driven by high-quality products and superior after-sales customer service. With its low labor cost base, years of spinning-machinery expertise, and recent moves to technologically upgrade its manufacturing processes and product lines, the company is working hard to transform itself into a major global contender.

In 1993, Shanghai Erfangji's revenues rose substantially. Given a stable political environment, Shanghai Erfangji is poised to improve on that record.

☆ 26 HAI SUN HUP ☆ GROUP LIMITED

HAI SUN HUP GROUP LIMITED   Stock exchange: OTC
Country: Singapore   Ticker symbol: HISHF
Industry: Transportation   Ratio (ADR:ORD): 1:5

ADR Trading Information. Hai Sun Hup Group Limited's ADRs initiated trading in the American OTC market in mid-December of 1993.

Company Market. Along with other Far Eastern countries, Singapore ranked as the fourth-strongest world economy as we said good-bye to 1994 and headed on toward the twenty-first century. Singapore is emerging as a major service center and supplier for Southeast Asia, a great boost for transportation revenues. The worldwide economic stagnation has put a damper on the revenues and earnings of transportation companies around the globe.

Company Profile. Hai Sun Hup Group Limited has grown since its founding in 1935 into one of Singapore's leading shipping groups. It offers a wide variety of transportation services, including sea transportation of automobile, oil, liquid-chemical, and container cargo; warehousing and distribution; sea and air freight forwarding; intra-island transport; courier services; port terminal operation; and marine supplies.

Extending its market reach and transportation capabilities, Hai Sun joint-ventures with Japanese and European shipping principals such as

Mitsui O.S.K. Lines, Ltd. and Intermaritime Ltd. (Germany). The company maintains regional offices in Malaysia, Thailand, Indonesia, and Hong Kong—all areas with high economic-growth potential. Hai Sun derives its revenues from three industry segments: ship owning, management, and chartering (58 percent); agencies, terminals, and logistics (39 percent); and trading (3 percent).

Management Talent.   Executive Chairman Ow Chio Kiat plays an active role in the shipping firm, with ownership of over 29 percent of the company's outstanding shares. He joined the Group in 1962 and assumed management in 1966. Other company directors have extensive transportation industry experience, both in and out of the company.

Financial Status.   The company has a better than 4:1 current-asset-to-current-liability ratio. During fiscal 1993, a private placement of nearly 20 million new shares generated over S$41 million, to fill company coffers and for investment in more specialized vessels to meet shipping demand.

Particular Strengths.   Hai Sun is strategically located to serve the transportation and logistics requirements of the expanding Indonesian and Chinese economies. Its key joint-venture agreements with major world transportation groups allow the company to tap new markets with less commitment of capital and a lower level of risk. Joint-venture trading partners already have established offices in key markets such as the United States, Africa, Europe, and Japan.

Hai Sun's broad range of transportation services gives the company a broad revenue and customer base to help it weather downturns in segments of the industry.

Financial statistics (figures in millions of S$, except per-share amounts):

For fiscal year ended March 31	1991	1992	1993
Revenues	134	155	162
Net income (loss)	19	22	25
Earnings per share	.129	.149	.127

Investment Assessment.   Despite the global recession, Hai Sun held its own in fiscal 1993 and 1994, with increased revenues and earnings. A rebound in the overall world economy; increased demand for transportation and logistics services from expanding Southeast and Far East Asia; new specialized vessels coming on-stream; and further penetration of major transportation markets via joint-venture arrangements—all these place Hai Sun in an excellent position to achieve strong gains.

☆ 27 TEVA ☆ PHARMACEUTICAL INDUSTRIES LIMITED

TEVA PHARMACEUTICAL		
INDUSTRIES LIMITED	Stock exchange:	NASDAQ
Country: Israel	Ticker symbol:	TEVIY
Industry: Pharmaceuticals	Ratio (ADR:ORD):	1:12

ADR Trading Information. Teva Pharmaceutical Industries ADRs have been traded in the United States for over a decade. The ADRs hit a 1992 high of $22½ per ADR in 1992, rose nearly 50 percent in 1993 to another new high of $33½ per ADR, then climbed to $34½ per ADR in early 1994.

Company Market. Teva Pharmaceutical Industries Limited competes in the pharmaceutical industry in Israel, Europe, and the United States with generic drug products.

The industry is characterized by stiff competition, from other generic drug producers and because of the entry of the major pharmaceutical companies into the generic drug segment via acquisitions.

In recent years, falsified testing information by some generic drug producers has tainted the industry, causing some consumers to switch back to brand-name drugs.

Company Profile. Founded over a half-century ago, Teva Pharmaceutical has grown into Israel's leading producer of pharmaceuticals, specializing in generic drugs. It generates its revenues from a variety of products: human pharmaceuticals (66 percent), chemicals (15 percent), hospital supplies (10 percent), veterinary pharmaceuticals (6 percent), and yeast and alcohol (3 percent).

Around 49 percent of sales are generated within Israel, the balance coming from North America (35 percent), Europe (9 percent), and the rest of the world (7 percent).

Over the years the company has grown through acquisitions, and beginning in 1986, Teva entered the large U.S. pharmaceutical market with an aggressive growth strategy. Expansion outside of Israel is fueling revenue growth in the 20-plus percent range.

Management Talent.   Chairman Moshe Shamir and President and Chief Executive Officer Eli Hurvitz have done an outstanding job of penetrating the U.S. and European markets.

Financial Status.   Improving earnings and margins are contributing to a healthy cashflow. Long-term debt is minimal, at $36 million, with plenty of bank credit for key acquisitions.

Particular Strengths.   Teva Pharmaceutical places a great deal of emphasis on research and development of new products. Its track record of obtaining U.S. Food and Drug Administration approval for new drugs has been impressive. With a number of major proprietary drugs coming off-patent over the next few years, Teva is well positioned to garner more market share.

Management has proven adept at entering new markets in the United States and abroad. Its blending of acquisitions into its corporate structure has gone well.

Financial statistics (figures in millions of $US, except per-ADR amounts):

For fiscal year ended Dec. 31	1991	1992	1993
Revenues	$321	$396	$502
Net income (loss)	23	32	57
Earnings per ADR	.46	.61	1.07
ADR price range/ADR:			
High	$10\frac{1}{8}$	$22\frac{5}{8}$	$33\frac{1}{2}$
Low	$5\frac{1}{2}$	$9\frac{5}{8}$	17

Investment Assessment.   Results for 1993 came in more than 30 percent higher than the already impressive 1992 revenues and earnings. Teva will continue to make inroads into the United States and other key markets with acquisitions, new generic products, and its own proprietary drugs.

Teva is a solid company seeking out unique market opportunities. A new Israeli 10% tax on stock profits beginning in 1995 caused their stock price to fall, making the shares even more attractive.

5
Scoring with Special Situations

Every industry reacts to economic, political, and other events in different ways, depending on certain factors such as its place in the current economic cycle, industry technological advances, the impact of interest rates on operations, and various other factors.

Likewise, certain companies within those industries are better positioned to take advantage of opportunities as they arise due to management quality, financial strength, market position, research and development efforts, etc.

To illustrate, the trend toward consolidation in the banking industry has accelerated growth of some super-regional financial institutions such as Banc One, KeyCorp, and Norwest. These have made significant inroads into new markets through an aggressive and successful acquisition strategy.

In the same vein, the health care industry is undergoing changes that will drastically alter existing underlying industry fundamentals. The proliferation of discount and generic drug outlets has changed the complexion of industry pricing policies that have stood for decades. The Clinton Administration's push on health care reform has already sent ripples through the industry and sent shell-shocked health care stock prices to lower levels.

Health care companies with unique market niches, extensive research and development programs, product-line breadth, efficient distribution networks, solid financials, and financial and operating flexibility are primed to perform well in any health care environment.

These and other industry trends not only present challenges to company management, they also herald significant opportunities to garner market share and improve revenues and earnings, as some companies fall by the wayside and others react too late or with the wrong strategies in light of the new industry realities.

Ferreting out the winners, in the ever-changing realm of corporate competition, can pay off big for investors also. Rising revenues, larger market share, increased earnings, and raised dividend payouts translate into surging stock prices and capital gains.

With that in mind, here's a list of companies covering a number of industries headed to the twenty-first century with their sights solidly set on substantial gains in their market position and operating and financial results.

Special Situation Candidates

COMPANY	INDUSTRY
Abbott Laboratories	Health Care/Pharmaceuticals
Banc One Corporation	Banking
Beckman Instruments, Inc.	Laboratory Instruments
Calgon Carbon Corporation	Carbon Products
Charter One Financial, Inc.	Thrift Financial Institution
Countrywide Credit Industries, Inc.	Mortgage Lender
Gentex Corporation	Automotive Mirrors/Fire Protection
KeyCorp	Banking
Merck & Company, Inc.	Health Care/Specialty Chemicals
Norwest Corporation	Banking
St. Jude Medical, Inc.	Medical Devices
Sensormatic Electronics Corp.	Electronic Security Systems

Now sit back and learn about each of these leaders of tomorrow. Each firm possesses attributes that will keep it ahead of the pack in terms of performance.

☆ 28 ABBOTT ☆ LABORATORIES

ABBOTT LABORATORIES   Stock exchange: NYSE
One Abbott Park Road   Ticker symbol: ABT
Abbott Park, IL 60064-3500   DRIP program: Yes

708-937-6100   Ownership:
                                      Institutional: + 50%
                                      Insiders: + 3%

Industry Review.   The health care and medical supplies industry is in
flux, given the proliferation of health care reform packages being promoted. To be sure there is a higher degree of risk in investing in the
health care business now than there was before the Clinton Administration set out to reform the health care industry.

While the final shape of this country's health care structure still can-
not be discerned, what is clear is that industry companies with substantial financial resources will fare better than firms with less financial
strength to seize market opportunities and weather temporary turbu-
lence as health care reforms take their final shape. Larger companies
with broader product lines also will be better able to absorb changes in
pricing under government guidelines, if enacted.

Yet regardless of what goes on at the governmental level, the trend
toward double-digit revenue and earnings gains will continue, spurred
on by increased product demand, an aging population, new products
coming on-stream, and penetration into new markets.

Company Profile.   Abbott Laboratories is a worldwide producer of
hospital products, diagnostics, nutritional products, and pharmaceuticals. The company is adept at turning out new products and churning
out record revenues and earnings. Its diverse operations provide a balanced approach to growth and stability in the company's performance
results. The company sells its many products in over 130 countries
worldwide.

Not waiting to see the final outcome of health care reform, Abbott has
been proactively cutting costs and improving operating efficiencies.
Long-term contracts with key hospital and health care purchasers provide a steady base of business for the years ahead.

Abbott outpaces all competitors in sales of infant formula and medical nutritionals in the United States, and also maintains a leading
global position in anesthetics and in several key diagnostic areas. The
company's Abbott Diagnostics Division is the recognized leader in the
field, with $2 billion of the $13 billion global diagnostics market. Eager
to sustain its leadership role, Abbott spends nearly 10 percent of annual
revenues on research and development efforts.

Abbott derives its business from four nearly equal segments: nutri-
tion (28 percent), diagnostics (26 percent), pharmaceutical (24 percent),
and hospital supply (22 percent).

Management Talent.   Chairman and Chief Executive Officer Duane L. Burnham rose from Vice Chairman and Chief Financial Officer to his present position in 1990, and first became a company officer in 1982. President and Chief Operating Officer Thomas R. Hodgson was first elected a company officer in 1980.

Financial Status.   With operating margins among the best in the industry, Abbott enjoys a solid balance sheet. Working capital stands at nearly $800 million, and long-term debt (around $300 million) consists of low-cost industrial revenue bonds and other debt securities totaling less than 4 percent of capital.

Cashflow.   With an average return on equity in the high 30 percent range, cashflow comes in at around $2.30 per share. The cash dividend has been rising at a double-digit clip for many years, and excess cash has been used for stock buybacks.

DRIP Details.   Abbott's dividend reinvestment program is at no cost to the shareholder, and permits additional cash investments of $10 to $5000 per quarter. For information, write to Abbott Shareholder Services, One Abbott Park Road, Abbott Park, IL 60064-3500, or call 708-937-3923.

Particular Strengths.   Consistency of performance has been Abbott's mainstay. For 22 consecutive years Abbott has increased shareholder's return on equity, which stood at over 38 percent in 1993. Leading market positions and heavy research-and-development expenditures will keep Abbott in the industry forefront in terms of performance.

Strategic joint ventures, such as the one with Takeda Chemical Industries, Ltd. of Japan, help Abbott to enter new markets and to tap the research expertise of other industry companies.

Solid financials, with low debt and nearly $150 million in investment securities, give Abbott plenty of operating flexibility.

Financial statistics (figures in millions, except per-share numbers):

For fiscal year ended December 31	1990	1991	1992	1993
Revenues	$6,159	$6,877	$7,852	$8,407
Net income (loss)	966	1,089	1,289	1,399
Earnings (loss)/share	1.11	1.27	1.47	1.69
Dividend/share	.42	.50	.60	.78
Long-term debt	135	125	110	310
Stock price range/share:				
High	23⅛	34¾	34⅛	30⅞
Low	15⅝	19⅝	28⅛	22⅝

Investment Assessment.   Abbott's stock price, along with that of other healthcare companies, has been hit by concern over the eventual outcome of healthcare reform legislation. The company is sound financially, has an excellent track record in research and development and product approval, and a dominant market position in key areas.

The company's sound fundamentals will continue to win out in the years ahead, with earnings increases up to the 15 percent range and higher stock prices over the long term.

☆ 29 BANC ONE ☆
CORPORATION

BANC ONE CORPORATION
100 East Broad Street
Columbus, OH 43271
614-248-5944

Stock exchange: NYSE
Ticker symbol: ONE
DRIP program: Yes
Ownership:
  Institutional: + 53%
  Insiders: + 10%

Industry Review.   Banking bottom lines are improving, as the size of nonperforming assets decreases and operating efficiencies take hold. However, the stock market has been selling off bank shares, as the interest-rate environment looks like it will start to heat up in the wake of Federal Reserve actions.

Industry consolidation, with superregionals buying their way into new markets and expanding their presence in old territories, moves ahead. The main risks are that some banks may end up paying too much for sought-after banking franchises, or that the match-up won't deliver the hoped-for operating and marketing synergies.

Bank earnings as a whole moved up strongly in 1993. How well they adapt to the new interest-rate scenario and maintain a quality loan portfolio will determine their level of performance in 1994 and beyond.

Company Profile.   Banc One ranks as a major superregional Midwest bank, but it has also been stretching its territory to include such lucrative markets as rebounding Colorado and Kentucky.

Run by several generations of McCoys, Banc One has carved out a profitable market through key acquisitions in states bordering Ohio, and it is now extending that successful strategy to other areas of the country. Its well-thought-out acquisition strategy seeks out markets in which it can immediately become one of the three top banks, with room to grow market share through innovative products and cross-selling of services.

Banc One benefits from operating synergies, setting up strict performance measures, and keeping local management focused on enhancing business with its customers via new products and services. The strategy has paid off handsomely, for Banc One's track record is unequaled. Over the past 10 years this Columbus, Ohio–headquartered financial institution has earned first place among the 25 largest U.S. banks in return on average assets, return on common equity, and average equity to assets.

Through 1993, Banc One's earnings per share have increased for 25 consecutive years, more than three times longer than any of the nation's other 25 largest banks. Its five-year average revenue growth rate exceeds 20 percent, while earnings per share have been increasing at a 13 percent annual pace. Adding diversity to the bank's operations, Banc One is a leading processor of debit/credit card transactions.

Management Talent. Chairman and Chief Executive Officer John B. McCoy assumed the chair in 1987, after having served as company president for three years. His family has guided Banc One for two generations. McCoy rules through partnership with his management team and local bank managers, giving them authority to run their operations but backing them up with innovative products and services and back-office efficiencies. It is up to them to meet or beat tough operating and financial-performance criteria.

Financial Status. Banc One's vital signs are good. Its loan portfolio credit quality is holding up, net interest margin is expanding, and the return on average assets also is improving.

DRIP Program. Participants in Banc One's dividend reinvestment program can invest between $10 to $5000 in cash per quarter, with no administration cost. For information on the DRIP program, call 1-800-753-7107.

Particular Strengths. Banc One has successfully pulled off a number of major banking acquisitions without negatively impacting earnings. Its entrance into new markets such as those of Colorado, Utah, and West Virginia, as well as further penetrations in Indiana, Kentucky, and other Midwest territories, strengthens its grip on the market.

With its over $80 billion in assets, Banc One has the clout to bid for choice acquisitions without having to overpay. Management has been adept at increasing its loan portfolio without taking on undue credit risk. Within the industry, its portfolio quality is seen as being stellar.

Financial statistics (figures in millions, except per-share numbers):

For fiscal year ended December 31	1990	1991	1992	1993
Assets	$27,654	$33,861	$58,249	$76,500
Net income (loss)	423	530	781	1,125
Earnings (loss)/share	2.01	2.33	2.62	3.25
Dividend/share	.72	.82	.93	1.13
Long-term debt	581	703	1,198	1,500
Stock price range/share:				
High	24⅛	38⅜	42¾	49¼
Low	13⅞	18⅛	33¾	35½

Investment Assessment. In 1994, Banc One's stock price dropped to a more than two-year low (around the $32-per-share level), due to concern over the bank's use of off-balance-sheet derivatives. Derivatives are confusing to the average investor, but if they are handled properly they play an important role in the portfolio management and overall profit performance of a bank. The evidence to date is that Banc One management knows its way around the derivative world, for its use of derivatives has worked to reduce risk and improve performance. The bank deals exclusively with top-tier derivative counter-parties/dealers, and requires cross-collateralization of its exposures.

Banc One's underlying fundamentals are strong, and the market reaction has been unduly negative in light of its superb performance. Over time, and with continued excellent results from Banc One, these fears will be calmed and the bank's stock price should surpass its former highs. (See Fig. 5-1, Banc One stock chart.)

☆ 30 BECKMAN ☆
INSTRUMENTS, INC.

BECKMAN INSTRUMENTS, INC.
2500 Harbor Boulevard
Fullerton, CA 92634
714-871-4848

Stock exchange: NYSE
Ticker symbol: BEC
DRIP program: No
Ownership:
    Institutional: + 53%
    Insiders: + 2%

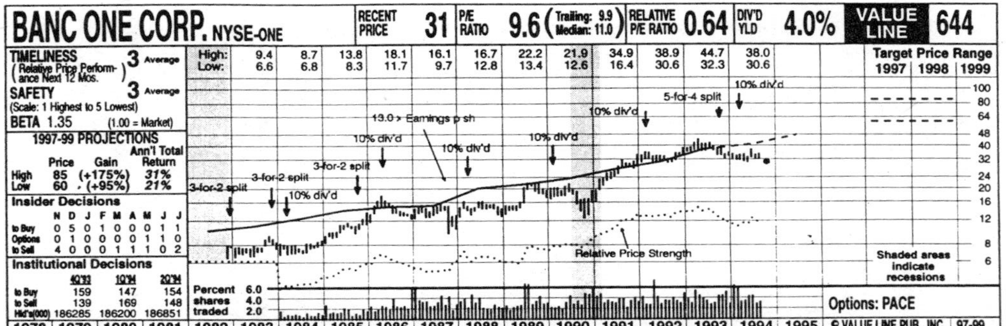

1978	1979	1980	1981	1982	1983	1984	1985	1986	1987	1988	1989	1990	1991	1992	1993	1994	1995	© VALUE LINE PUB., INC.	97-99
.46	.53	.59	.67	.78	.84	.95	1.10	1.16	1.19	1.57	1.67	1.82	2.12	2.39	2.93	*3.15*	*3.65*	Earnings per sh A E	*5.50*
.15	.18	.20	.22	.24	.28	.32	.38	.45	.49	.55	.63	.69	.76	.89	1.07	*1.24*	*1.36*	Div'ds Decl'd per sh B■	*1.80*
2.88	3.23	3.61	3.91	4.27	4.90	5.66	6.62	7.51	8.28	9.37	10.35	11.97	13.97	15.52	17.82	*19.75*	*21.15*	Book Value per sh C	*28.20*
56.98	56.97	56.24	63.43	84.75	103.45	109.45	116.59	166.52	179.96	215.03	217.81	240.23	253.83	319.11	380.69	*380.00*	*390.00*	Common Shs Outst'g D	*390.00*
6.4	5.8	5.5	6.7	7.4	9.1	8.1	10.6	12.5	11.7	9.5	10.7	9.9	12.5	14.0	13.0	*Bold figures are Value Line estimates*		Avg Ann'l P/E Ratio	*13.0*
.87	.84	.73	.81	.82	.77	.75	.86	.85	.78	.79	.81	.74	.80	.85	.76			Relative P/E Ratio	*1.00*
5.2%	5.9%	6.1%	4.9%	4.2%	3.7%	4.2%	3.3%	3.1%	3.5%	3.7%	3.5%	3.8%	2.9%	2.6%	2.8%			Avg Ann'l Div'd Yield	*3.0%*
						9106.1	10823	17372	18730	25274	26552	30336	46293	61417	79919	*88500*	*95000*	Total Assets ($mill)	*125000*
						5791.8	6598.1	11392	12752	17087	17658	20043	29659	37452	52927	*57500*	*62500*	Loans ($mill)	*75000*
						379.1	427.9	685.4	812.9	1060.5	1116.3	1240.9	1770.7	3164.9	4090.1	*4150*	*4300*	Net Interest Inc ($mill)	*4600*
						64.4	85.2	130.1	177.9	183.4	197.5	300.3	424.4	510.5	368.5	*275*	*275*	Loan Loss Prov'n ($mill)	*600*
						116.3	157.8	276.0	290.2	463.1	511.9	658.2	844.5	1159.1	1491.7	*1600*	*1750*	Noninterest Inc ($mill)	*2000*
						305.9	361.2	608.6	666.5	902.6	967.4	1102.7	1486.2	2652.8	3514.1	*3600*	*3800*	Noninterest Exp ($mill)	*4725*
						108.0	130.4	199.8	208.9	340.2	362.9	423.4	529.5	781.3	1120.6	*1200*	*1400*	Net Profit ($mill) E	*1950*
						13.7%	6.3%	10.3%	19.2%	22.3%	21.7%	22.1%	24.8%	32.7%	34.0%	*34.0%*	*34.0%*	Income Tax Rate	*32.5%*
						1.19%	1.20%	1.15%	1.12%	1.35%	1.37%	1.40%	1.14%	1.27%	1.40%	*1.55%*	*1.47%*	% Earned Total Assets	*1.55%*
						97.0	92.0	169.7	266.2	378.9	371.6	581.0	703.1	1197.5	1701.7	*2000*	*2000*	Long-Term Debt ($mill)	*2000*
						668.8	822.2	1300.0	1489.5	2040.8	2279.2	2899.5	3814.1	5213.5	7033.6	*7750*	*8500*	Net Worth ($mill)	*11000*
						7.3%	7.6%	7.5%	8.0%	8.1%	8.6%	9.6%	8.2%	8.5%	8.8%	*9.5%*	*10.0%*	% N W to Tot Assets	*9.0%*
						63.6%	61.0%	65.6%	68.1%	67.6%	66.5%	66.1%	64.1%	61.0%	64.5%	*65.0%*	*66.0%*	% Loans to Tot Assets	*60.0%*
						16.1%	15.9%	15.4%	14.0%	16.7%	15.9%	14.6%	13.9%	15.0%	15.9%	*15.5%*	*16.5%*	% Earned Net Worth	*18.0%*
						10.9%	10.5%	10.3%	8.1%	11.1%	10.0%	9.1%	9.2%	10.6%	10.5%	*11.5%*	*11.5%*	% Retained to Comm Eq	*12.0%*
						38%	38%	36%	42%	34%	38%	38%	38%	33%	36%	*37%*	*35%*	% All Div'ds to Net Prof	*33%*

BUSINESS: Banc One Corporation is among the largest banking organizations in Indiana, Ohio, Texas, and Wisconsin. Also owns banks in Illinois, Kentucky, and Michigan. Is a leading processor of debit/credit card transactions. Net loan losses last twelve months, 1.04% of average loans. Loan loss reserve, 1.98% of loans at 3/31/93; nonperforming assets, 1.75% of total loans. Loan portfolio breakdown (average) first quarter: commercial loans, 28%; real estate, 27%; consumer, 30%; other, 15%. Has about 32,700 employees; 58,114 shareholders. Insiders and subsidiaries own about 10% of the stock (3/94 proxy). Chairman & C.E.O.: John B. McCoy. President: Donald L. McWhorter. Inc.: Ohio. Address: 100 E. Broad St., Columbus, Ohio 43271. Telephone: 614-248-5944.

Figure 5-1. Banc One Corporation stock chart. *(Copyright 1994 by Value Line Publishing Inc. Reprinted by permission; all rights reserved.)*

Industry Review. As indicated in our discussion of Abbott Laboratories, the medical supplies and laboratory instruments business is in flux. Those companies with a more directed focus on specific market segments should perform well, as they garner market share from smaller companies with less human and financial resources to draw upon.

In light of budget pressures, many government-sponsored university and research institute programs have been hit hard by funding cuts.

Company Profile. Beckman Instruments started trading publicly after the 1988 spinoff from SmithKline Beckman. The company's origins date back to 1934, since which time Beckman has emerged as one of the world's leading manufacturers of laboratory instruments.

In response to the new (post-1988) market realities, Beckman restructured its operations in late 1993 to concentrate its strong franchise in clinical diagnostics and centrifugation, and direct more investment toward its biotechnology-based life-science business. The move created a significant one-time, fourth-quarter 1993 restructuring charge, but it cleared the decks for better future performance. The company trimmed nearly 11 percent of its work force, and streamlined operations in the process.

Management Talent. Chairman, President, and Chief Executive Officer Louis T. Russo now heads a leaner management team, devoted to directing its resources toward the company's core strengths and new opportunities in the lucrative life-science segment.

Financial Status. The company's reorganization and recent stock buy-back programs have negatively impacted both long-term debt and working capital positions. Long-term debt increased to over $100 million in 1993, from less than $60 million at the end of 1992.

Cashflow. Cashflow comes in at a little over $4 per share, and will improve as the company moves forward with a leaner organization. Long-term debt will be steadily reduced from the current high-water mark in excess of 30 percent of capitalization.

Particular Strengths. Now that management has bitten the bullet and refocused the company, Beckman Instruments can concentrate on its extensive technological expertise in the life sciences and diagnostic instrumentation businesses. In both of these business segments, the company has a strong track record of new-product introductions and increased market share.

Research and development expenditures also have grown steadily, increasing more than 90 percent from 1988 to over $90 million, or 10 percent of revenues by the end of 1993.

Financial statistics (figures in millions, except per-share numbers):

For fiscal year ended December 31	1990	1991	1992	1993
Revenues	$815	$858	$909	$890
Net income (loss)	36	38	44	47*
Earnings (loss)/share	1.26	1.32	1.53	1.69*
Dividend/share	.28	.28	.30	.36
Long-term debt	65	59	60	115
Stock price range/share:				
High	19	20⅝	24¼	28¼
Low	11⅞	13⅞	17⅝	19⅝

*Excludes restructuring charge of $115 million or $4.28 per share.

Investment Assessment. The fourth-quarter-1993 restructuring charge put a damper on Beckman's earnings and stock price. In the long run, the more focused strategy will deliver big dividends in the form of better margins and a stronger bottom line.

The heavier emphasis on the life-science segment will keep Beckman in the forefront of technology in this rapidly growing field, a good omen for future revenues and profits.

☆ 31 CALGON CARBON ☆ CORPORATION

CALGON CARBON CORPORATION
400 Calgon Carbon Drive
Pittsburgh, PA 15205
412-787-6700

Stock exchange: NYSE
Ticker symbol: CCC
DRIP program: No
Ownership:
   Institutional: + 43%
   Insiders: + 30%

Industry Review. Calgon Carbon operates in the specialty chemical arena but has had few major competitors, as the leading producer of granular activated carbon. However, low-cost producers of low-end activated-carbon products from abroad have been adding competitive pressures in that segment of the business.

Sluggish economic activity, both domestically and abroad, has cut into industry revenues and earnings in the past few years. In addition, plant expansions by Calgon Carbon and other producers have temporarily flooded the market with capacity and lowered price levels. However, a return to a more robust global economic environment will put the industry back on track.

Company Profile.   Calgon Carbon's activated-granular-carbon products help other companies to purify their products during their manufacturing process. Activated carbon is essential for clean water, air pollution control, and the purity of thousands of industrial and chemical products.

Calgon Carbon is the world's leading producer of granular activated-carbon products, with a 90 percent share of the U.S. public-water-treatment market and a 60 percent worldwide market share.

The company generates 58 percent of revenues from activated carbon and the balance from services (24 percent), equipment (11 percent), and charcoal/liquids (7 percent). Nearly half of revenues are from products and services sold to the industrial process market, 44 percent to the environmental segment, and the rest from consumer and other markets.

The United States accounts for 53 percent of sales and Western Europe another 37 percent, while 10 percent comes from other geographic markets.

The company operates eight activated-carbon manufacturing and six reactivation facilities in the United States, Belgium, Germany, Japan, and the United Kingdom. Its state-of-the-art research and development facility near the firm's Pittsburgh headquarters is the industry's largest and most technologically advanced.

Management Talent.   Industry veteran Thomas A. McConomy has been with Calgon Carbon for decades, and as President and Chief Executive Officer he also owns a significant stake in the company.

Financial Status.   Despite the downturn in the industry's fortunes in recent years, Calgon Carbon's balance sheet still looks pristine. Long-term debt is virtually nil, at less than $7 million. The company also enjoys a healthy current ratio of better than 4:1.

Cashflow.   Although cashflow dipped to under a $1-per-share level in 1993, it is expected to rebound in 1994 to the $1.05-per-share level. The company's cash position is fine, and the lack of any real debt positions Calgon Carbon well to ride out the present economic stagnation in good shape.

Particular Strengths. An industry-dominant position, financial strength, modern manufacturing facilities, a balanced client and geographical customer base, and solid research and development make Calgon Carbon a force to contend with in this industry.

Yet the company isn't sitting still waiting for things to happen. In response to weak international demand, Calgon Carbon cut its worldwide salaried staffing levels by 8 percent and restructured operations so as to reduce the number of manufacturing employees as well.

Financial statistics (figures in millions, except per-share amounts):

For fiscal year ended December 31	1990	1991	1992	1993
Revenues	$285	$308	$298	$269
Net income (loss)	38	38	18*	19*
Earnings (loss)/share	.94	.94	.44	.47†
Dividend/share	.15	.16	.16	.16
Long-term debt	11	28	7	7
Stock price range/share:				
High	25⅛	30¾	26¾	18⅞
Low	14⅝	17½	15¼	9⅞

*Includes one-time restructuring charges in 1993 of $1.73 million versus $5.20 million in 1992.
†After a one-time charge of $10.65 million or $.26 per share to absorb effects of accounting change.

Investment Assessment. Calgon Carbon, carved out of another featured company, Merck, came to market in 1987 and developed a devoted following as the company posted earnings gains of 30 percent on average before the worldwide slowdown hit.

The company's stock price rose from an initial offering price in 1987 of under $6 per share to an all-time high of $30¾ per share in 1991. Then the sky came crashing down. Revenues dropped by 10 percent from 1991 to 1993, and earnings per share were slashed by more than half. Calgon Carbon's stock dropped like a rock to a low of $9¾ per share in late 1993, before recovering a bit to the $13-per-share level in mid-1994. (See Fig. 5-2, Calgon Carbon Corporation stock chart.)

Now the stock is grossly underpriced, and improvement in the world economy will tip the scales in favor of higher revenues, earnings, and stock prices. Calgon Carbon represents a great turnaround candidate.

CALGON CARBON NYSE-CCC

TIMELINESS (Relative Price Perform- ance Next 12 Mos.)	4 Below Average
SAFETY (Scale: 1 Highest to 5 Lowest)	3 Average
BETA 1.30 (1.00 = Market)	
RECENT PRICE	12
P/E RATIO	11.1
Trailing: 26.7 Median: 28.6	
RELATIVE P/E RATIO	1.83
DIV'D YLD	1.3%
VALUE LINE	502

High: 11.1 15.3 23.8 25.1 30.8 26.8 18.9 15.3
Low: 5.6 8.8 12.1 14.6 17.5 15.3 9.9 11.4

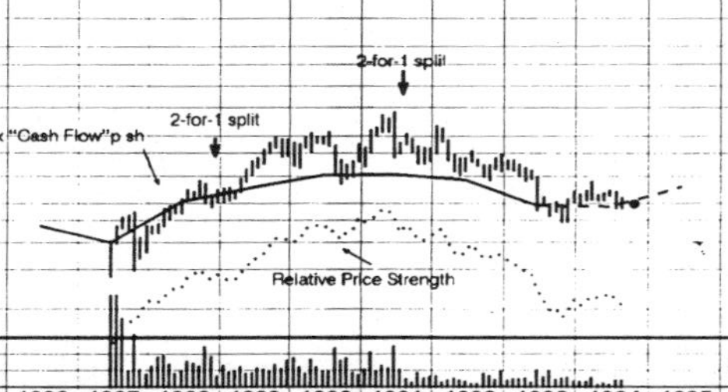

13.0 x "Cash Flow" p sh

2-for-1 split
2-for-1 split

Relative Price Strength

Shaded areas indicate recessions

Options: PHLE

Target Price Range
1997 1998 1999

1997-99 PROJECTIONS

	Price	Gain	Ann'l Total Return
High	30	(+150%)	27%
Low	19	(+60%)	13%

Insider Decisions

	N	D	J	F	M	A	M	J	J
to Buy	0	1	0	0	0	0	0	0	0
Options	0	1	0	0	0	3	0	0	0
to Sell	0	1	0	0	3	0	0	2	0

Institutional Decisions

	4Q93	1Q94	2Q94	
to Buy	39	31	35	Percent 21.0
to Sell	36	44	30	shares 14.0
Hld's(000)	18606	17393	18732	traded 7.0

Formed in 1942, Calgon Carbon Corp.'s predecessor business was owned by Merck from 1968 until April, 1985, when it was purchased by management in a leveraged buyout. An initial public offering of 10.4 mill. shares at a price of $5.50 per share (adjusted for splits) was completed in June, 1987 through Shearson Lehman and First Boston. IPO proceeds of $52.8 mill. were applied to acquisition debt. In 1988, the company purchased the net assets of the Degussa AG activated carbon and charcoal businesses for approximately $25.4 mill.

	1984	1985	1986	1987	1988	1989	1990	1991	1992	1993	1994	1995	© VALUE LINE PUB, INC.	97-99
Sales per sh	--	--	6.38	4.31	5.64	6.26	7.01	7.57	7.29	6.58	6.75	7.20	Sales per sh	9.60
"Cash Flow" per sh	--	--	.74	.62	.95	1.09	1.24	1.25	1.18	.91	.90	1.10	"Cash Flow" per sh	1.80
Earnings per sh(A)	--	--	.29	.48	.74	.87	.98	.94	.77	.47	.40	.55	Earnings per sh(A)	1.20
Div'ds Decl'd per sh(B)	--	--	--	.03	.05	.11	.15	.16	.16	.16	.16		Div'ds Decl'd per sh(B)	.24
Cap'l Spending per sh	--	--	.11	.40	.60	1.17	1.73	.59	.37	.40			Cap'l Spending per sh	.65
Book Value per sh	--	--	1.32	2.27	3.00	3.99	4.92	5.67	5.84	6.03	6.15	6.30	Book Value per sh	8.60
Common Shs Outst'g(C)	--	--	21.65	39.63	40.07	40.51	40.64	40.75	40.90	40.95	40.00	39.00	Common Shs Outst'g(C)	39.00
Avg Ann'l P/E Ratio	--	--	--	17.9	16.3	20.2	21.2	24.1	24.9	29.8			Avg Ann'l P/E Ratio	20.0
Relative P/E Ratio	--	--	--	1.20	1.35	1.53	1.57	1.54	1.51	1.76	Bold figures are		Relative P/E Ratio	1.55
Avg Ann'l Div'd Yield	--	--	--	.3%	.4%	.6%	.7%	.7%	.8%	1.1%	Value Line estimates		Avg Ann'l Div'd Yield	1.0%
Sales ($mill)	--	--	138.2	170.7	226.1	253.4	284.9	308.4	298.4	269.4	270	280	Sales ($mill)	375
Operating Margin	--	--	27.0%	27.6%	26.4%	25.7%	25.7%	24.1%	23.0%	19.6%	17.5%	19.0%	Operating Margin	25.0%
Depreciation ($mill)	--	--	5.4	7.9	8.6	9.0	10.8	13.0	16.7	18.2	19.5	20.0	Depreciation ($mill)	23.0
Net Profit ($mill)	--	--	11.4	17.6	29.5	35.2	39.6	38.1	31.6	19.2	16.5	22.0	Net Profit ($mill)	47.0
Income Tax Rate	--	--	52.1%	46.3%	39.2%	36.5%	37.4%	37.2%	35.8%	37.8%	35.0%	35.0%	Income Tax Rate	35.0%
Net Profit Margin	--	--	8.2%	10.3%	13.0%	13.9%	13.9%	12.4%	10.6%	7.1%	6.1%	7.9%	Net Profit Margin	12.5%
Working Cap'l ($mill)	--	--	26.7	44.2	71.2	90.6	82.1	77.0	74.6	94.6	100	105	Working Cap'l ($mill)	195
Long-Term Debt ($mill)	--	--	58.7	22.5	27.0	17.7	11.2	27.7	6.8	6.5	6.0	5.0	Long-Term Debt ($mill)	5.0
Net Worth ($mill)	--	--	36.3	90.0	120.4	161.7	199.8	230.9	238.8	247.1	245	245	Net Worth ($mill)	335
% Earned Total Cap'l	--	--	16.5%	19.6%	21.3%	19.1%	19.8%	14.9%	13.1%	7.7%	6.5%	9.0%	% Earned Total Cap'l	13.5%
% Earned Net Worth	--	--	31.3%	19.6%	24.5%	21.8%	19.8%	16.5%	13.2%	7.8%	6.5%	9.0%	% Earned Net Worth	14.0%
% Retained to Comm Eq	--	--	37.1%	18.0%	22.7%	16.7%	13.7%	10.5%	5.1%	4.0%	6.5%		% Retained to Comm Eq	11.0%
% All Div'ds to Net Prof	--	--	7%	8%	7%	13%	15%	17%	21%	34%	38%	28%	% All Div'ds to Net Prof	20%

BUSINESS: Calgon Carbon is the leading producer of granular activated carbon, which is used for removing organic chemical compounds from liquids and gases. It sells related services and systems too. Customers are in the industrial process market (about 49% of '93 sales), which includes original equipment manufacturers, food processors, and chemical and pharmaceutical firms, and in the environmental market (44%), which encompasses industrial and municipal customers. Calgon also sells charcoal (7%). '93 deprec. rate: 6.5%. Foreign sales: 40% of total. Employs 1,500, has 1,500 shñldrs. Insiders hold 30.3% of shs., 81.0% of voting rights (4/93 proxy). Pres. & C.E.O.: T.A. McConomy. Inc.: DE. Addr.: P.O. Box 717, Pittsburgh, PA 15230-0717. Tel.: 412-787-6700.

Figure 5-2. Carbon stock chart. (Copyright 1994 by Value Line Publishing Inc. Reprinted by permission; all rights reserved.)

☆ 32 CHARTER ONE ☆ FINANCIAL, INC.

CHARTER ONE FINANCIAL, INC.   Stock exchange: NASDAQ
1215 Superior Avenue   Ticker symbol: COFI
Cleveland, OH 44114   DRIP program: Yes
216-589-8320   Ownership:
                                       Institutional: + 59%
                                       Insiders: + 10%

Industry Review.   Quality savings-and-loan and thrift associations
such as Charter One Financial Inc. were tainted by the savings and loan
debacle in the late eighties. While high-flying savings-and-loans ven-
tured into risky loans and investments and eventually became insol-
vent or were taken over by federal agencies and subsequently either
closed down or sold off, savvy savings-and-loan and thrift managers
quietly went about their business of making money.

There are still plenty of savings-and-loans in dire financial straits,
and then there are the premier companies with top management delivering solid growth and earnings in a variety of economic scenarios
ranging from bust to boom.

Company Profile.   Charter One Financial is the largest thrift banking
institution and the seventh-largest federally insured financial institution in Ohio, with 99 offices located throughout the Cleveland-Akron-
Toledo-Youngstown market area. In the past decade, Charter One has
expanded its asset base and market reach significantly through well-
placed acquisitions. The company converted from a chartered mutual
savings bank to a publicly-held stock company in 1988.

Charter One can boast of in excess of $5.8 billion in total assets, and
an exceptionally strong loan portfolio constructed by a conservative
management not prone to making mistakes. One-to-four family residential loans make up the bulk of the portfolio (69 percent), while the
balance comes from consumer (10 percent), commercial real estate (10
percent), business (3 percent), and other (8 percent) loans.

Management Talent.   Director, President, and Chief Executive
Officer Charles John Koch has been an officer since 1987. He took over
the financial institution's reins from his father, Charles Joseph Koch,
now Chairman and Chief Planning Officer.

Financial Status. A quality loan portfolio, efficient operations, and an expanding interest-rate spread point to solid financials. Charter One's net income in 1993 surged 42 percent (excluding the positive effect of adopting new accounting standards) to $61.4 million.

DRIP Program. Under the Charter One dividend reinvestment program, shareholders may invest between $10 to $5000 cash per quarter in company stock without incurring any administrative expenses. For information on the DRIP program, contact Charter One's Investor Relations Department at 12315 Superior Avenue, Cleveland, OH 44114, or call 216-589-8320.

Particular Strengths. The company's key performance ratios are strong, and improving. Recent acquisitions such as Women's Federal Savings Bank (Cleveland) and branches of Citizens Federal Bank's Ohio Equitable Savings Bank division (Canton area) work to expand market depth and increase net worth.

Charter One is making several other moves to improve performance. It is widening its entrance into the business lending arena, which offers opportunities for better yields. In the past two years it has more than doubled permanent loan originations for housing, and has reduced the ratio of nonperforming assets by nearly 29 percent. On another front, checking deposits have more than doubled in the past five years, and now account for almost 10 percent of total savings.

Financial statistics (figures in millions, except per-share amounts):

For fiscal year ended December 31	1990	1991	1992	1993
Assets	$3,772	$4,359	$4,261	$5,215
Net income (loss)	23*	40	43	61
Earnings (loss)/share	1.24*	2.10	2.20	2.67*
Dividend/share	.25	.28	.31	.42
Long-term debt		231	305	604
Stock price range/share:				
High	8⅜	14¼	20	25
Low	4¼	5⅝	11⅜	17

*Before effects of accounting change.

Investment Assessment. Interest-rate worries have sent Charter One's stock price down nearly 20 percent from its all-time high of $25 per share. The concerns are unfounded. Charter One will keep its impressive earnings record intact by clamping down on expenses, improving operations, enhancing its loan portfolio, and plain old solid management.

Look for Charter One's stock price to rebound, as improved earnings are backed up by strategic acquisitions and market penetration. An earnings kicker could come with a successful bid for TransOhio Savings Bank, whose $1.4 billion in deposits will be put up for bid by the Resolution Trust Company in 1994.

☆ 33 COUNTRYWIDE ☆ CREDIT INDUSTRIES, INC.

COUNTRYWIDE CREDIT
  INDUSTRIES, INC.
155 North Lake Avenue
Pasadena, CA 91101-1857
818-304-8400

Stock exchange: NYSE
Ticker symbol: CCR
DRIP program: Yes
Ownership:
  Institutional: + 92%
  Insiders: + 4%

Industry Review.   Concerns over rising interest rates have rippled through the stock prices of financial service companies, sending share prices sharply lower and creating oversold positions in quality companies with sound fundamentals.

Ignoring the gyrations of Wall Street, industry companies keep right on delivering sound earnings reports. Low interest rates in recent years have allowed financial service firms to strengthen their balance sheets and build shareholder value.

Without a doubt, higher interest rates will put a damper on future earnings prospects, but improved credit quality and sharpened operations by the most efficient companies in the industry should help to offset any negative impact.

Company Profile.   By far the largest player in the industry, Countrywide Credit Industries, Inc. dominates the mortgage business by buying and selling upwards of $50 billion of home mortgages annually, as well as by collecting servicing and administration fees on a whopping $78 billion worth of mortgages each year. Its share of the national single-family-residential mortgage market has more than quadrupled, from 1 percent in 1990 to over 4 percent in 1993.

Coming off a record fiscal 1994 (ended February 23), Countrywide boosted earnings per share nearly 20 percent (to $2.96 per share) on surging revenues.

Mortgage banking accounts for 88 percent of its annual revenues, with the rest coming from homeowner and mortgage life insurance sales and a real estate investment trust.

To date, the company has done a good job of hedging its interest-rate risk through interest-rate call options. It also has reduced its risk posture by securitizing and selling its loan production while retaining the right to service the loans.

In 1993, Countrywide Credit purchased a new facility near Dallas, Texas, with the capacity for 1000 employees. It's the first major expansion of the firm's loan-servicing and data-processing operations outside of California.

Management Talent. Chairman and President David S. Loeb and Director and Executive Vice President Angelo R. Mozilo cofounded Countrywide Credit in 1969. They head an aggressive management team of seasoned industry veterans.

Financial Status. Sixteen consecutive quarters of earnings growth and a more than quadrupling of revenues have helped to push the firm's net worth to over $840 million in fiscal 1994, from under $200 million in fiscal 1991.

Cashflow. Cashflow also has improved significantly, from less than $1 per share in fiscal 1991 to over $3 per share in fiscal 1994.

DRIP Program. The dividend reinvestment program permits purchase of additional shares of company stock with dividends. Purchases of stock under the DRIP program are made at a 4 percent discount from the current market price. For information on Countrywide Credit's DRIP program, contact either the company's Investors Relations Department—MSN9-19, P.O. Box 7137, 155 North Lake Avenue, Pasadena, CA 91109-7137, 818-304-7523—or Chemical Bank, Dividend Reinvestment Department, P.O. Box 24850, Church Street Station, New York, New York 10249, 212-613-7147.

Particular Strengths. Countrywide Credit's proven ability to more than replace refinancing revenues with fees earned from its growing loan-servicing portfolio promises to prop up earnings. In addition, the company's expansion plans will boost market share and mortgage loan revenues, even in the face of rising interest rates.

Overall, Countrywide's mortgage portfolio carries a relatively low (average, 7.4 percent) coupon rate, which should discourage any mass refinancings.

Financial statistics (figures in millions, except per-share amounts):

For fiscal year ended February 28	1991	1992	1993	1994
Loan production	$4,577	$12,156	$32,388	$52,459
Revenues	135	246	506	756
Income (loss)	22	60	140	179
Earnings (loss)/share	.48	.89	1.65	1.97
Dividend/share	.12	.15	.25	.29
Long-term debt	154	383	735	1,197
Stock price range/share:	1990	1991	1992	1993
High	6	26⅝	29⅞	35
Low	3⅜	5⅝	16¼	22⅞

Investment Assessment.   After a meteoric rise, from less than $4 per share in 1990 to a peak of $35 per share in 1993, Countrywide Credit's stock price retreated more than 28 percent to a $15-per-share level. Given a gradual increase in interest rates, the firm's deftness in offsetting refinancings through higher loan-servicing revenues, and additional market penetration, Countrywide Credit is sure to hold its own in the long run. The bottom line: a great turnaround situation for patient investors.

☆ 34 GENTEX ☆
CORPORATION

GENTEX CORPORATION
600 North Centennial Street
Zeeland, MI 49464
616-772-1800

Stock exchange: NASDAQ
Ticker symbol: GNTX
DRIP program: No
Ownership:
   Institutional: + 51%
   Insiders: + 13%

Industry Review.   The U.S. automotive industry has snapped back with a vengeance. Spurred by rising sales via innovative leases, world-class quality vehicles, and modernized high-tech manufacturing facilities as well as by significantly increased design and research and development expenditures and strategic supplier partnerships, the domestic automobile industry has regained market share from the Japanese and other major importers to the North American market. Obviously, the improving fortunes of domestic automotive manufacturers has been beneficial to domestic auto-parts suppliers as well.

Another trend working in favor of domestic automobile parts suppliers is the locating of vehicle manufacturing facilities in the United States by foreign companies, thus expanding sales opportunities.

In the automotive electro-optical (mirror) market, Gentex enjoys a virtual monopoly with its specialized mirror. It has gone to court numerous times to protect its patents, and has won injunctions against its major domestic competitor, Donnelly Corporation, prohibiting them from marketing several electrochromic mirror products worldwide. Yet the market remains highly fragmented, with Gentex supplying around 3 percent of all mirror units, to go on 45 million vehicles produced worldwide on an annual basis. The overall market for electrochromic mirrors is expected to grow to in excess of 20 percent through the year 2000.

Gentex also operates in the fire protection industry against a number of competitors. Stricter building standards, and passage of the Americans With Disabilities Act (ADA) enforcing new fire-code standards, will lead to increased industry revenues as new building and renovation projects get under way.

Company Profile. Gentex Corporation first introduced the electrochromic (dimming rearview) mirror to the automotive industry, and it remains the leading supplier of these mirrors to the worldwide automotive industry. Increased emphasis on automotive safety means higher sales of the electrochromic mirror.

Gentex's expanded line of interior and exterior "Night Vision Safety" mirrors are currently offered as standard or optional equipment on over 55 domestic and foreign vehicles.

The company derives 76 percent of annual revenues from its automotive products group, with the balance coming from the firm's fire protection products group (around 23 percent) and precision glass components group (less than 2 percent).

Fire protection products include a strobe warning light, primary evacuation voice/tone speakers, and photoelectric smoke detectors. Gentex's estimated market share of the fire protection smoke detector and signaling device segment is around 5 percent.

The precision glass group manufactures glass components for the company's mirror products and for the office-machine and electronic-test-equipment markets.

Management Talent.   Chairman and Chief Executive Officer Fred Bauer founded Gentex in 1974 as a manufacturer of residential smoke detectors. Under Bauer's guidance, the company acquired the rights to a prototype automatic interior rearview mirror in 1981, and later developed electrochemistry options to improve on this mirror concept.

Bauer and his management team have led Gentex to the industry's dominant position. The company produces in excess of 1.2 million electrochromic mirrors, as opposed to the only 20,000 from all of its competitors combined.

Financial Status.   The firm's balance sheet is healthy, with no long-term debt whatsoever. Cash and short-term investments total over $13 million, and the company's current ratio stands at an enviable 5:1.

Cashflow.   With projected revenues going into the twenty-first century growing in excess of 25 percent and gross margins topping 30 percent, Gentex has plenty of cashflow for research and development and new-product introductions.

Particular Strengths.   Gentex's inroads as supplier to the world's major automobile manufacturers provides significant growth opportunities, as its mirror products gain greater acceptance and market penetration. For example, Chrysler Corporation announced in early 1994 that it will purchase Gentex's interior automatic-dimming mirrors through the 1999 model year. This trend toward long-term supplier partnership relationships makes it difficult for competitors to make any significant dent in Gentex's market position as industry leader.

In the foreign market, Gentex expanded its Japanese client base when a third Japanese automobile manufacturer committed to purchase the company's Night Vision Safety mirror for its 1995 model year. Gentex supplies mirror products to all major domestic automobile manufacturers, and it has won the highest-quality awards from Chrysler, Ford, and General Motors.

The company's revenue and earnings wild card lies in its fire protection group. That segment experienced sales gains in excess of 65 percent during 1993, paced by several recent new-product introductions.

Finally, Gentex invests nearly 8 percent of revenues in research and development, to extend its electrochromic expertise into nonmirror applications such as sunroofs, windows, etc. Down the road, this could lead to product-line diversification and new market opportunities in industries outside of the automotive arena.

One caveat needs to be considered. Rumors abound about the possibility of another company producing a mirror superior to Gentex's.

While that possibility exists, the nature of the industry's long-term contract relationships, and the length of time it would take a competitor to provide proof of its superior product, means it would be years, even decades, before that could negatively impact Gentex's revenues and earnings.

Financial statistics (figures in millions, except per-share amounts):

For fiscal year ended December 31	1990	1991	1992	1993
Revenues	$21	$27	$45	$64
Net income (loss)	1	2	5	10
Earnings (loss)/share	.075	.105	.315	.59
Dividend/share	—	—	—	—
Long-term debt	6	6	—	—
Stock price range/share:				
High	7⅛	6¹¹⁄₁₆	13	35¼
Low	2⁹⁄₁₆	2⁷⁄₁₆	6⁹⁄₁₆	10⅛

Investment Assessment. With its dominant market position in two highly fragmented industries and plenty of room to grow market share, Gentex is poised for explosive growth. The company isn't resting on its laurels, either. An aggressive research and development program and new-product introduction campaign will help Gentex to expand future revenues and earnings. General Motors honored Gentex as a "Worldwide Supplier of the Year" in 1993.

Gentex's stock price declined substantially in the second quarter of 1994, possibly due to rumors of new mirror technology. As discussed earlier, this concern appears to be overblown. Gentex's stock price dropped more than 30 percent, from a 52-week high of $35¼ per share to under the $24-per-share level. Yet this company represents a solid play on the automotive industry in the twenty-first century.

☆ 35 KEYCORP ☆

KEYCORP
127 Public Square
Cleveland, OH 44114-1306
216-689-3000

Stock exchange: NYSE
Ticker symbol: KEY
DRIP program: Yes
Ownership:
  Institutional: + 53%
  Insiders: —%

Industry Overview. For a discussion of the overall banking industry, refer to the industry review section for Banc One earlier in this chapter. The KeyCorp/Society Corporation merger in March 1994 accelerated the industry's consolidation, and in the process created the nation's 10th largest bank holding company, with combined assets totaling more than $58 billion and operations in 18 states stretching from Alaska to Maine.

Company Profile. The merger of KeyCorp and Society Corporation appears to be a match made in heaven. The two banking organizations formerly operated in different markets but will now form the tenth largest bank holding company in the country.

One-time restructuring charges in the fourth quarter of 1993 associated with the merger will pave the way for a smooth merger and deliver an estimated $80 to $105 million in annual savings, beginning in 1995.

Cross-marketing of each of the bank's specialty products and services offers plenty of opportunity for revenue and earnings growth. In addition, KeyCorp's acquisition strategy continues unabated. In March 1994 the bank strengthened its position in the Colorado market with the completion of its acquisition of Commercial Bancorp of Colorado, with nearly $400 million in assets.

Management Talent. KeyCorp's chief executive, Victor J. Riley, Jr., took over the reins as Chairman and Chief Executive Officer of the merged company. Succession plans already in place will install Society's President and Chief Executive Officer, George W. Gillespie, as the bank holding company's Chairman and Chief Executive Officer when Riley retires in 1995.

The new firm has plenty of talented bank managers, to draw strength from both entities in forging the melding of their two organizations.

Financial Status. The combined financial clout will give KeyCorp added negotiating clout in strategic bank acquisitions, as it moves to bolster its strength in current markets and expand into new banking territories. Combined 1993 earnings totaled $791 million, with a return on average assets of 1.39 percent and a return on average total equity at 18.9 percent.

DRIP Details. KeyCorp's dividend reinvestment program allows for additional cash investment in company stock in amounts from $10 to

$10,000 per month. For information on the DRIP program, contact Shareholder Relations at KeyCorp, 127 Public Square, Cleveland, OH 44114-1306.

Particular Strengths. This merger of equally well-run, top-performing banking organizations should proceed exceedingly smoothly, since there are no real poor-performing segments to prop up or rebuild. Each can draw upon the strengths of the other in building a consolidated national banking powerhouse.

Asset quality is improving with the cleaning out of poor loans associated with Society's earlier takeover of the troubled Ameritrust in Cleveland.

Financial statistics (figures in millions, except per-share amounts; all figures before effect of merger with Society in 1994):

For fiscal year ended December 31	1990	1991	1992	1993
Assets	$19,266	$23,156	$25,457	$32,648
Net income (loss)	148	188	246	363
Earnings (loss)/share	2.31	2.57	3.17	3.84
Dividend/share	.89	.95	1.04	1.19
Long-term debt	381	511	655	911
Stock price range/share:				
High	19½	29⅝	39⅛	46
Low	11¼	13⅞	27⅛	32¾

Investment Assessment. KeyCorp already holds major market shares in many of its banking territories. The addition of new banking products and service lines, greater financial clout, and expanded territories will make it a stronger national competitor and a force to be reckoned with in the future.

The market has virtually ignored the positive impact of the synergies created within this merger, and instead focused on potential problem areas that really should not materialize. Since hitting a peak of $46 per share in 1993, KeyCorp's stock price has dropped to near the $30-per-share level. (See Fig. 5-3, KeyCorp stock price.) The market will respond more positively as the new financial giant comes through with higher earnings.

KEYCORP NYSE-KEY

RECENT PRICE **33** | P/E RATIO **9.2** (Trailing: 10.8 Median: 8.5) | RELATIVE P/E RATIO **0.59** | DIV'D YLD **4.2%** | VALUE LINE **2023**

TIMELINESS (Relative Price Performance Next 12 Mos.) **3** Average
SAFETY (Scale: 1 Highest to 5 Lowest) **3** Average
BETA 1.05 (1.00 = Market)

1997-99 PROJECTIONS

	Price	Gain	Ann'l Total Return
High	65	(+95%)	21%
Low	45	(+35%)	12%

Insider Decisions

	O	N	D	J	F	M	A	M	J
to Buy	0	1	0	0	0	0	0	1	0
Options	0	0	3	0	2	2	4	2	0
to Sell	0	0	1	0	0	0	0	2	0

Institutional Decisions

	4Q'93	1Q'94	2Q'94
to Buy	65	135	123
to Sell	94	140	118
Hld's(000)	51489	110730	111769

	1983	1984	1985	1986	1987	1988	1989	1990	1991	1992	1993	1994
High:	7.6	9.1	13.7	17.9	20.0	18.9	20.3	17.6	26.3	33.4	37.3	33.6
Low:	5.4	7.1	8.9	13.5	13.3	15.5	16.5	12.0	15.3	24.3	27.4	28.9

Target Price Range: 1997 | 1998 | 1999

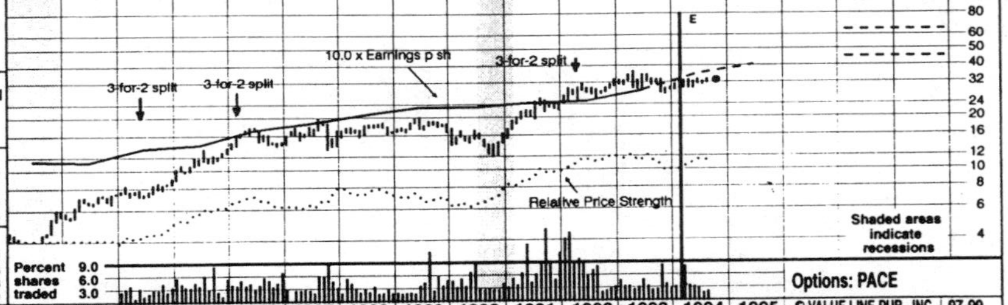

Options: PACE

1978	1979	1980	1981	1982	1983	1984	1985	1986	1987	1988	1989	1990	1991	1992	1993	1994	1995	© VALUE LINE PUB., INC.	97-99
1.10	1.09	1.06	.98	1.15	1.13	1.36	1.41	1.72	1.88	2.10	2.32	2.32	2.45	2.51	2.89	*3.60*	*4.05*	Earnings per sh A	*5.50*
.26	.30	.33	.36	.38	.40	.43	.46	.48	.60	.68	.80	.88	.92	.98	1.12	*1.28*	*1.40*	Div'ds Decl'd per sh B■	*1.80*
8.47	7.62	8.26	8.98	9.63	10.34	10.16	10.90	12.14	13.47	14.98	16.58	15.34	16.90	15.49	17.53	*20.15*	*23.05*	Book Value per sh C	*36.00*
15.96	26.86	26.89	25.47	25.56	25.74	34.94	44.28	44.81	44.09	44.36	43.50	65.54	66.06	116.73	241.55	*246.00*	*250.00*	Common Shs Outst'g D	*280.00*
4.8	4.5	4.0	4.4	3.9	5.9	5.8	8.1	9.0	8.8	8.2	7.9	6.5	8.8	11.5	11.0	Bold figures are		Avg Ann'l P/E Ratio	*10.0*
.65	.65	.53	.53	.43	.50	.54	.66	.61	.59	.68	.60	.48	.56	.70	.65	Value Line		Relative P/E Ratio	*.75*
4.9%	6.2%	7.8%	8.4%	8.4%	6.0%	5.4%	4.0%	3.1%	3.7%	3.9%	4.4%	5.9%	4.3%	3.4%	3.5%	estimates		Avg Ann'l Div'd Yield	*3.3%*
						5835.4	8749.1	9061.0	9077.3	10010	10903	15110	15405	24978	59631	*65000*	*70000*	Total Assets ($mill)	*95000*
						3383.9	5272.9	5386.2	5476.7	5948.2	6719.9	9895.2	9417.3	15699	39269	*44000*	*48500*	Loans ($mill)	*62000*
						193.6	263.4	323.2	329.1	359.8	425.8	624.3	686.8	1130.4	2679.0	*2725*	*2950*	Net Interest Inc ($mill)	*4000*
						13.6	18.6	19.4	18.1	24.9	51.6	94.7	79.9	147.4	211.7	*150*	*185*	Loan Loss Prov'n ($mill)	*280*
						51.2	85.9	124.6	145.2	146.2	161.5	238.5	225.1	501.5	1001.7	*935*	*1075*	Noninterest Inc ($mill)	*1350*
						178.3	268.2	326.5	334.5	351.2	390.2	605.9	598.0	1046.0	2385.1	*2150*	*2275*	Noninterest Exp ($mill)	*2650*
						43.6	56.7	84.1	90.9	100.1	110.0	155.2	163.0	301.2	709.9	*895*	*1025*	Net Profit ($mill)	*1550*
						17.5%	9.4%	17.4%	25.3%	23.0%	24.4%	4.4%	30.3%	31.3%	34.5%	*34.0%*	*35.0%*	Income Tax Rate	*35.0%*
						.75%	.65%	.93%	1.00%	1.00%	1.01%	1.03%	1.06%	1.21%	1.19%	*1.40%*	*1.45%*	% Earned Total Assets	*1.65%*
						77.8	108.8	188.5	186.0	182.5	122.2	183.2	177.1	886.1	1763.9	*1700*	*1900*	Long-Term Debt ($mill)	*2500*
						354.8	532.4	568.9	618.8	689.5	746.2	1005.2	1116.7	1868.1	4393.6	*5115*	*5920*	Net Worth ($mill)	*10235*
						6.1%	6.1%	6.3%	6.8%	6.9%	6.8%	6.7%	7.2%	7.5%	7.4%	*8.0%*	*8.5%*	% N W to Tot Assets	*11.0%*
						58.0%	60.3%	59.4%	60.3%	59.4%	61.6%	65.5%	61.1%	62.9%	65.9%	*67.5%*	*69.5%*	% Loans to Tot Assets	*65.5%*
						12.3%	10.7%	14.8%	14.7%	14.5%	14.7%	15.4%	14.6%	16.1%	16.2%	*17.5%*	*17.5%*	% Earned Net Worth	*15.0%*
						8.4%	7.7%	10.9%	10.5%	10.2%	10.1%	9.6%	9.2%	10.8%	10.3%	*11.5%*	*11.5%*	% Retained to Comm Eq	*10.5%*
						32%	35%	30%	32%	32%	34%	38%	37%	35%	39%	*36%*	*35%*	% All Div'ds to Net Prof	*33%*

BUSINESS: KeyCorp was formed by the merger of Society Corp and KeyCorp on March 1, 1994. Has more than 1,300 offices in 18 states. Geographic distribution of net income: Northeast, 27%; Great Lakes region, 49%; Rocky Mountain region, 6%; Northwest, 18%. Loan portfolio breakdown as of 12/31/93: commercial, 22%; commercial real estate, 16%; construction, 3%; residential mortgage, 28%; consumer, 23%; other, 8%. Net loan losses, .56% of average loans in '93; loan loss reserve, 1.89% of gross loans at 6/30/94; nonperforming assets, 1.17%. About 29,810 empl.; comm. stkhldrs, N.A.. Insider ownership: 1.7% of comm. (4/94 proxy). Chrmn.: V.J. Riley, Jr. Pres.: R.W. Gillespie. Inc.: OH. Address: 127 Public Square, Cleveland, OH 44114-1306. Tel.: 216-689-3000.

Figure 5-3. KeyCorp stock chart. (*Copyright 1994 Value Line Publishing Inc. Reprinted by permission; all rights reserved.*)

☆ 36 MERCK & ☆ COMPANY, INC.

MERCK & COMPANY, INC.
P.O. Box 100
Whitehouse Station, NJ 08889-0100
908-423-1000

Stock exchange: NYSE
Ticker symbol: MRK
DRIP program: Yes
Ownership:
    Institutional: + 41%
    Insiders: + 1%

Industry Review.   For a more detailed description of the industry, see the industry review section under Abbott Laboratories earlier in this chapter.

As indicated there, the industry is encountering cost-control measures and possible sweeping health care reform legislation. In a move to adjust to the changing industry environment, Merck acquired the mail-order drug firm Medco Containment in a late-1993, $6 billion deal, and in early 1994 announced a nationwide program to offer 10 to 20 percent discounts on generic drugs through a company subsidiary.

Company Profile.   Merck, the nation's largest pharmaceutical firm, manufactures both human and animal health care products and specialty chemicals. Major contributors to company revenues and earnings are a broad array of products including cardiovasculars, anti-ulcerants, antibiotics, vaccines, animal health and crop protection products, and anti-inflammatories and analgesics.

The company employs over 6500 people and spends over $1.2 billion annually in its research and development efforts. A major player in the international market, Merck generates around 46 percent of overall company revenues from sales outside of the United States. In a move to further penetrate the international market, Merck finalized an agreement with Johnson and Johnson in 1993 to extend into Europe the U.S. joint venture originally formed in 1989.

New products in the pipeline promise to restore Merck's winning ways with a new streak of consecutive years of record revenues and earning per share. Healthy margins deliver net income at around 25 percent of revenues, on average.

Management Talent.   Chairman and Chief Executive Officer P. Roy Vagelos has been stewarding Merck since 1986, and recently elected

President and Chief Operating Officer Richard J. Markham sports years of company experience on both the domestic and international fronts in various positions. Highly regarded industry veteran Raymond Gilmartin has been chosen to replace Vagelos in late 1994.

Financial Status.   Long-term debt has held steady for the past three years at around $490 million. Working capital is healthy, and more than adequate for the expansion of research and development and entrance into new markets.

Cashflow.   Cashflow is approaching $3 per share, while cash dividends have been increasing at a better than 10 percent pace.

DRIP Details.   Merck's dividend reinvestment program allows for additional stock purchases, in cash amounts from $25 to $50,000 per year. Administrative costs are absorbed by the company. For information on the company's DRIP program, contact Merck & Company, Inc., Stockholder Services Department, P.O. Box 100-WS3AB-40, One Merck Drive, Whitehouse Station, NJ 08889-0100.

Particular Strengths.   Merck's recent expansion into the cost-containment area of the health care industry with the Medco acquisition and the launching of its discount generic drug program rounds out the company's strategy. It's a bold move to meet the challenges of the industry head-on, and it should pay off in the long run.

Look for more international expansion, such as the late-1993 new plant in China to produce a hepatitis B vaccine in that country where an estimated 100 million people carry the disease. Revenues from developed countries will pace near-term growth, but the company is firmly establishing itself in emerging nations, where long-term growth potential is enormous.

Merck's efficient distribution network, aggressive research and development efforts, and world-class manufacturing facilities will hold the company in good stead on the worldwide competitive front.

Financial statistics (figures in millions, except per-share amounts):

For fiscal year ended December 31	1990	1991	1992	1993
Revenues	$7,672	$6,603	$9,663	$10,315
Net income (loss)	1,781	2,121	2,447	2,690
Earnings (loss)/share	1.52	1.83	2.12	1.87
Dividend/share	.64	.44	.92	1.03
Long-term debt	124	494	495	495

Stock price range/share:

High	$30\frac{3}{8}$	$55\frac{3}{4}$	$56\frac{5}{8}$	$44\frac{1}{8}$
Low	$22\frac{1}{4}$	$27\frac{3}{8}$	$40\frac{1}{2}$	$28\frac{5}{8}$

Investment Assessment. Market worries over healthcare reform and disappointing 1993 results caused investors to shed Merck stock and drive its price down from a 1993 high of $44\frac{1}{8}$ per share to nearly a 52-week low of around $30 per share. That's nearly $27 per share, or 47 percent below its all-time high (reached in early 1992) of $56\frac{5}{8}$ per share. (See Fig. 5-4, Merck & Company, Inc. Stock Chart.)

Merck is an A-1 healthcare company that will surmount the difficulties facing the industry. As such, it is a solid investment for the twenty-first century.

☆ 37 NORWEST ☆ CORPORATION

NORWEST CORPORATION	Stock exchange: NYSE
Norwest Center	Ticker symbol: NOB
Sixth and Marquette	DRIP program: Yes
Minneapolis, MN 55479	Ownership:
612-667-1234	Institutional: + 73%
	Insiders: + 2%

Industry Review. For a more detailed discussion of the banking industry, refer to the industry review section under Banc One earlier in this chapter.

Company Profile. Norwest Corporation's nearly $51 billion in assets positions it as the nation's fifteenth largest bank holding company. The company has been on the acquisition trail, picking up more than 20 banks in nine Upper Midwest and Rocky Mountain states stretching from Indiana to Wyoming. Overall, its territory covers 13 states.

The Minneapolis-headquartered banking firm serves territories with stable and improving economies. It is the leading bank in the Upper Midwest, and is making major inroads into the Rocky Mountain region.

MERCK & CO. NYSE-MRK

RECENT PRICE	P/E RATIO	RELATIVE P/E RATIO	DIV'D YLD	VALUE LINE
35	14.3 (Trailing: 15.0, Median: 18.0)	0.99	3.4%	1274

TIMELINESS 3 Average (Relative Price Performance Next 12 Mos.)
SAFETY 1 Highest (Scale: 1 Highest to 5 Lowest)
BETA 1.10 (1.00 = Market)

1997-99 PROJECTIONS

	Price	Gain	Ann'l Total Return
High	80	(+130%)	25%
Low	65	(+85%)	19%

Insider Decisions
Institutional Decisions

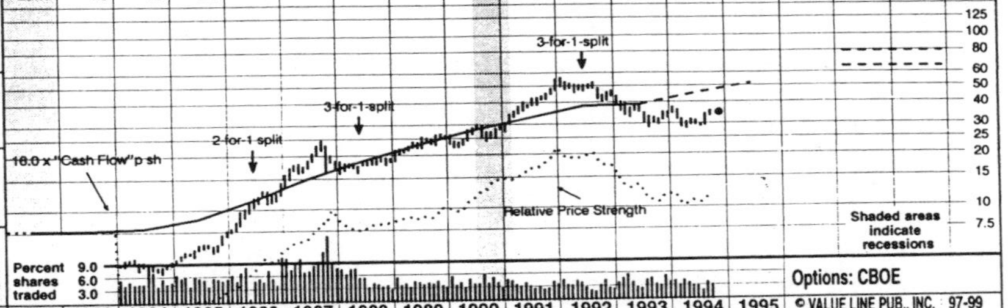

Target Price Range 1997 1998 1999

Price scale: 125 100 80 60 50 40 30 25 20 15 10 7.5

3-for-1 split, 3-for-1 split, 2-for-1 split
16.0 x "Cash Flow" p'sh
Relative Price Strength
Shaded areas indicate recessions
Options: CBOE

© VALUE LINE PUB., INC.

Per-share and ratio data

	1984	1985	1986	1987	1988	1989	1990	1991	1992	1993	1994	1995	97-99
Sales per sh	2.74	2.81	3.36	4.28	4.99	5.52	6.61	7.42	8.44	8.37	11.90	13.35	18.80
"Cash Flow" per sh	.50	.56	.71	.94	1.19	1.45	1.75	2.06	2.42	2.45	2.80	3.25	4.50
Earnings per sh A	.37	.43	.55	.77	1.02	1.26	1.52	1.83	2.12	2.33	2.38	2.70	4.00
Div'ds Decl'd per sh B■	.17	.18	.21	.27	.43	.55	.64	.77	.92	1.03	1.14	1.24	1.80
Cap'l Spending per sh													.80
Book Value per sh	1.91	1.96	2.09	1.79	2.40	2.97	3.30	4.24	4.37	7.99	9.30	10.65	15.00
Common Shs Outst'g C	1331.0	1263.1	1227.6	1182.0	1190.2	1186.2	1161.0	1159.5	1144.7	1253.9	1225.0	1250.0	1225.0
Avg Ann'l P/E Ratio	13.2	14.5	19.8	25.2	18.0	18.6	17.4	22.0	22.9	15.1			18.0
Relative P/E Ratio	1.23	1.18	1.34	1.68	1.49	1.41	1.29	1.41	1.39	.89			1.40
Avg Ann'l Div'd Yield	3.6%	2.9%	2.0%	1.5%	2.3%	2.3%	2.4%	1.9%	1.9%	2.9%			2.5%

(Bold figures are Value Line estimates)

Financial data

	1984	1985	1986	1987	1988	1989	1990	1991	1992	1993	1994	1995	97-99
Sales ($mill)	3559.7	3547.5	4128.9	5061.3	5939.5	6550.1	7671.5	8602.7	9662.5	10498	14950	16675	23000
Operating Margin	26.6%	28.3%	29.9%	31.2%	34.9%	37.5%	37.9%	39.2%	39.5%	41.0%	34.0%	34.5%	34.5%
Depreciation ($mill)	151.6	163.6	193.9	204.9	210.0	221.7	254.0	263.8	321.4	386.5	530	550	625
Net Profit ($mill)	493.0	539.9	675.7	906.4	1206.8	1495.4	1781.2	2121.7	2446.6	2687.2	3010	3385	4910
Income Tax Rate	37.7%	37.0%	37.0%	35.5%	35.5%	34.5%	34.0%	33.0%	31.3%	30.7%	33.5%	33.5%	33.5%
Net Profit Margin	13.8%	15.2%	16.4%	17.9%	20.3%	22.6%	23.2%	24.7%	25.3%	25.6%	20.1%	20.3%	21.6%
Working Cap'l ($mill)	1076.5	1106.6	1094.3	798.3	1480.3	1502.5	939.2	1496.5	782.4	d161.1	755	1675	2145
Long-Term Debt ($mill)	179.1	170.8	167.5	167.4	142.8	117.8	124.1	493.7	495.7	1120.8	820	470	170
Net Worth ($mill)	2544.2	2634.0	2569.1	2116.7	2855.8	3520.6	3834.4	4916.2	5002.9	10022	11700	13305	18200
% Earned Total Cap'l	18.4%	19.5%	25.0%	40.0%	40.5%	41.2%	45.1%	39.6%	44.8%	24.4%	24.5%	25.0%	27.0%
% Earned Net Worth	19.4%	20.5%	26.3%	42.8%	42.3%	42.5%	46.5%	43.2%	48.9%	26.8%	26.0%	25.5%	27.0%
% Retained to Comm Eq	10.6%	11.6%	15.5%	27.0%	24.6%	24.0%	26.9%	25.0%	27.6%	15.1%	14.0%	13.5%	14.5%
% All Div'ds to Net Prof	46%	42%	38%	35%	42%	44%	42%	42%	43%	44%	48%	46%	45%

BUSINESS: Merck & Co., Inc. is a leading manufacturer of human and animal health care products and specialty chemical products. Important product names include Vasotec, Prinivil (angiotensin converting enzyme (ACE) inhibitor agents for high blood pressure and angina); Mevacor, Zocor (cholesterol-lowering agents); Primaxin, Mefoxin (antibiotics); Pepcid (anti-ulcer agent); Recombivax HB (hepatitis B vaccine); and Prilosec (gastrointestinal). Int'l business: 44% of sales, 18% of pretax profits. R&D, 11.2% of sales; labor costs, 25%. '93 depr. rate: 5.4%. Est'd plant age: 10 yrs. Has 47,100 empls., 231,300 stkhldrs. Dir. own 1% of stock (394 proxy). Chairman & C.E.O.: P.R. Vagelos. Inc.: NJ. Address: P.O. Box 100, Whitehouse Station, NJ 08889-0100. Tel. 908-423-1000.

Figure 5-4. Merck & Company stock chart. *(Copyright 1994 by Value Line Publishing Inc. Reprinted by permission; all rights reserved.)*

It leads the nation's 50 largest banks in terms of revenues generated per dollar of assets, and has the fourth best noninterest income ranking.

Norwest maintains a strong performance track record. Its balance sheet is healthy, and its nonperforming assets are low. The firm's better than 17 percent return on equity stands among the best in the industry.

The mortgage group services some $28 billion in mortgages, and Norwest owns one of the nation's largest mortgage companies, Norwest Mortgage.

Management Talent. Chairman Lloyd Johnson and President and Chief Executive Officer Richard M. Kosacevich have grown Norwest through key acquisitions, and by paying close attention to customer needs and delivering quality banking products and services.

Financial Status. Norwest takes an extremely conservative stance when it comes to reporting earnings. Discretionary expenses charged off in recent years have masked the true earning power of this financial institution.

The company maintains big capital levels and large loan-loss reserves to guard against unexpected earnings drops, and has generated compounded earnings growth at around the 16 percent level since 1988.

The bank holding company has made a dramatic turnaround from the eighties, when its balance sheet was loaded up and its income statement weighted down with poor-performing Third World loans and a disastrous agricultural loan portfolio. Evidence of Norwest's significant improvement is illustrated by the firm's garnering recognition as the nation's "Bank of the Year," an award in 1992 from *Bank Management* magazine. Analysis criteria included return on equity, return on assets, capital strength, credit quality, productivity measures, and market assessment and market strength. Norwest's composite score topped that of the remaining 100 largest bank holding companies in America.

DRIP Details. Norwest's dividend reinvestment program operates at no cost to the shareholder. It permits additional purchases of Norwest common stock in amounts ranging from $25 to $30,000 per quarter. For information on the company's DRIP program, contact Norwest Corporation, Investor Relations, Norwest Center, Sixth and Marquette, Minneapolis, MN 55479, 612-667-1234.

Particular Strengths. Adding considerable stability to Norwest's earnings posture, the company's nonbank business segments contribute around 45 percent of earnings annually.

The company places heavy emphasis on marketing its broad product line via a nationwide distribution network. It operates more like a true retailer; in fact, it even refers to its far-flung banking, finance, and mortgage operations as "stores."

The company's full-scale push into Arizona, Colorado, Montana, and other Western states should provide ample growth and operating efficiencies for years to come.

All three of Norwest's major business segments are rising sharply. The firm's customer focus on consumers and small-to-medium size businesses adds revenue and earnings stability, while its growing geographical diversification reduces risks associated with regional economic downturns.

A balanced loan portfolio consists of 41 percent residential mortgages, 25 percent consumer loans, 21 percent commercial and industrial loans, and 13 percent commercial real estate and other loan categories.

Financial statistics (figures in millions, except per share numbers):

For fiscal year ended December 31	1990	1991	1992	1993
Assets	$348,607	$40,293	$44,557	$50,782
Net income (loss)	136	422	447	654
Earnings (loss)/share	.51	1.45	1.49	2.10
Dividend/share	.43	.47	.59	.64
Long-term debt	2,967	3,579	4,468	6,802
Stock price range/share:				
High	11⅞	18⅜	22⅛	29
Low	6⅞	9⅜	16⅝	20⅝

Investment Assessment. Jittery, interest-rate-sensitive investors dropped Norwest's stock price over 17 percent, from its 1993 high of $29 per share to the $24-per-share level after two interest-rates hikes in the first quarter of 1994.

Unfortunately, these investors are ignoring the solid prospects for Norwest, with its diversified loan portfolio, balanced earnings from nonbank business segments, and an expanding franchise with a number of successful acquisitions in a variety of new markets.

Expect Norwest to improve on its streak over the past 5 years of 100 percent earnings per share growth, 120 percent dividend growth, and an average internal return on equity of over 19 percent.

The firm's quality loan portfolio, quality management, quality territory, and quality track record all add up to an overall quality investment.

☆ 38 ST. JUDE ☆ MEDICAL, INC.

ST. JUDE MEDICAL, INC.
One Lillehei Plaza
St. Paul, MN 55117
612-483-2000

Stock exchange: OTC
Ticker symbol: STJM
DRIP program: No
Ownership:
   Institutional: + 52%
   Insiders: + 2%

Industry Review. The medical sector of the market virtually went into cardiac arrest during 1993, as concerns over healthcare reform mounted. This came on the heels of an anemic 1992 for medical stocks, which itself followed the boom years for the sector of 1990 and 1991.

Also negatively impacting the perceived fortunes of medical companies was a slowdown in the approval process of the Food and Drug Administration (FDA).

Looking ahead, the underlying fundamentals of well-managed medical companies with excellent research and development, a good product line, and good finances will win out with higher earnings, and subsequently, higher stock prices. After all, health care expenditures have consistently risen over the years, from under 10 percent of gross domestic product (GDP) in 1981 to nearly 15 percent in 1993.

More specific to St. Jude Medical, Inc.'s market, the interventional cardiology segment has experienced exceptional growth, to a current market of around $1 billion annually. Within the heart-valve business, five major manufacturers compete for market share worldwide. The heart-valve market is estimated to be around $500 million in size, and growing at somewhere between 8 to 10 percent per year.

Company Profile. St. Jude Medical, Inc. leads the pack as the world's largest mechanical heart valve manufacturer, with over 500,000 of its valves installed around the world and nearly 50 percent of market share. The company has made moves to expand its product line with an equity investment in InControl, Inc., a developer of an implantable defibrillator product.

The company has embarked on a diversification strategy that will focus the company on new medical-device products and markets, as well as cause it to make a bigger push into the tissue segment of the valve marketplace, form more strategic partnerships and joint ventures, and invest in emerging technology companies.

St. Jude Medical operates manufacturing facilities in Massachusetts; Quebec, Canada; Brussels, Belgium; and Caguas, Puerto Rico. Its new facility in St. Paul, Minnesota, for the production of carbon components for its new mechanical heart valve, promises to boost production and trim operating costs. The company also maintains sales offices throughout the United States, Europe, and Japan. International markets generate over 40 percent of annual revenues.

In addition to heart valves, St. Jude Medical and its subsidiaries manufacture and sell balloon pumps, centrifugal blood pumps, balloon catheters, annuloplasty rings, and aortic valved grafts.

Management Talent.   Ronald A. Matricaria took over as President and Chief Operating Officer of St. Jude Medical in 1993, while Lawrence A. Lehmkuhl moved from those positions to the chairmanship. Matricaria brings on-board extensive industry experience with the medical-device business at Eli Lilly, and is seen as the impetus behind St. Jude Medical's diversification strategy. Another noteworthy addition to the St. Jude management team is Dr. Bruce C. Ward, Vice President–Technology of the St. Jude Medical Division, with his significant product-development experience gained at Pfizer, Inc. and American Hospital Supply Corporation.

Financial Status.   St. Jude Medical maintains a fine financial posture. The company's coffers are overflowing with over $350 million in cash and marketable securities.

This treasure trove will permit St. Jude Medical to enter into joint ventures, make acquisitions, develop new products in-house, and expand markets without having to resort to costly outside financing.

Cashflow.   With a current ratio in excess of 10:1 and cashflow at over $5.50 per share, St. Jude has ample cash for operations and research and development. The Board of Directors discontinued the card in mid-1994 to repay acquisition debt on recent acquisition.

Particular Strengths.   New President and Chief Executive Officer Ronald Matricaria is rejuvenating St. Jude Medical and exploring new frontiers, similar to when the firm designed and developed the prosthetic heart valve back in 1977.

The new direction will decrease the firm's heavy dependence on one product and allow it to enter faster-growing medical markets with new products.

The company's considerable financial resources, research and development efforts, state-of-the-art manufacturing facilities, and strong earnings base will be key factors in the success of this new strategy.

Financial statistics (figures in millions, except per-share amounts):

For fiscal year ended December 31	1990	1991	1992	1993
Revenues	$175	$210	$240	$253
Net income (loss)	65	84	102	110
Earnings (loss)/share	1.35	1.75	2.12	2.32
Dividend/share	—	—	.30	.40
Long-term debt	—	—	—	—
Stock price range/share:				
High	36½	55½	55½	42¼
Low	18½	30⅛	27½	25

Investment Assessment.   The current disenchantment with the medical sector of the market will eventually disappear. St. Jude made a major diversification move in June 1994, with the $500 million acquisition of Siemen's pacemaker business. In June 1994, the company's stock traded at more than $28 per share lower than its 1993 all-time high of $55½ per share. (See Fig. 5-5, St. Jude Medical, Inc. stock chart.) Trading around 12 times earnings and sporting an 18 percent growth rate, St. Jude Medical is substantially undervalued.

☆ 39 SENSORMATIC ☆ ELECTRONICS CORPORATION

SENSORMATIC ELECTRONICS
   CORPORATION
500 N.W. 12th Avenue
Deerfield Beach, Florida 33442-1795
305-420-2000

Stock exchange: NYSE
Ticker symbol: SRM
DRIP program: No
Ownership:
   Institutional: + 86%
   Insiders: + 3%

ST. JUDE MEDICAL NDQ-STJM

RECENT PRICE 35 | P/E RATIO 16.1 (Trailing: 15.7 Median: 16.0) | RELATIVE P/E RATIO 1.10 | DIV'D YLD 1.1-Nil% | VALUE LINE 230

TIMELINESS 3 Average (Relative Price Performance Next 12 Mos.)
SAFETY 3 Average (Scale: 1 Highest to 5 Lowest)
BETA 1.45 (1.00 = Market)

1997-99 PROJECTIONS	Price	Gain	Ann'l Total Return
High	70	(+100%)	20%
Low	50	(+45%)	11%

Insider Decisions

	O	N	D	J	F	M	A	M	J
to Buy	0	0	0	0	0	0	0	0	0
Options	0	0	0	0	0	0	0	0	0
to Sell	0	0	0	0	0	0	0	0	0

Institutional Decisions

	4Q'93	1Q'94	2Q'94
to Buy	56	53	53
to Sell	69	78	78
Hld's(000)	19438	21210	23276

	1983	1984	1985	1986	1987	1988	1989	1990	1991	1992	1993	1994
High:	3.7	2.4	2.8	4.4	7.6	10.8	25.3	36.5	55.5	55.5	42.3	35.8
Low:	1.9	1.0	0.9	2.3	3.7	5.8	9.7	18.5	30.1	27.5	25.0	24.8

Target Price Range 1997 | 1998 | 1999

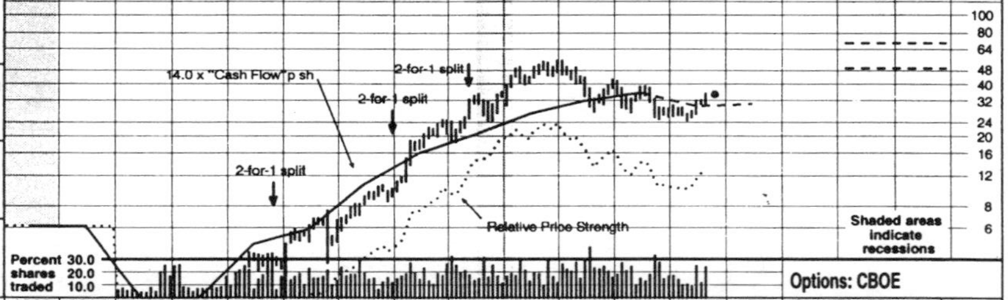

Options: CBOE

1978	1979	1980	1981	1982	1983	1984	1985	1986	1987	1988	1989	1990	1991	1992	1993	1994	1995	© VALUE LINE PUB., INC.	97-99
.06	.25	.38	.41	.54	.67	.95	.70	1.58	1.59	2.47	3.17	3.72	4.43	5.04	5.44	5.45	5.50	Sales per sh	10.00
.00	.05	.04	.07	.08	.13	.17	.00	.35	.42	.77	1.16	1.47	1.93	2.30	2.56	2.20	2.20	"Cash Flow" per sh	4.35
.00	.05	.04	.06	.07	.12	.14	d.03	.30	.41	.71	1.07	1.35	1.75	2.12	2.32	2.20	2.20	Earnings per sh (A)	4.00
--	--	--	--	--	--	--	--	--	--	--	--	--	--	.30	.40	.40	.40	Div'ds Decl'd per sh (B)	.65
.00	.01	.05	.01	.03	.07	.07	.02	.03	.07	.02	.15	.20	.16	.25	.35	.45	.50	Cap'l Spending per sh	.80
.06	.14	.19	.28	.36	.85	.97	.95	1.30	2.05	2.81	3.98	5.41	7.28	9.03	10.43	11.95	13.75	Book Value per sh (C)	22.20
30.07	31.46	31.70	32.62	32.67	38.06	36.96	37.26	38.37	45.08	46.14	46.73	47.04	47.36	47.52	46.41	46.00	45.50	Common Shs Outst'g (D)	45.00
NMF	23.4	64.8	44.9	37.0	24.4	12.1	--	11.9	14.2	14.1	16.8	21.0	26.5	18.8	14.0	Bold figures are Value Line estimates		Avg Ann'l P/E Ratio	15.0
NMF	3.39	8.61	5.46	4.08	2.06	1.13	--	.81	.95	1.17	1.27	1.56	1.69	1.14	.82			Relative P/E Ratio	1.15
--	--	--	--	--	--	--	--	--	--	--	--	--	--	.8%	1.2%			Avg Ann'l Div'd Yield	1.1%

1984	1985	1986	1987	1988	1989	1990	1991	1992	1993	1994	1995		97-99
34.9	26.1	60.5	71.8	114.1	148.0	175.2	209.8	239.6	252.6	250	250	Sales ($mill)	450
22.5%	NMF	38.0%	41.8%	41.8%	44.3%	46.6%	51.4%	54.3%	55.5%	55.5%	55.0%	Operating Margin	56.5%
.8	1.3	1.5	1.8	2.0	3.4	4.3	7.2	7.8	9.0	10.0	11.0	Depreciation ($mill)	15.0
5.3	d1.1	12.0	17.3	33.5	50.9	64.7	84.0	101.7	109.6	101	100	Net Profit ($mill)	180
40.5%	--	47.6%	41.1%	33.0%	26.5%	25.7%	25.5%	25.5%	24.5%	30.0%	30.0%	Income Tax Rate	30.0%
15.1%	NMF	19.9%	24.1%	29.3%	34.4%	36.9%	40.0%	42.4%	43.4%	40.4%	40.0%	Net Profit Margin	40.0%
28.0	28.1	64.6	80.9	113.0	157.1	218.5	301.1	377.3	409.0	420	450	Working Cap'l ($mill)	400
--	--	26.1	.5	--	--	--	--	--	--	Nil	Nil	Long-Term Debt ($mill)	Nil
36.0	35.3	49.8	92.3	129.7	186.0	254.4	344.7	429.0	484.2	550	625	Net Worth ($mill)	1000
14.7%	NMF	15.9%	19.3%	25.8%	27.4%	25.4%	24.4%	23.7%	22.6%	18.5%	16.0%	% Earned Total Cap'l	18.0%
14.7%	NMF	24.2%	18.8%	25.8%	27.4%	25.4%	24.4%	23.7%	22.6%	18.5%	16.0%	% Earned Net Worth	18.0%
14.7%	NMF	24.2%	18.8%	25.8%	27.4%	25.4%	24.4%	20.4%	18.8%	15.0%	17.0%	% Retained to Comm Eq	16.5%
--	--	--	--	--	--	--	--	14%	17%	17%	17%	% All Div'ds to Net Prof	16%

BUSINESS: St. Jude Medical, Inc. is the world's leading manufacturer of mechanical heart valves. Its pyrolytic, carbon-coated, bileaflet valve has been distributed commercially in the U.S. since 1982; sold abroad since 1977. Biolmplant Canada, Inc., a subsidiary acquired in September 1986, makes tissue heart valves. Also makes intra-aortic balloon pumps, centrifugal blood pumps, and annuloplasty rings. Facilities are located in Minnesota, Massachusetts, Montreal and Puerto Rico. 1993 depreciation rate: 13.6%. R&D: 4.3% of sales. Has 722 employees; 5,391 shareholders. Insiders own 1.8% of stock (3/94 proxy). Chairman: L.A. Lehmkuhl. President & C.E.O.: R.A. Matricaria. Inc.: Minnesota. Address: One Lillehei Plaza, St. Paul, MN 55117. Telephone: 612-483-2000.

Figure 5-5. St. Jude Medical, Inc. stock chart. *(Copyright 1994 by Value Line Publishing Inc. Reprinted by permission; all rights reserved.)*

Industry Review.   The electronics industry serves a diverse industry base with a wide variety of products. Likewise, product margins also vary considerably, depending on the electronic product's uniqueness, its intended use, and the degree of competition in specialized industry sectors.

Prospects for the electronic security and electronic article-surveillance segment look promising. Companies continue to expend large sums to reduce the cost of internal theft and shoplifting. In addition, the rising trend toward more workplace violence gives added impetus to higher spending for security in order to protect company property and employees.

The electronic security industry is also going through a consolidation, with the larger, better-financed firms acquiring smaller operations. This promises to provide economies of scale and operating efficiencies.

Company Review.   Sensormatic Electronics Corporation ranks as the world loss-prevention leader. It supplies electronic security systems to both retail and nonretail customers. Products and services include closed-circuit television, exception monitoring systems, and electronic article-surveillance systems.

The company has been aggressive on the acquisition front. Revenues have grown from less then $200 million in fiscal 1990 to over $600 million for fiscal 1994 (ended June 30). In 1993, Sensormatic acquired Automated Loss Prevention Systems, its largest European competitor. The move nearly doubled its presence in the European market. It also acquired total control of Security Tag, an American loss-prevention firm with operations in the United States and overseas.

Further increasing its penetration of overseas markets, the company announced in February 1994 its plans to create its first European electronic manufacturing operation. Overall, European operations contribute around 50 percent of annual company revenues.

Sensormatic's broad customer base provides a great deal of diversification. It serves Fortune 500 companies, retailing giants, and smaller customers. Department/specialty stores account for 30 percent of company revenues, followed by hypermarkets (15 percent), industrial (13 percent), discount/mass merchandisers (12 percent), food stores (9 percent), home improvement (9 percent), and other (12 percent). Expanding market opportunities in hospital, industrial, retail, and casino security systems make for a bright future.

Management Talent.   Founder, Chairman, President, and Chief Executive Officer Ronald G. Assaf heads a seasoned management team adept at creating new electronic loss-prevention and security systems and developing new markets.

Financial Status.   Gross margins in excess of 50 percent keep Sensormatic's cash flowing and its balance sheet strong. Cashflow per share has nearly doubled, to over $2 per share in fiscal 1994 from $1.06 per share in fiscal 1991.

The company sports in excess of $100 million in cash and marketable securities, and nearly $200 million in working capital. The company issued $135 million in debt in conjunction with the 1993 European acquisition. In addition, another $115 million in 7 percent Convertible Subordinated Debentures is due on May 15, 2001.

Particular Strengths.   As the worldwide industry leader, Sensormatic has the resources to expand via acquisition and market penetration. The company also pays attention to new-product introduction. Its engineering and research and development expenditures have increased over 65 percent since fiscal 1991, to nearly $14 million in fiscal 1993.

The company already provides security technology to 49 of the world's top 50 retailers, and it's making inroads into the industrial and other commercial markets. In January 1994, Home Depot began installing Sensormatic's universal Product Protection source-tagging program in its 260-plus stores.

Financial statistics (figures in millions, except per-share amounts):

For fiscal year ended May/June 30	1990	1991	1992	1993
Revenues	$191	$239	$310	$487
Net income (loss)	20	25	32	54
Earnings (loss)/share	.49	.60	.73	.97
Dividend/share	.17	.20	.20	.20
Long-term debt	20	149	151	308
Stock price range/share:				
High	$10\frac{7}{8}$	$20\frac{1}{4}$	$21\frac{7}{8}$	35
Low	$6\frac{5}{8}$	$9\frac{1}{4}$	15	20

Investment Assessment.   Sensormatic management has set some lofty goals for itself over the next five years. It plans to expand revenues to the $1 billion level, a nearly 66 percent rise over today's revenues. On top of that, management intends to achieve return on equity approaching 17 percent, and return on assets of 15 percent.

There's plenty of room for growth. Currently, Sensormatic has barely touched the large market potential in Latin America and Asia, which account for only 5 percent of company revenues. The company's inroads into the hard-goods sector, and commercial and industrial security requirements, also represent huge sales opportunities.

Sensormatic has earned its growth-stock status and high-price-earnings multiple. Look for this trend to continue. With the stock trading at a full 25 percent below its all-time high, you won't find many more attractive bargains on companies targeted for strong growth in the twenty-first century.

Search out other special situations to help to improve your portfolio performance. A little upfront work can pay off big in capital gains down the road.

6
Enlightening Utility and Energy Stocks

Utility and energy stocks represent a unique opportunity for investors to lock in attractive yields and retain upside potential for capital gains, as the economy picks up steam and industry increases its demand for energy.

Outside of the utility arena on the natural-gas front, clean energy mandates from the Clinton Administration promise to provide the impetus for higher natural-gas consumption. With natural-gas prices at lows not seen in a number of years, prices are poised to rise, with an increase in demand brought on by a reviving economy.

Likewise, alternative energy companies such as geothermal, cogeneration, and coal gasification energy producers stand to benefit from the push for cleaner energy sources. Look for significantly higher revenues and earnings in this expanding energy sector.

The following utility and energy stocks are positioned to perform well in the decades ahead, for a variety of reasons including unique market and competitive positions, well-run operations, solid finances, effective marketing and distribution, large reserves, and increasing operating efficiencies. For a discount offer on the investment newsletter *Utility & Energy Portfolio*, see the final pages of this book.

COMPANY	UTILITY AND ENERGY SEGMENT
California Energy Co., Inc.	Geothermal/ind. power producer
Central Vermont Pub. Ser. Corp.	Electric utility
Cincinnati Bell Inc.	Telephone/telecomm.
Destec Energy, Inc.	Cogen./coal gasif.
Magma Power Co.	Geothermal energy
Piedmont Natural Gas Co.	Natural gas utility
Southwestern Bell Corp.	Telephone/telecomm.
Southwestern Energy Co.	Diversified natural gas Co.
United Water Resources	Water utility
Washington Water Power Co.	Water utility

Due to industry and stock market conditions, many of these stocks are trading far below their highs despite higher earnings, expanding market share, and stronger financials. Now's the time to establish positions in these quality companies, in order to achieve large capital gains in the coming years.

☆ 40 CALIFORNIA ☆ ENERGY

CALIFORNIA ENERGY
   COMPANY, INC.   Stock exchange: NYSE
10831 Old Mill Road   Ticker symbol: CE
Omaha, NE 68154   DRIP program: No
402-330-8900   Ownership:
                                        Institutional: + 44%
                                        Insiders: + 2%

Company Profile.   California Energy Company, Inc. is a growing independent energy producer, targeting the geothermal energy market with leases of strategic geothermal development properties in the western United States.

Headquartered in Omaha, Nebraska, and with strong ownership ties to that city's large construction and mining company, Peter Kiewit Sons' Inc. (subsidiary Kiewit Energy owns in excess of 36 percent of the geothermal firm's common stock), California Energy operates five geothermal facilities producing more than 250 megawatts (MW) of power.

In addition, the company established a subsidiary, CE International, to manage its offshore project development and operations activities in

September 1993. Another expansion thrust included the acquisition of Ben Holt Company, a Pasadena-based engineering firm with international experience in the design of geothermal plants.

CE has a 30-year lease with the United States Department of the Navy to explore for, develop, and generate electricity from geothermal resources located on 5000 acres of the Naval Weapons Center at China Lake, California. CE owns about 50 percent and is the managing partner of the Coso Project, operating under this lease. Other geothermal operations include newly acquired leases and wells from Unocal on 26,000 acres of geothermal properties, and a pilot program being developed under the Bonneville Power Administration. California Energy also plans to explore other power-generation opportunities in wind, hydro, and gas-fired operations.

Management Talent.   Chairman and Chief Executive Officer Walter Scott has also served as Chairman and President of Peter Kiewit Sons', Inc. since 1979. President and Chief Operating Officer Richard R. Jaros previously served as Vice President for Mergers and Acquisitions of Kiewit Holdings, a subsidiary of Kiewit.

Financial Status.   Enhancing its financial prowess, California Energy moved from the American Stock Exchange to The New York Stock Exchange in August of 1993. A June 1993 $100,000 issue of 5 percent convertible subordinated debentures added to corporate liquidity and working capital. Most of the company's other long-term debt consists of collateralized project loans, with debt-service reserve funds and contingency funds.

Cashflow.   Cashflow has been steadily improving, reaching around $1.60 per share in 1993. The company currently doesn't pay any cash dividends on common stock, preferring to reinvest the cash in improving operations and growth.

Particular Strengths.   California Energy is one of the nation's leading geothermal companies. While the Coso Project refinancing dampened 1992 earnings, the company still posted record earnings that year and again in 1993. The deal was recognized by *Institutional Investor* as one of the "Deals of the Year," reducing the average interest rate to around 7.8 percent and slashing future interest payments.

The company recently scored a major coup, having been selected by the Philippine National Oil Company to negotiate arrangements to build, operate, and own for 10 years two geothermal plants in the Philippines. The total combined cost of the projects is estimated to exceed $350 million. CE joined forces with Kiewit Diversified Group, Inc. in a bid for one of the projects.

CE is widely regarded as the geothermal industry low-cost producer. On top of that, California Energy controls nearly two-thirds of the geothermal resources anticipated to be developed during the next decade.

Financial statistics (figures in millions, except per-share amounts):

For fiscal year ended December 31	1990	1991	1992	1993
Revenues	$97	$116	$128	$149
Net income (loss)	12	27	39*	43*
Earnings (loss)/share	.44	.75	.92*	1.00*
Dividend/share	—	—	—	—
Long-term debt	259	256	300	383
Stock price range/share:				
High	14½	16⅝	17⅜	21¾
Low	6½	7	11⅜	15¾

*Before deduction of $5 million or 13 cents per share extraordinary item in 1992, and before credit of $4.1 million or 11 cents per share due to accounting change in 1993.

Investment Assessment. Despite higher earnings and an increased interest in alternative energy sources such as geothermal, CE's stock traded at around $18 per share in early 1994, near the midpoint of its 52-week trading range.

Look for continued double-digit growth for the next 5 to 10 years. Higher revenues and earnings make this stock a solid long-term investment.

☆ 41 CENTRAL ☆ VERMONT

CENTRAL VERMONT
  PUBLIC SERVICE CORP.
77 Grove Street
Rutland, VT 05701
802-773-2711

Stock exchange: NYSE
Ticker symbol: CV
DRIP program: Yes
Ownership:
  Institutional: + 16%
  Insiders: + —%

Company Profile. Central Vermont Public Service Corporation services with electric power about half of Vermont's residents, plus another 10,000 New Hampshire residents in 13 towns. Customers include a diverse mixture of commercial, industrial, and residential accounts. Large commercial and industrial customers include General Electric, Eveready Battery Company, and Ben & Jerry's Homemade, Inc.

Central Vermont also operates a nonregulated energy-related subsidiary, Catamount Energy Corporation, with $28 million of investments in cogeneration and alternative energy plants, such as a 20-megawatt woodchip-fueled facility in Vermont and a part-interest in an 85-megawatt cogeneration plant in Maine. Another subsidiary, SmartEnergy, distributes energy-efficient products such as the "GreenPlug," an energy-saving device that controls the amount of electricity delivered to an appliance. SmartEnergy also is involved in an electric-car demonstration with the State of Vermont and other Vermont utilities

Management Talent. President and Chief Executive Officer Thomas C. Webb is battening down the hatches to make his company more cost-efficient. In addition to directing cost savings through more efficient operations, Thomas has delegated the duties of officers who recently left the utility to existing management.

Financial Status. Central Vermont boasts strong financials. Its percentage of total capital deriving from common stock equity amounts to over 55 percent, significantly higher than the 42 percent industry average. In late 1993, the company issued $43 million of first-mortgage bonds, with a weighted average rate of 6.2 percent, to repay higher cost debt. Over the past five years the utility has cut its average interest rate from nearly 10 to around 7.6 percent. Both rating agencies covering Central Vermont reaffirmed their investment-grade rating for its long-term debt.

Cashflow. Cashflow has been ample to fund operations and construction and plant expenditures, with some use of outside debt. As indicated earlier, the company takes a conservative debt position. The Board raised the common stock dividend slightly in 1993 (by 3 cents on an annual basis) to $1.42 per share.

DRIP Details. Central Vermont's DRIP program allows the utility's shareholders to acquire additional shares of company common stock via cash investments in amounts of $50 to $2000 per month. For information on the company's DRIP, contact Shareholder Services, Central

Vermont Public Service Corporation, 77 Grove Street, Rutland, Vermont 05701, 802-747-5406.

Particular Strengths.   Stringent cost controls are targeted to squeeze $20 million out of annual expenses by the end of 1995. Employee task forces are seeking ways to streamline operations in the capital construction process and to combine operating districts while improving customer service.

The nonregulated side of Central Vermont's business is growing, and stands to be a benefactor of the National Energy Policy Act of 1992 by investment in projects that had previously been restricted in their ability to deliver power.

Financial statistics (figures in millions, except per-share amounts):

For fiscal year ended December 31	1990	1991	1992	1993
Revenues	$233	$235	$275	$279
Net income (loss)	16.5	17.5	21.4	21.3
Earnings (loss)/share	1.62	1.65	1.71	1.64
Dividend/share	1.37	1.39	1.39	1.42
Long-term debt	130	130	107	122
Stock price range/share:				
High	$19\frac{5}{8}$	$22\frac{7}{8}$	25	$25\frac{3}{4}$
Low	$14\frac{1}{2}$	17	$19\frac{1}{2}$	$20\frac{1}{8}$

Investment Assessment.   Central Vermont has been active on the economic development front, joining forces with both the regional and state economic-development efforts to attract new industry to Vermont. These efforts, combined with an economic revival in Vermont will help to boost revenues and keep regulated earnings at the maximum allowable percentage.

Expanding diversification in the utility's nonregulated business segment could provide a nice kicker to Central Vermont's earnings in the future. In 1993, this segment contributed 14 cents to Central Vermont's total earnings per share.

The company's earnings are due for a rebound with a rate increase. In the wake of two-year lows in the Dow Jones Utility average, Central Vermont's stock hit a new 52-week low and yielded above 10.9 percent. The stock is an attractive long-term buy for the conservative investor with both income and capital-gains objectives.

☆ 42 CINCINNATI BELL ☆

CINCINNATI BELL, INC.
201 East Fourth Street
P.O. Box 2301
Cincinnati, OH 45201
513-397-9900

Stock exchange: NYSE
Ticker symbol: CSN
DRIP program: Yes
Ownership:
   Institutional: + 30%
   Insiders: + 0%

Company Profile. Cincinnati Bell, Inc. supplies telephone service to Cincinnati and nearby counties in Indiana and Kentucky, with nearly 850,000 access lines. The telecommunications company also recently expanded its telemarketing operations with the acquisition of WATS Marketing in March 1994.

Cincinnati Bell is busy restructuring its major operations and focusing its resources. To that end, the company sold its residence equipment business line to AT&T Consumer Products in February 1993, and late in 1993 prepared for the sale of CBIS Federal, the company's integrator of automated data processing systems and components for the federal government.

In a move geared to improve operating profits on the firm's telephone operations, the company filed a $16 million rate increase with the Public Utilities Commission of Ohio. In 1994, the PUCO granted Cincinnati Bell a 3.75 percent rate increase, to be instituted over a three-year period. In addition the company requested greater flexibility in bringing new services to its market area.

Management also has turned its attention to cutting costs. Starting in 1992 and continuing through 1993, management ranks have been reduced by nearly 20 percent. Quality-improvement programs and proactive maintenance have worked to trim customer trouble calls by more than 10 percent.

Management Talent. Chairman Dwight H. Hibbard and President, Chief Operating Officer, and Chief Executive Officer John T. LaMacchia have their work cut out for them. In a changing of the guard, LaMacchia took over the Chief Executive position from Hibbard in October 1993. Management's handling of the company's transition and its restructuring will be the key for a successful turnaround.

Financial Status. Cincinnati Bell has been in a downward spiral since 1990, culminating in a fourth-quarter-1993 loss in excess of $106 million, with restructuring charges and provision for a loss on the sale of CBIS Federal. As a result of the acquisition of WATS Marketing, Dun & Bradstreet lowered the company's note rating from Single A to Single A minus.

Cashflow. Cashflow is on the rebound from a downtrend beginning in 1989, and should approach the $3.30-per-share level in 1994. The company's common-stock cash dividend stands at 20 cents per share, and hasn't been raised since early 1991.

DRIP Details. Cincinnati Bell's DRIP program allows company shareholders to purchase with cash up to $5000 per month in additional company common stock. The company absorbs all administrative expenses. For information, contact Cincinnati Bell Shareholder Dividend Reinvestment and Stock Purchase Plan, KeyCorp, Corporate Trust, P.O. Box 65477, Cleveland, OH 44101, or call 800-542-7792.

Particular Strengths. Cincinnati Bell's strength lies beneath all the bad news and restructuring charges negatively impacting earnings in recent years, and driving the company's stock price down to lows not seen since 1988. The company's core telephone business is gaining in strength and improving operating profits.

The acquisition of WATS Marketing removes a direct competitor and gives Cincinnati Bell a stronger foothold in the telemarketing market. On the information-systems front, CBIS revenues have been steadily increasing, and that company subsidiary leads the market in providing billing systems for the explosive cellular telephone industry.

Financial statistics (figures in millions, except per-share amounts):

For fiscal year ended December 31	1990	1991	1992	1993
Revenues	$996	$1,064	$1,101	$1,090
Net income (loss)	91	43	35	(57)*
Earnings (loss)/share	1.44	.63	.50	(.93)*
Dividend/share	.76	.80	.80	.80
Long-term debt	437	445	350	523
Stock price range/share:				
High	$27\frac{7}{8}$	$25\frac{3}{8}$	$20\frac{7}{8}$	$24\frac{3}{8}$
Low	$17\frac{5}{8}$	$17\frac{7}{8}$	$15\frac{3}{8}$	$16\frac{1}{8}$

*Includes charges of $88 million or $1.30 per share for divesting of federal operations.

Investment Assessment. Management has cleared the clutter of poor-performing operations that dragged down company earnings. Now that the restructuring has been put into motion, Cincinnati Bell should be able to channel resources to its more successful endeavors. The company represents a classic turnaround in progress. As earnings improve and Cincinnati Bell lowers its debt level and interest expenses and further penetrates the information systems and telemarketing markets, a rebounding stock price will reach new highs.

☆ 43 DESTEC ENERGY ☆

DESTEC ENERGY, INC.
2500 City West Boulevard
Houston, TX 77042
713-735-4000

Stock exchange: NYSE
Ticker symbol: ENG
DRIP program: No
Ownership:
    Institutional: + 19%
    Insiders: + 73%

Company Profile. This Houston-based power producer, Destec Energy, Inc., provides electric power, thermal energy, and synthetic fuel gas for use in energy production. It is one of the largest nonutility power producers in the nation, with interests in a dozen operating power projects. In addition, several other projects in various phases of development, and four projects under construction representing an additional 1200 megawatts of power capacity, promise to more than double the firm's 1992 energy output.

Destec also continues to explore international opportunities, specifically in locations where Dow Chemical Company has a large presence (Destec is the successor to a part of the energy business developed by Dow). Dow continues to own in excess of 70 percent of Destec common shares. Other interest in Destec's prospects includes two insiders purchasing company stock in December 1993.

In late 1993, Destec inked a power agreement with Metropolitan Edison Company to provide power from a $160 million, 150-MW combined cycle power project in Pennsylvania, expected to be operational in 1997. The company also purchased a 50 percent interest in the 85-MW Black Mountain cogeneration facility in Nevada.

Management Talent. Chairman Robert McFedries and President and Chief Executive Officer Charles F. Goff both possess extensive industry experience. Management has proven itself talented in seeking out and developing successful alternative energy projects.

Financial Status. Destec enjoys a healthy current ratio in excess of 4:1. Nearly $250 million in cash and cash equivalents give the company plenty of operating flexibility. Through 1997, Destec will receive guaranteed payments from the federal government for the sale of syngas, as an incentive for research and development of syngas technologies and syngas production.

Cashflow. Strong working capital and cash flow from projects coming on-stream provide adequate cashflow for operations. Project partnerships and third-party financing of non-recourse-project debt allow Destec to develop new projects without loading itself down with debt and consuming cashflow.

Particular Strengths. Destec continues its aggressive expansion program, with new power projects scheduled to begin operation in the next few years and others under consideration. The company also owns fee lands and oil and gas leases in Louisiana, New Mexico, and Texas.

As developer, builder, and operator of the power facilities, Destec not only earns operating revenues from the facilities but also collects fees in conjunction with its project engineering and developing activities.

Financial statistics (figures in millions, except per-share amounts):

For fiscal year ended December 31	1990	1991	1992	1993
Revenues	$412	$437	$508	$674
Net income (loss)	70	81	99*	103
Earnings (loss)/share	1.56	1.39	1.59*	1.67
Dividend/share	—	—	—	—
Long-term debt	153	46	35	33
Stock price range/share:				
High	—†	28⅝	22¾	19¼
Low	—†	15	13	13½

*Includes $11 million or 18 cents per share gain associated with a change in accounting.
†Initial public offering March 15, 1991, at $20 per share.

Investment Assessment. Destec is a major player in the alternative energy industry segment. Its history of successful power projects and rising revenues will deliver improved earnings per share. The stock hit an all-time low in 1994 at $10\frac{1}{2}$ per share, and trades far below the $28\frac{5}{8}$-per-share peak seen shortly after its initial public offering in 1991.

Destec is a strong company with a secure position in this growing industry. The stock is a solid long-term investment.

☆ 44 MAGMA POWER ☆

MAGMA POWER COMPANY	Stock exchange: NASDAQ
4365 Executive Drive	Ticker symbol: MGMA
Suite 900	DRIP program: No
San Diego, CA 92121	Ownership:
619-622-7800	Institutional: + 50%
	Insiders: + 2%

Company Profile.   Magma Power Company ranks as the largest geothermal power producer in the world. The company manages the operation of geothermal power facilities in which it maintains a significant ownership interest.

In the largest exchange of geothermal assets ever, Magma Power acquired three geothermal power plants from Unocal in 1993, as well as geothermal interests and leases in California and Nevada for $225 million.

International geothermal development is ongoing. In 1993, Magma Power signed an agreement covering the development of a $280 million, 231-MW power facility in the Philippines. In addition, a memorandum of understanding was signed regarding a geothermal power development in Indonesia.

Overall, the company operates seven geothermal power plants in California, and holds geothermal leaseholds and fee interests in other parts of California and Nevada.

Management Talent.   Both Chairman Paul M. Pankratz and President and Chief Executive Officer Ralph W. Boeker came to Magma Power with years of experience at Dow Chemical Company. Dow Chemical owns 39 percent of Magma Power's outstanding common shares.

Financial Status.   In February 1994, Magma Power completed a
$130 million project-financing on the three geothermal thermal-power
facilities acquired from Unocal. The six-year loan replaces the one-year
bridge-financing associated with the acquisition.

Magma Power has over $30 million in marketable securities. Long-
term debt is decreasing, from its peak of $97 million in 1990 to around
$75 million in 1994.

Cashflow.   Working capital and sharply increasing cashflow are providing ample capital for operations, project development, and acquisitions. Bank credit is used to finance major projects.

Particular Strengths.   The company is just starting to benefit from
the synergies generated by the Unocal asset acquisition. Expansion into
overseas markets adds a whole new dimension to company revenue
and earnings prospects. In March 1994, Magma Power joined forces
with Dow Engineering Company in a five-year supplier partnership
agreement, under which Dow Engineering will provide state-of-the-art
plant-construction and process-engineering technologies to Magma
Power projects.

Magma Power has a long history of running its facilities in excess of
rated capacity. During 1993, the company improved on those efficiencies by running its plants at 115 percent of contract capacity near year-
end, up from 104 percent earlier in the year.

**Financial statistics (figures in millions, except per-share
amounts):**

For fiscal year ended December 31	1990	1991	1992	1993
Revenues	$86	$95	$109	$167
Net income (loss)	30	34	36*	52
Earnings (loss)/share	1.32	1.44	1.59*	2.17
Dividend/share	—	—	—	—
Long-term debt	120	109	96	212
Stock price range/share:				
High	37½	34¼	32¼	41½
Low	21½	22½	19¼	29¾

*Before positive effects of $18 million or $.77 per share accounting change.

Investment Assessment.   Earnings per-share growth is moving
ahead strongly. Look for Magma Power to earn over $2.50 per share in
1994 and more than $2.90 per share in 1995.

The future looks brighter. Under the California Public Utilities
Commission's Biennial Resource Plan Update (BRPU), Magma Power

MAGMA POWER NDQ-MGMA | RECENT PRICE **29** | P/E RATIO **11.8** (Trailing: 12.2 / Median: 34.0) | RELATIVE P/E RATIO **0.77** | DIV'D YLD **Nil** | VALUE LINE **1869**

TIMELINESS (Relative Price Performance Next 12 Mos.) **3** Average
SAFETY **3** Average (Scale: 1 Highest to 5 Lowest)
BETA .50 (1.00 = Market)

1997-99 PROJECTIONS

	Price	Gain	Ann'l Total Return
High	105	(+260%)	38%
Low	70	(+140%)	25%

Insider Decisions

	O	N	D	J	F	M	A	M	J
to Buy	0	0	0	0	0	1	1	0	0
Options	0	0	0	1	2	0	1	0	0
to Sell	0	0	1	1	2	0	1	0	0

Institutional Decisions

	3Q'93	4Q'93	1Q'94
to Buy	49	42	31
to Sell	23	25	34
Hld's(000)	10967	10726	9965

Target Price Range 1997 1998 1999

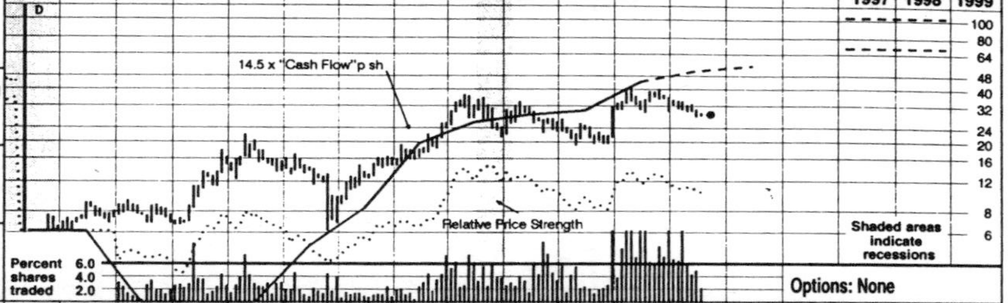

Options: None

1978	1979	1980	1981	1982	1983	1984	1985	1986	1987	1988	1989	1990	1991	1992	1993	1994	1995	© VALUE LINE PUB., INC.	97-99
					9.1	9.4	18.1	22.3	17.3	16.8	26.0	37.5	34.3	32.3	41.5	35.3		High	
					5.5	6.9	6.8	12.4	6.3	8.9	14.9	21.5	22.3	19.3	29.8	28.0		Low	
1.32	1.42	1.69	2.57	.03	.12	.15	.16	.66	.78	.95	2.86	3.74	4.14	4.74	6.97	*7.90*	*8.55*	Revenues per sh	*18.00*
.44	.68	1.02	1.75	d.29	d.35	d.14	d.09	.05	.35	.58	1.37	1.80	1.99	2.10	3.08	*3.55*	*3.80*	"Cash Flow" per sh	*7.20*
.35	.57	.89	1.52	d.34	d.40	d.20	d.16	d.13	.20	.43	1.01	1.32	1.44	1.59	2.17	*2.45*	*2.65*	Earnings per sh A	*4.40*
--	--	--	--	--	--	--	--	--	--	--	--	--	--	--	--	--	*Nil*	Div'ds Decl'd per sh	*Nil*
.95	.77	1.24	1.56	.24	.10	1.32	2.25	.18	3.06	4.48	1.99	.31	.69	.52	.35	*1.05*	*1.15*	Cap'l Spending per sh	*2.50*
2.61	3.36	4.78	6.31	.78	.37	2.35	3.05	3.45	5.16	5.77	6.81	8.41	9.90	12.28	14.67	*17.10*	*19.80*	Book Value per sh B	*30.00*
9.52	9.67	9.99	9.99	9.99	9.99	15.13	15.95	16.78	20.44	21.96	22.05	22.90	22.93	22.98	23.99	*24.00*	*24.00*	Common Shs Outst'g C	*25.00*
28.1	25.3	29.5	27.6	--	--	--	--	--	63.7	31.0	18.8	22.9	19.3	14.4	16.4	*Bold figures are Value Line estimates*		Avg Ann'l P/E Ratio	*20.0*
3.83	3.66	3.92	3.35	--	--	--	--	--	4.26	2.57	1.42	1.70	1.23	.87	.97			Relative P/E Ratio	*1.55*
--	--	--	--	--	--	--	--	--	--	--	--	--	--	--	--			Avg Ann'l Div'd Yield	*Nil*
						2.3	2.6	11.1	15.9	20.9	63.1	85.6	94.9	109.0	167.1	*190*	*205*	Revenues ($mill)	*450*
						NMF	NMF	NMF	39.3%	45.8%	65.5%	66.7%	64.7%	62.8%	63.6%	*65.5%*	*67.0%*	Operating Margin	*60.0%*
						.6	1.1	2.9	3.2	3.4	7.8	11.0	11.7	11.9	21.7	*25.0*	*26.0*	Depreciation ($mill)	*70.0*
						d2.6	d2.5	d2.2	4.0	9.3	22.3	30.2	33.9	36.4	52.1	*60.0*	*65.0*	Net Profit ($mill)	*110.0*
						--	--	--	36.6%	17.5%	17.1%	17.8%	17.6%	26.8%	30.4%	*31.0%*	*33.0%*	Income Tax Rate	*33.0%*
						NMF	NMF	NMF	25.2%	44.5%	35.3%	35.2%	35.8%	33.4%	31.2%	*31.6%*	*31.7%*	Net Profit Margin	*24.4%*
						.2	4.0	.9	14.8	46.7	70.2	77.8	92.5	74.5	69.7	*90.0*	*215*	Working Cap'l ($mill)	*425*
						.5	--	--	25.5	67.9	96.3	97.2	88.6	85.8	189.2	*150*	*215*	Long-Term Debt ($mill)	*215*
						35.6	48.6	58.0	105.4	126.7	150.1	192.6	226.9	282.3	351.9	*410*	*475*	Net Worth ($mill)	*750*
						NMF	NMF	NMF	3.1%	5.8%	10.8%	11.9%	11.7%	10.8%	10.2%	*11.5%*	*10.5%*	% Earned Total Cap'l	*12.5%*
						NMF	NMF	NMF	3.8%	7.3%	14.9%	15.7%	15.0%	12.9%	14.8%	*14.5%*	*13.5%*	% Earned Net Worth	*14.5%*
						NMF	NMF	NMF	3.8%	7.3%	14.9%	15.7%	15.0%	12.9%	14.8%	*14.5%*	*13.5%*	% Retained to Comm Eq	*14.5%*
						--	--	--	--	--	--	--	--	--	--	*Nil*	*Nil*	% All Div'ds to Net Prof	*Nil*

BUSINESS: Magma Power Co. designs, builds, and manages geothermal power plants in which it retains an ownership interest. Owns geothermal leaseholds in Nevada and California. Holds 50%-stake in four plants in southern Calif. with combined nameplate capacities of 148 MW. Acq'd. three operating geothermal plants from Unocal, 3/93; acq'd. Peak Power Corp., 5/93. Has 30-year contracts to sell electricity to Southern Calif. Edison, with price fixed first ten yrs. 1993 depr. rate: 6.8%. Has 340 empls.; 7,500 stkhldrs. Insiders own 1.6% of stock; Dow Chemical, 21%; B.C. McCabe Foundation, 11.5%; First Star, 9.5% (5/94 Proxy). Chrmn.: Paul M. Pankratz. Pres. & C.E.O.: Ralph W. Boeker. Inc.: NV. Addr.: 4365 Executive Dr., Ste. 900, San Diego, CA 92121. Tel.: 619-622-7800.

Figure 6-1. Magma Power Company stock chart. *(Copyright 1994 by Value Line Publishing Inc. Reprinted by permission; all rights reserved.)*

already has garnered contracts for several development projects for new generating capacity utilizing renewable-energy resources.

Despite record revenues and earnings in 1993 and bright prospects ahead, Magma Power's stock trails along near its 52-week low. (See Fig. 6-1, Magma Power Company stock chart.) Like Destec Energy, Magma Power is a great way to take a position in the alternative energy segment. California energy made a bid to acquire Magma Power Company in October 1994.

☆ 45 PIEDMONT ☆ NATURAL GAS

PIEDMONT NATURAL
  GAS COMPANY   Stock exchange: NYSE
1915 Rexford Road   Ticker symbol: PNY
P.O. Box 33068   DRIP program: Yes
Charlotte, NC 28233   Ownership:
704-364-3120   Institutional: + 22%
                               Insiders: +—%

Company Profile. Piedmont Natural Gas Company serves over 528,600 residential, commercial, and industrial natural-gas and propane customers in North Carolina, South Carolina, and Tennessee. The company's nonutility operations include acquisition, marketing and transportation of natural gas to large-volume purchasers, retailing of residential and commercial gas appliances, and propane sales.

Management Talent. Chairman, President, and Chief Executive Officer John H. Maxheim leads a management team that has achieved record revenues, earnings, and customer growth in 1993.

Financial Status. Piedmont's finances continue to improve. Both Standard & Poor's and Moody's upgraded the firm's debt ratings in 1993 to A and A-2, respectively. Under a $150 million shelf registration in 1993, Piedmont sold two separate debt issues totaling $90 million. Proceeds were used to reduce existing short-term debt and, as a result, lower interest costs.

Cashflow.   Combined with long-term debt, cashflow provides ample funds for operations and capital expenditures.

DRIP Details.   Piedmont Natural Gas operates a DRIP program at no administrative cost to the shareholder. Current stockholders may purchase additional shares of Piedmont common stock for cash amounts ranging from $25 to $3000 per month. Making the DRIP program even more attractive, the company allows shareholders to purchase the stock at a 5 percent discount from market price. To receive information on Piedmont's dividend reinvestment program, contact the Corporate Secretary, Piedmont Natural Gas Company, 1915 Rexford Road, P.O. Box 33068, Charlotte, North Carolina 28233, 704-364-3120, or the Dividend Reinvestment Agent, Wachovia Bank of North Carolina, N.A., Corporate Trust Department, P.O. Box 3001, Winston-Salem, North Carolina 27102, 800-633-4236.

Particular Strengths.   Piedmont's service area reflects a robust economic environment, with large markets such as Charlotte, Nashville, Winston-Salem, and the Spartanburg/Greenville area anchoring strong customer growth. For the fifth year in a row, customer growth exceeded 25,000, or 5.5 percent.

In addition to a strong economic base, a growing non-utility sector enhances future earnings potential. Propane sales increased over 9 percent in fiscal 1993 (ended October 31).

A projected interstate pipeline, possibly ready by late 1994, will boost the company's ability to foster growth and better serve its customers.

Financial statistics (figures in millions, except per-share amounts):

For fiscal year ended October 31	1990	1991	1992	1993
Revenues	$404	$412	$460	$553
Net income (loss)	26	21*	35	38
Earnings (loss)/share	1.22	.88*	1.39	1.45
Dividend/share	.83	.87	.91	.65
Long-term debt	174	221	231	278
Stock price range/share:				
High	14⅞	16⅞	20½	26⅜
Low	12¾	12⅞	15½	18⅞

*Results negatively impacted by the warmest winter in Piedmont Natural Gas's history.

Investment Assessment.   In April 1994, Piedmont Natural Gas filed for a 3.6 percent rate increase, and also requested a boost in its allowable rate of return to 10.41 percent from 8.74 percent. Combined with an expanding customer base, a rate increase would help to boost earnings for 1994 and beyond.

Piedmont's cash dividend is growing at a better than 6 percent pace. The stock yields around 5 percent. It's an excellent choice for those seeking to earn an attractive yield while waiting for the stock market to reward good performance.

☆ 46 SOUTHWESTERN ☆ BELL

SOUTHWESTERN BELL CORPORATION
175 East Houston
P.O. Box 2933
San Antonio, TX 78299
210-351-2044

Stock exchange: NYSE
Ticker symbol: SBC
DRIP program: Yes
Ownership:
   Institutional: + 37%
   Insiders: + —%

Company Profile. Baby Bell Southwestern Bell Corporation provides telephone service to a five-state region (Arkansas, Kansas, Missouri, Oklahoma, and Texas) with over 13 million access lines. It's a major player in the key international telecommunications markets, with a controlling interest (with two international partners), in Telefonos de Mexico. Other international operations include cable television interests in Israel and the United Kingdom, and directory interests in Australia and Israel.

The company has been a leader in the cellular and mobile communications industry, a business slated to grow between 15 and 20 percent annually, compared to the industry average of 3 to 5 percent growth in regulated telephone business.

Rounding out Southwestern Bell's diversified operations is its advertising and publishing segment, which publishes over 400 Yellow Pages directories.

Management Talent. Chairman and Chief Executive Officer Edward E. Whiteacre, Jr., and his management team, have made an admirable jump by moving Southwestern Bell into high-growth areas. The collapse of the proposed $4.9 billion U.S. cable television partnership with Cox Cable Communications in April 1994 signaled Southwestern Bell's prudent approach to new ventures. In the wake of new Federal Communications Commission (FCC) regulations rolling back cable TV rates, the partnership as originally structured lacked the cashflow to make it viable.

Whiteacre and team will now seek other ventures more suitable to Southwestern Bell's cashflow, revenue, and earnings expectations.

Financial Status. Southwestern Bell is a premier performer in the Baby Bell group. Since coming out from under the Ma Bell umbrella in 1984, the company has provided the best overall return to shareholders of any Bell company. Over the past 10 years, both net income and cash dividends have grown at a compound annual rate of 5.5 percent. An investment of $100 invested in Southwestern Bell stock in 1984 was worth $733 at the end of 1993.

The company's net profit margin has been improving steadily since 1990, and reached a record high of around 13.5 percent in 1993.

Cashflow. Record earnings and higher margins are providing plenty of working capital and cashflow for operations and acquisitions. Clear evidence of Southwestern Bell's significant amount of capital resources was reflected in the $1.6 billion the company stood ready to commit to the cable partnership with Cox.

DRIP Details. Southwestern Bell Corporation's DRIP program allows shareholders to purchase additional shares of company stock for cash, in amounts ranging from $50 to $50,000 per year with no administrative or commission costs. For information, contact Southwestern Bell, Shareowner Services, P.O. Box 2009, Houston, Texas 77252-2009, 800-351-7221, or Southwestern Bell Corporation, c/o The Bank of New York, Church Street Station, P.O. Box 11272, New York, New York 10277-0123.

Particular Strengths. Southwestern Bell will continue to search for appropriate ventures through which it can expand its revenue and earnings base. Despite the called-off partnership with Cox in the United States, Southwestern Bell and Cox are going forward and pursuing a cable partnership in the United Kingdom.

Also on the international front, the company is investigating opportunities in the privatization of foreign telephone companies. Typically, foreign markets offer higher growth potential, since the household-telephone-service penetration level is far below the 94 percent rate in the United States. The company owns a 10 percent stake in Telefonos de Mexico.

Customer growth in Southwestern Bell's cellular operations has been growing by leaps and bounds. It leads the cellular industry in penetration rate and has been adding new customers at a rate in excess of 40 percent annually, with a 57 percent increase in the first quarter of 1994.

Financial statistics (figures in millions, except per-share amounts):

For fiscal year ended December 31	1990	1991	1992	1993
Revenues	$9,113	$9,332	$10,015	$10,690
Net income (loss)	1,101	1,076*	1,302	1,435†
Earnings (loss)/share	1.84	1.93*	2.17	2.39†
Dividend/share	1.38	1.42	1.46	1.51
Long-term debt	5,483	5,675	5,716	5,459
Stock price range/share:				
High	32⅜	32⅞	37⅜	47
Low	23⅝	24½	28⅜	34¼

*Before decrease of $81 million or $.27 per share, related to early extinguishment of debt.

†Before extraordinary charge of $153 million or 25 cents per share, for early extinguishment of debt and charge of $2,127 million or $3.55 per share.

Investment Assessment. Southwestern Bell represents a solid, conservative, income investment, with a capital gains kicker. Yielding around 4 percent, and with dividends growing at an average annual rate of nearly 3 percent, the telecommunications company provides a steadily rising income stream to investors.

On top of that, the company's investments in the cellular and international telecommunications markets gives shareholders a stake in high-growth areas, and capital gains as the stock market responds to higher earnings. The stock trades well below its all-time high of $47 per share. (See Fig. 6-2, Southwestern Bell Corporation stock chart.)

SBC COM'CATIONS NYSE-SBC

RECENT PRICE 40	**P/E RATIO** 22.8 (Trailing: 15.7 / Median: 12.0) 14.1	**DIV'D YLD** 4.0%

VALUE LINE 767

High: 10.4 11.9 14.8 19.4 21.3 32.2 32.4 37.4 47.0 44.3
Low: 9.7 9.2 11.4 13.2 16.5 19.4 23.6 28.4 36.8

TIMELINESS 3 Average (Relative Price Performance Next 12 Mos.)
SAFETY 1 Highest (Scale: 1 Highest to 5 Lowest)
BETA .85 (1.00 = Market)

1997-99 PROJECTIONS
	Price	Gain	Ann'l Total Return
High	55	(+40%)	12%
Low	45	(+15%)	7%

Insider Decisions
N D J F M A M J J
to Buy 0 0 0 0 1 0 0 0 0
Options 0 0 0 0 0 0 0 0 0
to Sell 0 0 0 1 0 0 0 0 1

Institutional Decisions
	4Q23	1Q24	2Q24
to Buy	177	175	175
to Sell	175	240	177
Hld's(000)	215917	220454	219714

Percent shares traded 6.0 4.0 2.0

1.51 x Dividends p sh divided by Interest Rate
3-for-1-split
2-for-1 split
Relative Price Strength
Shaded areas indicate recessions

Target Price Range 1997 1998 1999

Options: PACE

© VALUE LINE PUB, INC.

	1984	1985	1986	1987	1988	1989	1990	1991	1992	1993	1994	1995	97-99
Revenues per sh	12.04	13.26	13.18	13.32	14.07	14.52	15.19	15.55	16.70	17.81	19.25	20.50	26.10
"Cash Flow" per sh	3.39	3.85	4.02	4.49	4.83	4.96	4.66	4.87	5.24	5.73	6.20	6.55	7.85
Earnings per sh A	1.51	1.67	1.71	1.74	1.77	1.82	1.84	1.93	2.17	2.39	2.70	2.90	3.70
Div'ds Decl'd per sh B	.93	1.00	1.07	1.16	1.24	1.30	1.38	1.42	1.46	1.51	1.56	1.63	1.90
Cap'l Spending per sh C	3.02	3.50	3.28	2.47	2.03	2.47	2.97	3.04	3.58	3.70	3.60	3.80	3.80
Book Value per sh C	11.71	12.38	13.04	13.63	14.15	13.92	14.31	14.76	15.51	12.68	13.65	14.95	19.75
Common Shs Outst'g D	597.19	597.72	599.76	600.90	600.83	601.17	599.74	600.32	599.75	600.23	602.00	602.00	602.00
Avg Ann'l P/E Ratio	6.8	7.8	9.8	10.9	10.8	14.0	14.8	14.2	14.8	16.7		13.0	
Relative P/E Ratio	.63	.63	.66	.73	.90	1.06	1.10	.91	.90	.99		1.00	
Avg Ann'l Div'd Yield	9.1%	7.7%	6.4%	6.1%	6.5%	5.1%	5.1%	5.2%	4.6%	3.8%		4.0%	
Revenues ($mill) A	7191.3	7925.0	7902.4	8002.6	8452.7	8729.8	9112.9	9331.9	10015	10690	11575	12235	15700
Net Profit ($mill)	883.1	996.2	1022.7	1047.1	1060.1	1092.8	1101.4	1156.5	1301.7	1435.2	1625	1745	2225
Income Tax Rate	39.6%	39.7%	41.0%	34.2%	24.8%	26.1%	28.5%	29.7%	30.4%	30.3%	34.0%	35.0%	35.0%
Net Profit Margin	12.3%	12.6%	12.9%	13.1%	12.5%	12.5%	12.1%	12.4%	13.0%	13.4%	14.0%	14.0%	14.0%
Long-Term Debt Ratio	41.4%	40.3%	38.6%	40.8%	37.2%	39.5%	39.0%	39.0%	38.1%	41.8%	41.0%	40.5%	38.0%
Common Equity Ratio	58.6%	59.7%	61.4%	59.2%	62.8%	60.5%	61.0%	61.0%	61.9%	58.2%	59.0%	59.5%	62.0%
Total Capital ($mill)	11929	12398	12730	13840	13543	13822	14064	14535	15020	13068	13975	15120	19155
Net Plant ($mill)	15394	16140	16727	16740	16304	16078	16322	16510	16899	17092	18270	19550	23800
% Earned Total Cap'l	9.4%	10.0%	9.9%	9.3%	9.7%	9.8%	9.7%	9.9%	10.4%	12.8%	13.0%	13.0%	13.0%
% Earned Net Worth	12.6%	13.5%	13.1%	12.8%	12.5%	13.1%	12.8%	13.1%	14.0%	18.9%	20.0%	19.5%	18.5%
% Earned Comm Equity	12.6%	13.5%	13.1%	12.8%	13.5%	13.1%	12.8%	13.1%	14.0%	18.9%	20.0%	18.9%	18.5%
% Retained to Comm Eq	4.8%	5.4%	4.9%	4.3%	4.9%	4.8%	4.3%	4.5%	5.6%	8.3%	8.5%	8.5%	9.0%
% All Div'ds to Net Prof	62%	62%	67%	67%	61%	63%	67%	66%	60%	58%	58%	56%	51%

Bold figures are Value Line estimates

BUSINESS: SBC Communications, Inc. is one of the seven regional holding companies formerly owned by the American Telephone & Telegraph Co. Owns 10.2% of the assets of the former AT&T and 10% of Telmex. Provides telecommunications service in Arkansas (6.2% of access lines), Kansas (8.7%), Missouri (16.5%), Oklahoma (10.6%), and Texas (58%). Access lines in service: 13.5 mill. '93 revenue breakdown: local service, 48.5%; access charges, 25%; toll, 9%; directory advertising, 8%; other, 9.5%. Has 37 telco employees/10,000 access lines. '93 depr. rate: 7.1%. Est'd plant age: 5.5 yrs. Has 58,400 employees, 963,355 shareholders. Chmn and C.E.O.: E. Whitacre, Jr. Inc.: DE. Address: 175 E. Houston, P.O. Box 2933, San Antonio, TX 78299. Telephone: 210-351-2044.

Figure 6-2. Southwestern Bell Corporation stock chart. (Copyright 1994 by Value Line Publishing Inc. Reprinted by permission; all rights reserved.)

☆ 47 SOUTHWESTERN ☆ ENERGY

SOUTHWESTERN ENERGY COMPANY
1083 Sain Street
P.O. Box 1408
Fayetteville, Arkansas 72702-1408
501-521-1141

Stock exchange: NYSE
Ticker symbol: SWN
DRIP program: Yes
Ownership:
   Institutional: + 56%
   Insiders: + 2%

Company Profile.   Southwestern Energy Company is a diversified natural gas company engaged in oil and natural gas exploration and production in Arkansas, Louisiana, other states, and the Gulf of Mexico. The company carries on an active exploration program, with a more than 30 percent increase scheduled for 1994. Its gas distribution network serves customers in Arkansas and Missouri.

Management Talent.   Chairman and Chief Executive Officer Charles E. Scharlu and President Dan B. Grubb have exhibited strong management tactics, with six consecutive years of rising earnings despite an environment marked by extremely soft gas prices.

Financial Status.   Three years of record revenues and earnings, capped by a surge in revenues and earnings in 1993, have substantially strengthened Southwestern Energy's balance sheet. Long-term debt decreased by over 14 percent, or nearly $20 million, and working capital increased to $18 million.

Cashflow.   Cashflow from continuing operations rose in excess of 40 percent in 1993 and more than doubled the 1991 cashflow figure, to over $70 million.

DRIP Details.   Southwestern Energy Company's DRIP program allows shareholders to purchase additional shares of company stock for cash, in amounts from $25 to $1000 per month, without incurring any commission or administrative expenses. For information, contact Southwestern Energy Company, c/o First Chicago Trust Company, P.O. Box 2598, Jersey City, New Jersey 07303-2598, 800-446-2617.

Particular Strengths. Significant increases in reserves, exploration, and gas production point to higher revenues and earnings in the coming decade. Backed by an efficient distribution system, Southwestern Energy can widen its market penetration.

There are some industry risks, such as pending rate cases and cost overruns on the new NOARK pipeline, that could negatively impact short-term earnings, but the company's bright long-term prospects promise to overshadow those problems with rising earnings.

With company business segments operating on all cylinders, Southwestern Energy is well structured to capitalize on rising gas prices.

Financial statistics (figures in millions, except per-share amounts):

For fiscal year ended December 31	1990	1991	1992	1993
Revenues	$117	$136	$144	$175
Net income (loss)	14	20	22	27*
Earnings (loss)/share	.57	.78	.87	1.05*
Dividend/share	.19	.19	.20	.22
Long-term debt	123	131	433	124
Stock price range/share:				
High	12	12¾	14	21⅞
Low	9⅜	9⅛	9¼	12⅛

*Excludes a gain of $8 million or $.39 cents per share due to the effect of an accounting change.

Investment Assessment. Southwestern Energy's stock has been trading not far above its 52-week trading low, despite strong fundamentals. With a recovering economy, higher gas prices, sharply expanding exploration activities, and rising revenues and earnings, this diversified energy company should be one of the industry's stellar performers.

A 50 percent rise in the stock price is not out of reach over the next few years. In the meantime, take advantage of the cash dividend, which in the past two years has been boosted an average of 8 percent.

☆ 48 UNITED WATER ☆ RESOURCES

UNITED WATER RESOURCES
200 Old Hook Road
Harrington Park, New Jersey 07640
201-784-9434

Stock exchange: NYSE
Ticker symbol: UWR
DRIP program: Yes
Ownership:
   Institutional: + 14%
   Insiders: +—%

Company Profile.   United Water Resources is a holding company with subsidiaries involved in water-related services and real estate operations. Its water utilities serve approximately 1 million people in northern New Jersey and southern New York. The company has been in business for over 125 years, and its unbroken string of cash dividends on its common stock stretches back to 1886.

Using its expertise acquired over a century in the water utility business, United Water Resources operates a network of environmental testing laboratories and sewage companies, in addition to its water companies.

Management Talent.   Chairman Robert A. Gerber and President and Chief Executive Officer Donald L. Correll are guiding United Water Resources into the twenty-first century. In 1993 the company created a new mission statement, designed to transform the firm into the premier water services company in the United States. A major step in that direction is the ongoing merger with GWC Corporation, discussed in more detail in a moment.

Financial Status.   United Water Resources has constructed a solid financial base upon which to grow into the nation's world-class water utility. In 1993 the company issued new low-cost debt, and retired debt with higher interest-rate burdens. With substantially all of its major capital-expenditure projects completed in the mid-to-late 1980s, United Water Resources is looking at significantly reduced capital outlays in the 1990s, counter to the water-industry trend. That translates into a competitive advantage, and more flexibility to use excess cash for acquisitions.

Cashflow.   Cashflows from income-producing real estate properties help to boost overall cashflow and working-capital levels. The cash dividend on common stock yields an attractive 7 percent, or close to it.

DRIP Details.   The United Water Resources DRIP program permits the cash purchase of additional company shares by shareholders in amounts of $25 to $3000 per quarter. There are no administrative costs or commissions for this service, and the company common stock may be purchased at a 5 percent discount to its current market price. For information on the dividend reinvestment plan, contact United Water Resources, c/o First Interstate Bank, Ltd., P.O. Box 60975, Terminal Annex, Los Angeles, California 90060, 800-522-6645.

Particular Strengths.   United Water Resources runs a first-class operation, with top-notch facilities that are well maintained. Earnings rebounded nicely in 1993 to $1.03 per share, after the weather-induced lower earnings of $.87 per share encountered in 1992.

The big impetus for future revenues and earnings lies in the anticipated benefits of the merger with GWC Corporation, a Wilmington, Delaware, water utility with operations in 14 states. The $200 million acquisition doubles United Water Resources's size, and made the firm the second-largest water utility in the United States. More importantly, it gives it immediate access to markets outside of New Jersey and New York.

Lyonnaise des Eaux-Dumez, one of Europe's largest water purveyors and providers of environmental services and public-works construction, will own 26.2 percent of United Water Resource's stock. It previously owned around 82 percent of GWC stock.

In 1993, GWC earned $1.40 per share on revenues of around $125 million, compared with earnings of $1.05 per share on revenues of $117 million in 1992.

Financial statistics (figures in millions, except per-share amounts; figures do not take into account the 1994 acquisition of GWC Corporation):

For fiscal year ended December 31	1990	1991	1992	1993
Revenues	$165	$162	$165	$200
Net income (loss)	18	16	16	20
Earnings (loss)/share	1.10	.96	.87	1.03
Dividend/share	.88	.91	.92	.92
Long-term debt	251	302	294	277
Stock price range/share:				
High	$16\frac{1}{2}$	$16\frac{5}{8}$	$16\frac{5}{8}$	$15\frac{7}{8}$
Low	$9\frac{7}{8}$	$10\frac{7}{8}$	13	14

Investment Assessment.   Rebounding earnings, excellent financials, and the merger with GWC Corporation should rejuvenate interest in United Water Resources. The company's stock price has treaded water over the past several years, with less than 4 points dividing its 52-week highs and lows.

The dynamic effects of the merger could well transform United Water Resources into an industry giant with unlimited growth potential. Look for a surge in earnings and in the company's stock price.

☆ 49 WASHINGTON ☆ WATER POWER

THE WASHINGTON WATER POWER COMPANY	Stock exchange: NYSE
1411 East Mission Avenue	Ticker symbol: WWP
Spokane, Washington 99202-2600	DRIP program: Yes
509-489-0500	Ownership:
	Institutional: + 17%
	Insiders: + —%

Company Profile.   Washington Water Power Company represents a diversified energy company. Its operations range from the generation, transportation, and distribution of electric energy, primarily deriving from water power, to the distribution and transportation of natural gas to non-utility operations such as waste-product power generation, freight-bill factoring, and a wholly-owned private investment firm.

Management Talent.   Paul A. Redmond has been Chairman and Chief Executive Officer since May 1988, and he assumed the additional position of President with the retirement of James R. Harvey in February 1994. Management has made substantial progress in corporate diversification and expansion of nonutility revenues, which are growing at an 18 percent annual rate.

Standard and Poor's ranked Washington Water Power in the top 25 competitively positioned U.S. utilities, based on financial performance and favorable business prospects.

Financial Status.   Both utility and non-utility revenues continue to expand, providing enhanced cashflow at around the $2.50-per-share level in 1993. Long-term debt of $540 million represents under 45 percent of total capital. Internally generated funds and outside financing will provide cashflow for planned capital expenditures of $110 million annually over the next five years.

DRIP Details.   Washington Water Power's DRIP program permits up to $100,000 cash investment in company shares annually, at no administrative or commission cost to program participants. For information, contact Shareholder Services, Washington Water Power Company, P.O. Box 3647, Spokane, Washington 99220-3647, 509-489-0500 or 800-727-9170.

Particular Strengths.   Traditionally, Washington Water Power has maintained a higher dividend payout than the industry average, and I expect this trend to continue. Its better than 8 percent yield also tops many other utility companies. The company's non-utility investments are having a growing impact on annual earnings.

Financial statistics (figures in millions, except per-share numbers):

For year ended December 31	1990	1991	1992	1993
Revenues	$554	$567	$558	$641
Net income (loss)	79	63	68	74
Earnings (loss)/share	1.73	1.34	1.37	1.44
Dividend/share	1.24	1.24	1.24	1.24
Long-term debt	559	632	597	647
Stock price range/share:				
High	15½	16⅞	18⅜	21
Low	13⅜	14⅛	16	17⅜

Investment Assessment.   A return to better weather patterns, enhanced nonutility operations, and lower long-term debt costs spell much-improved earnings prospects for Washington Water Power. The firm's high yield adds a degree of safety and stock-price support in a down market.

The utility and energy companies we have looked at in this chapter represent a variety of ways to add a charge to your overall portfolio return through attractive yields and long-term capital gains. Washington Water Powers' merger with Sierra Pacific is a good move. The new company will be called Resources West Energy.

7

Funding Your Portfolio

Mutual funds represent an easy way to diversify your portfolio while obtaining professional and specialized management. In the past few years, the number of available mutual funds has proliferated to the point where there are more mutual funds to choose from than there are individual stocks traded on U.S. exchanges.

In addition to the traditional domestic growth and income funds, there now exists a wide variety of global and international funds to aid you in your diversification efforts and to upgrade your overall investment performance. These range from open-end mutuals, seeking to capitalize on opportunities around the world, to closed-end funds targeting specific growth opportunities in single country, region, or even industry sectors.

Open-end mutual funds issue and redeem shares daily, based on a price determined from the combined value of the underlying shares or net asset value (NAV). Closed-end funds, on the other hand, issue a fixed number of outstanding shares and trade on a stock exchange, just like individual securities. At any given time their shares may trade at a discount or premium to the NAV, due to future prospects of the fund's holdings, investor sentiment, or other economic factors.

Solid reasons to expand your investments to the international and global arenas include the facts that over half of all equities trade outside of the United States, and that the average international fund rose over 38 percent in 1993, compared to less than 8 percent for the S&P 500. It only makes good investment sense to invest a portion of your portfolio in markets outperforming the U.S. markets and offering greater economic growth potential.

Just as you would investigate an individual stock's future prospects, you need to look beyond a mutual fund's past performance. Study the management style in light of anticipated economic changes; review its list of portfolio holdings with an eye to where the fund is headed; and match the fund's investment strategy to your own risk posture and investment goals.

Don't get bogged down in the heated debate over whether or not to invest in load funds, but let your investment return be your guideline. If a load fund outperforms its no-load counterparts, what's the difference if you pay a load charge? The main criterion is whether or not you are better off after you have considered the load charges in your net investment return. The same thinking holds true for expenses and expense ratios.

Here are some key questions to ponder when evaluating a fund. Is the manager responsible for past performance still at the helm? Has the fund's asset growth hampered its ability to move in and out of investments and sectors quickly, one of the reasons for its success to date? How well does the fund perform in different economic environments?

With that in mind, here are a dozen open- and closed-end funds with the management talent and investment strategy geared to deliver high returns in the decades ahead.

FUND NAME	FUND TYPE	OBJECTIVE/ STYLE	INVEST. SECTOR
Dreyfus Growth & Inc.	Open	Gr. & inc.	U.S. & intl. secur.
EuroPacific Growth	Open	Growth	International
Fidelity Contrafund	Open	Value	Undervalued situation
Invesco Strat. Leisure	Open	Cap appre.	Leisure industry
Keystone Amer. Global	Open	Growth	Small/medium global co.
T Rowe Price New Asia	Open	Growth	Asia large & small cap co.
Putnam Vista	Open	Growth	U.S. and foreign (max 20%)
SBSF Fund	Open	Total ret.	Com., conver., pref. stocks
Scudder Global	Open	Growth	U.S. & global secur.
Vanguard Intl. Growth	Open	Growth	International secur.
Warburg Pincus Intl.	Open	Growth	International secur.
Swiss Helvetia	Closed	Growth	Switzerland
Herzfeld Caribbean Basin	Closed	Growth	Caribbean

☆ 50 DREYFUS GROWTH ☆ & INCOME

DREYFUS GROWTH &
INCOME FUND
144 Glenn Curtiss Boulevard
Uniondale, New York 11556-0144
800-645-6561
Ticker symbol: DGRIX
Objective/style:
  Growth & income
Portfolio turnover: 85%
Investment adviser: Dreyfus Corporation*
Portfolio manager: Richard Hoey

Year begun:	1991
Assets:	$1.1 billion
Min. investment:	$2500
IRA:	$750
Load:	None
Annual exp. ratio:	1.24%

*Merger with Mellon Bank Corporation in progress in mid-1994.

Returns
Since inception (12/31/91): 37.97% thru 3/31/94
One-year: 9.20% thru 3/31/94

Representative Major Holdings

COMPANY	INDUSTRY	HQ
Occidental Petro CV	Energy	U.S.
UAL, CL ACV Pfd.	Transportation	U.S.
Brand	Basic ind.	U.S.
Chemical Bank, CV Pfd.	Financial	U.S.
Masco	Consumer	U.S.

Investment Strategy. Uses a mix of cyclical and interest-rate-sensitive stocks to delivery high total returns through a combination of capital appreciation and high-yielding investments.

Nearly 60 percent of the portfolio is invested in common stocks, with cyclical, finance, telecommunications, consumer, technology, and energy companies receiving higher relative weightings. While this fund's track record is short, it has performed well and is backed by solid Dreyfus investment experience.

Dreyfus has made a wholesale shift in its investments. None of the top five holdings listed above was even in the portfolio as recently as two years ago.

☆ 51 EUROPACIFIC ☆ GROWTH

EUROPACIFIC GROWTH FUND
333 South Hope Street, 52nd Floor
Los Angeles, California 90071-1447
800-421-9900
Ticker symbol: AEPGX
Objective/style: Growth
Portfolio turnover: 10%
Investment adviser: Capital Research & Management Company
Portfolio manager: Team Managed

Year begun: 1984
Assets: $5.8 billion
Min. investment: $250
Load: 5.75% max.
Annual exp. ratio: 1.10%

Returns

One-year: 43.1% thru 1/31/94
Three-year: 18.9% thru 1/31/94
Five-year: 15.6% thru 1/31/94

Representative Major Holdings

COMPANY	INDUSTRY	HQ
News Corp.	Pub. & broadcasting	Australia
ASEA/BBC Brown Boveri	Elec. & electronics	Swe./Switz.
Nestle SA	Food products	Switz.
Telefonos de Mexico	Telecomm.	Mexico
Tele. Corp. of New Zea.	Telecomm.	New Zeal.
Munchener Ruckver.	Insurance	Germany

Investment Strategy. EuroPacific employs a wide diversification strategy, with an investment mix of market sectors and worldwide geographic locations. Holdings include over 250 companies headquartered in more than 25 countries outside of the United States. The fund's comanagers are bottom-up investors utilizing various growth and valuation yardsticks to select individual securities. Investments run the gamut from large-cap international companies to emerging small-cap firms.

Recently, the portfolio holdings derived 45 percent of its assets from Europe, 9 percent from Japan, and 17 percent from other Pacific Rim nations. Telecommunications made up nearly 10 percent of the portfolio, with electrical and electronics stocks comprising another 7 percent and broadcasting and publishing nearly 7 percent.

☆ 52 FIDELITY ☆ CONTRAFUND

FIDELITY CONTRAFUND	Year begun:	1967
82 Devonshire Street	Assets:	$5.8 billion
Boston, Massachusetts 02109	Min. investment:	$2500
800-544-8888	IRA:	$500
Ticker symbol: FCNTX	Load:	3.00% max.
Objective/style: Value	Annual exp. ratio:	1.13%

Portfolio turnover: 230%
Investment adviser: Fidelity Management & Research Company
Portfolio manager: Will Danoff

Returns
One-year: 21.4% thru 12/31/93
Three-year: 29.7% thru 12/31/93
Five-year: 26.5% thru 12/31/93

Representative Major Holdings

COMPANY	INDUSTRY	HQ
DSC Comm. Corp.	Telecomm.	U.S.
Texas Inst. Inc.	Electronics	U.S.
Chrysler Corp.	Automotive	U.S.
Nomura Secur. Co. Ltd.	Securities	Japan
Adv. Micro Devices, Inc.	Electronics	U.S.

Investment Strategy.   This fund seeks enhanced growth via uncovering undervalued situations, turnarounds in the making, and other special situations not recognized by the market. The top 10 holdings accounted for nearly 11 percent of the fund's more than 760 investments. Major sectors include technology (16 percent), energy (14 percent), insurance/finance (7 percent), retail (6 percent), and utilities (3 percent).

Nearly 20 percent of the fund's holdings derived from foreign securities, with energy-related Canadian companies representing nearly 7 percent of the fund assets. Japanese stocks were heavily weighted with brokerage firms.

Energy stocks are taking on a more prominent role in the portfolio, with less emphasis being placed on leisure and entertainment.

☆ 53 INVESCO ☆
STRATEGIC LEISURE

INVESCO STRATEGIC LEISURE
7800 East Union Avenue, Suite 800
P.O. Box 173706
Denver, Colorado 80217-3706
800-525-8085
Ticker symbol: FLISX
Objective/style: Capital appreciation
Portfolio turnover: 148%
Investment adviser: INVESCO
    Funds Group, Inc.
Portfolio manager: Tim Miller

Year begun: 1984
Assets: $283 million
Min.
investment: $1000
IRA: $250
Load: None
Annual exp.
    ratio: 61%

Returns
One-year: 17.53% thru 3/31/94
Three-year: 34.89% thru 3/31/94
Five-year: 21.14% thru 3/31/94

Representative Major Holdings

COMPANY	INDUSTRY	HQ
Hasbro Inc.	Toy	U.S.
Mirage Resorts	Lodging/gaming	U.S.
Viacom Inc., CL B	Broadcasting	U.S.
Kroger Company	Supermarkets	U.S.
Cone Mills Corp.	Textiles	U.S.

Investment Strategy.   INVESCO Strategic Leisure invests in equity securities in consumer-sensitive sectors such as entertainment, recreation, restaurants, retailers, toys, newspapers, gaming, and other leisure goods.

The fund had a terrific run-up in value in 1993, with gaming issues leading the way. Since then management has shifted toward other leisure sectors, as gaming stocks reached their peak and increased the fund's presence in the multimedia sector. (See Fig. 7-1, INVESCO Strategic Leisure Fund chart.)

An economic rebound, with consumers possessing additional disposable income, bodes well for this aggressive fund. Since its inception

INVESCO STRATEGIC LEISURE

	INV. OBJECTIVE	YIELD	NAV	ASSETS($MIL)	VALUE LINE 847
FLISX	Other Specialty	0.0%	22.42	254.6	

FUND DESCRIPTION: INVESCO Strategic Leisure Fund seeks capital appreciation. The fund invests primarily in the equity securities of companies principally engaged in the design, production, or distribution of products or services related to the leisure time activities of individuals. The leisure sector includes the following industries: sporting goods, recreational equipment,

toys, games, photographic equipment and supplies, musical instruments, and recordings; motion picture and broadcasting companies; companies engaged in operating hotels or motels, sports arenas, gambling casinos, amusement or theme parks, or restaurants. Note: Prior to July 1, 1993, the fund was named Financial Strategic Leisure Fund.

ISSUE DATE
11/1/94

EXPENSE STRUCTURE

Management Fee	0.75%
12b-1 Fee	None
1st Yr. Red. Fee	None
Sales Load	Pct.
Maximum	None
at $25K	None
at $100K	None
at $500K	None
Minimum	None

Total Return
Performance of $10K Investment
Initial Investment (3/1/84): $10,000.
Value at 9/30/94: $65,914.
Fund
S&P500
Bottom Graph is Relative Strength of Fund Versus Peer.
Shaded areas indicate recessions.

Rising Line – Stronger Than Peer

Declining Line – Weaker Than Peer

HISTORICAL ARRAY	1990	1991	1992	1993	1984	1985	1986	1987	1988	1989	1990	1991	1992	1993	9/94
Bid Price (NAV)					8.49	11.18	10.69	9.29	11.94	14.34	11.93	15.94	18.55	23.28	22.42
Dividends ($)					0.06	0.04	0.00	0.00	0.00	0.21	0.03	0.00	0.00	0.00	0.00
12-Mo. Div. Yield (%)					0.70	0.35	0.00	0.00	0.00	1.27	0.26	0.00	0.00	0.00	0.00
Cap. Gains ($)					0.00	0.00	2.76	1.43	0.00	1.99	0.68	2.12	0.99	1.89	0.00
Expense Ratio (%)					1.50	1.50	1.50	1.50	1.89	1.38	1.84	1.86	1.51	1.14	1.08
Exp.Ratio Rel. to Peer					0.80	1.17	1.03	1.05	0.92	0.70	0.94	0.95	0.83	0.65	0.62
Turnover (%)					23	160	458	376	136	119	89	122	148	116	55
Net Assets ($Mil.)					0.3	1.2	2.8	2.7	5.6	12.6	5.1	14.4	40.1	304.5	254.6
Total Return (%)						32.2	18.8	0.7	28.5	38.3	-11.0	52.7	23.4	35.7	-3.7
+/- S&P 500 (%)						0.1	0.4	-4.5	11.7	6.8	-7.8	22.2	15.6	25.6	-5.0
+/- to Peer (%)						-4.9	-3.5	-0.1	6.3	16.5	-0.1	23.2	14.0	18.0	-2.2
Quintile Perf. Rel. to Peer						3	2	3	2	1	1	3	1	1	1	1	1	3

Figure 7-1. INVESCO Strategic Leasure Fund chart. (Copyright 1994 by Value Line Publishing Inc. Reprinted by permission; all rights reserved.)

over a decade ago, it has posted excellent returns, providing itself adept at foreseeing changes in investor sentiment and shedding over-valued situations before their eventual tumble could hinder portfolio performance. A broad diversification helps to reduce the risk of any one leisure sector negatively impacting results.

☆ 54 KEYSTONE ☆
AMERICA GLOBAL

KEYSTONE AMERICA GLOBAL
   OPPORTUNITIES CL A
99 High Street
P.O. Box 2121
Boston, Massachusetts 02106-2121
800-343-2898
Ticker symbol: KAGOX
Objective/style: Growth
Portfolio turnover: 64%
Investment adviser: Keystone Custodian Funds
Portfolio manager: Roland W. Gillis

Year begun:	1988
Assets:	$51 million
Min. investment:	$1000
Load:	5.75% max.
Annual exp.	
ratio:	2.84%

Returns
One-year: 37.7% thru 12/31/93
Three-year: 26.4% thru 12/31/93
Five-year: 15.0% thru 12/31/93

Representative Major Holdings

COMPANY	INDUSTRY	HQ
EMC Corporation	Off. & bus. equip.	U.S.
Parametric Technology	Off. & bus. equip.	U.S.
Best Buy Company	Retail	U.S.
NetManage, Inc.	Software services	U.S.
Tricord Systems	Off. & bus. equip.	U.S.

Investment Strategy. A relatively new fund, Keystone America Global Opportunities draws on Keystone's extensive investment experience stretching back to 1932. The connection has paid off handsomely, with steadily progressing performance result. In 1993, the fund earned over 37 percent. (See Fig. 7-2, Keystone America Global Opportunities Fund.)

Tapping into foreign opportunities, the fund utilizes the expertise of Credit Lyonnaise, a major international financial firm, for security selection and portfolio management of its overseas investments. In recent months, the portfolio managers have beefed up their foreign holdings with the addition of Latin American, Japanese, and Far Eastern companies.

The fund uses a bottom-up investment strategy, seeking strong growth opportunities in attractive emerging small-cap stocks. Major sector holdings include retail (12 percent), building (12 percent), office and business equipment (11 percent), and telecommunications (8 percent).

☆ 55 T. ROWE PRICE ☆
NEW ASIA

T. ROWE PRICE NEW ASIA FUND
100 East Pratt Street
P.O. Box 89000
Baltimore, Maryland 21202
800-638-5660
Ticker symbol: PRASX
Objective/style: Growth
Portfolio turnover: 40%
Investment adviser: Price-Fleming
Portfolio manager: David Warren/Martin Wade

Year begun:	1990
Assets:	$1.2 billion
Min. investment:	$2500
IRA:	$1000
Load:	None
Annual exp. ratio:	1.29%

Returns
One-year: 66.0% thru 1/31/94
Three-year: 28.7% thru 1/31/94

Holdings

COMPANY	INDUSTRY	HQ
Technology Resources Ind.	Telecomm.	Malaysia
Hong Kong Telecommunications	Telecomm.	Hong Kong
Granite Industries	Concrete	Malaysia
Aokam Perdana Berhad	Timber & wood prod.	Malaysia
Malaysian Helicopters	Helicopter mfr.	Malaysia

KEYSTONE AMERICA GLOBAL OPP A KAGOX

INV. OBJECTIVE	YIELD	NAV	ASSETS($MIL)	VALUE LINE	1029
Global Equity	0.0%	19.42	71.1		

FUND DESCRIPTION: Keystone America Global Opportunities Fund's investment objective is capital growth. The fund invests primarily in equity securities of small to medium sized companies (generally under $1 billion in market capitalization) that are in the relatively early stages of development. Investments can be in the securities of U.S. and foreign country companies. At least

65% of the fund's assets must be invested in securities in at least three different countries, one of which may be the United States. The fund uses a joint venture approach in selecting its securities; domestic investments are managed by Keystone, while Credit Lyonnais manages the fund's foreign holdings.

Total Return
Performance of $10K Investment
Initial Investment 6/30/88: $9,425.
Value at 9/30/94: $22,761.
Fund ___
MSCI WORLD ___
Bottom Graph is Relative Strength of Fund Versus Peer.
Shaded areas indicate recessions.

Rising Line – Stronger Than Peer
Declining Line – Weaker Than Peer

EXPENSE STRUCTURE

Management Fee	1.00%
graded to	0.08%
12b-1 Fee	0.25%
1st Yr. Red. Fee	None

Sales Load	Pct.
Maximum	5.75
at $25K	5.75
at $100K	3.75
at $500K	1.50
Minimum	0.00

HISTORICAL ARRAY

	1990	1991	1992	1993	9/94
Bid Price (NAV)	10.44	12.15	13.54	18.48	19.42
Dividends ($)	0.23	0.09	0.00	0.00	0.00
12-Mo. Div. Yield (%)	2.07	0.63	0.00	0.00	0.00
Cap. Gains ($)	0.08	1.35	0.00	0.16	0.00
Expense Ratio (%)	2.00	2.03	2.50	2.61	1.46
Exp.Ratio Rel. to Peer	1.00	1.05	1.31	1.41	0.85
Turnover (%)	51	134	75	34	15
Net Assets ($Mil)	1.5	2.2	10.9	41.0	71.1
Total Return (%)	-7.1	31.7	11.4	37.7	5.1
+/- MSCI WORLD (%)	9.9	13.4	16.7	15.1	-1.1
+/- to Peer (%)	3.0	12.2	10.8	7.6	3.8
Quintile Perf. Rel. to Peer	2	1	1	2	1

(other columns in array: 1982 | 1983 | 1984 | 1985 | 1986 | 1987 | 1988 | 1989)

	1988	1989
Bid Price (NAV)	10.82	11.49
Dividends ($)	0.35	0.03
12-Mo. Div. Yield (%)	3.04	0.24
Cap. Gains ($)	0.00	0.00
Expense Ratio (%)	1.50	2.00
Exp.Ratio Rel. to Peer	0.81	1.07
Turnover (%)	19	13
Net Assets ($Mil)	1.1	1.4
Total Return (%)		7.2
+/- MSCI WORLD (%)		-9.2
+/- to Peer (%)		-13.2
Quintile Perf. Rel. to Peer		5

Figure 7-2. Keystone American Global Opportunities Fund chart. (*Copyright 1994 by Value Line Publishing Inc. Reprinted by permission; all rights reserved.*)

Investment Strategy. In the past year, the portfolio managers of T. Rowe Price New Asia Fund have made a decided shift in its holdings to take a more aggressive position in Malaysia, with 5 of its top 6 holdings originating in that country. Overall, nearly 28 percent of the fund's holdings were in Malaysia. Other major holdings included equities from Hong Kong (27 percent), Singapore (14 percent), and Australia (8 percent).

Malaysia, along with Singapore and Indonesia, appears to be primed for substantial investment gains, given the good underlying economic foundations of rising gross domestic product, strong export growth, and low inflation.

Leading investment sectors include real estate (16 percent), banking (14 percent), transport and storage (7 percent), media (6 percent), and machinery and engineering (6 percent).

The fund invests in both large- and small-cap companies domiciled or with primary operations in Asia, excluding Japan. It also targets investments in China, Sri Lanka, Pakistan, and Indochina as opportunities arise.

The T. Rowe Price New Asia Fund has consistently outperformed its counterparts in the Pacific equity investment arena, beating them by over 20 percent in 1993. Management has been successful at anticipating new investment opportunities before its competitors, moving funds to investments in more promising companies/sectors/countries within the Asian region.

☆ 56 PUTNAM VISTA ☆

PUTNAM VISTA FUND CL A
One Post Office Square
Boston, Massachusetts 02109
800-225-1581
Ticker symbol: PVISX
Objective/style: Growth
Portfolio turnover: 121%
Investment adviser: Putnam Management Company
Portfolio manager: Jennifer Silver

Year begun: 1968
Assets: $525 million
Min. investment: $500
Load: 5.75% max.
Annual exp. ratio: 96%

Returns
One-year: 17.5% thru 12/31/93
Three-year: 23.8% thru 12/31/93
Five-year: 17.3% thru 12/31/93

Representative Major Holdings

COMPANY	INDUSTRY	HQ
Cisco Systems, Inc.	Software	U.S.
Harcourt General	Specialty consumer	U.S.
Leggett & Platt Inc.	Home furnishings	U.S.
Hercules Inc.	Chemical	U.S.
Applied Materials, Inc.	Electronics	U.S.

Investment Strategy. Putnam Vista Fund seeks mid-cap companies with above-average growth potential, coupled with a breadth of industries and a lower risk posture than the typical growth fund.

Major fund holdings include banks (8 percent), retail (6.5 percent), health care (6.3 percent), business services (5.95 percent), and electronics (5.0 percent).

Portfolio manager Silver's mid-cap investment strategy assumes a lower risk posture than investing in less financially strong small-cap firms. In addition, she seeks more undervalued situations, since many investment managers shun mid-cap stocks in favor of either large- or small-cap companies. With less interest in the mid-cap sector, there's less research, and therefore the chance for undervalued situations. Likewise, she avoids having to overpay for specific investments.

Taking a bottom-up approach, Silver employs a variety of quantitative yardsticks to ferret out reasonable values and earnings growth momentum.

☆ 57 SBSF FUND ☆

SBSF FUND
45 Rockefeller Plaza, 33rd Floor
New York, New York 10111
800-422-7273
Ticker symbol: SBFFX
Objective/style: Total return
Portfolio turnover: 70%
Investment adviser: Spears, Benzak, Salomon & Farrell
Portfolio manager: Louis R. Benzak

Year begun: 1983
Assets: $121 million
Min. investment: $5000
 IRA: $500
Load: None
Annual exp. ratio: 1.10%

Returns

One-year: 20.4% thru 12/31/93
Three-year: 15.2% thru 12/31/93
Five-year: 14.8% thru 12/31/93

Representative Major Holdings

COMPANY	INDUSTRY	HQ
American Inter. Group	Insurance	U.S.
Horsham Corporation	Metals & mining	Canada
Gannett Company	Pub. & enter.	U.S.
Avatar Holdings, Inc.	Real estate	U.S.
Capital Cities ABC, Inc.	Pub. & enter.	U.S.

Investment Strategy. SBSF does a fine balancing act between seeking above-average returns during strong markets and preserving capital during bear markets. The majority of its portfolio is in common stocks tempered by degrees of convertible, preferred, and government debt securities, depending on the economic environment.

Management moves deftly in and out of undervalued situations, cyclical stocks, out-of-favor industries and cash, as circumstances dictate. This fund is a good conservative holding, delivering an attractive total return with a low-risk posture.

☆ 58 SCUDDER GLOBAL ☆

SCUDDER GLOBAL FUND
175 Federal Street
Boston, Massachusetts 02110
800-225-2470
Ticker symbol: SCOBX
Objective/style: Growth
Portfolio turnover: 65%

Year begun: 1986
Assets: $963 million
Min. investment: $1000
IRA: $500
Load: None
Annual exp. ratio: 1.48%

Investment adviser: Scudder, Stevens & Clark, Inc.
Portfolio manager: William E. Holzer

Returns

One-year: 31.1% thru 12/31/93
Three-year: 15.6% thru 12/31/93
Five-year: 13.9% thru 12/31/93

Representative Major Holdings

COMPANY	INDUSTRY	HQ
Muenchener Rueck. AG	Insurance	Germany
Int.-Nederlanden Group	Banking/insur.	Nether.
Union Bank of Switzerland	Banking	Switz.
Bayerische Ver. AG	Banking	Germany
Pacific Telesis Group	Telecom	U.S.

Investment Strategy. Scudder global growth seeks long-term capital growth by identifying economic trends, promising technologies, and specific product and country opportunities that will deliver above-average gains.

The portfolio manager has the flexibility to be 100 percent invested in securities from outside or, as circumstances warrant, inside the United States. It invests in companies from industrialized, developed, and emerging nations. The geographical diversification of the portfolio reflected a 38 percent position in U.S. and Canadian securities, 37 percent in European firms, and 14 percent in the Pacific Basin, excluding Japan.

Scudder has been a major player in the international investment arena for over 40 years, which is a big plus when it comes to knowing the markets and recognizing foreign opportunities.

Lately, the fund has taken a high-profile stake in the financial/banking/insurance sector, with four of its top five holdings serving those markets worldwide.

This fund represents a conservative way for investors to participate in the international market and still retain impressive returns without a high degree of risk.

☆ 59 VANGUARD ☆
INTERNATIONAL GROWTH

VANGUARD
   INTERNATIONAL GROWTH   Year begun: 1985
P.O. Box 2600   Assets: $2.1 billion
Valley Forge, PA 19482   Min. investment: $3000
800-662-7447   IRA: $500
Turnover: 51%   Load: None
Ticker symbol: VWIGX   Annual exp. ratio: 59%

Objective/style: Growth
Portfolio turnover: 51%
Investment adviser: Vanguard Group
Portfolio manager: Richard R. Foulkes

Returns

One-year: 51.3% thru 1/31/94
Three-year: 13.2% thru 1/31/94
Five-year: 10.1% thru 1/31/94

Representative Major Holdings

COMPANY	INDUSTRY	HQ
Ito-Yokado Company Ltd.	Retail chain	Japan
Sekisui House Ltd.	Inv. banking	Japan
SIP	Telecomm.	Italy
STET	Telecomm.	Italy
Matsushita Electric Ind. Co.	Electronics & elec.	Japan

Investment Strategy. In 1993, Vanguard International Growth rebounded from two straight years of relatively bad performance. Long-time portfolio manager Foulkes has moved to companies and regions sensitive to adjustments in interest rates. Examples include the Italian telecommunications companies, SIP and STET. He has also made significant stakes in Japan, where a rebounding economy promises to uncover some undervalued situations in the wake of the beating the Japanese market has taken recently.

Over the long run, Foulkes has been very successful in taking the contrarian view. Consider the poor performances in 1991 and 1992 as being anomalies. Vanguard International is back on track.

☆ 60 WARBURG PINCUS ☆ INTERNATIONAL

WARBURG PINCUS INTER-
   NATIONAL EQUITY CL A
466 Lexington Avenue
New York, New York 10017
800-257-5614
Ticker symbol: CUIEX
Objective/style: Growth

Year begun: 1989
Assets: $570 million
Min. investment: $2500
   IRA: $500
Load: None
Annual exp. ratio: 1.48%

Portfolio turnover: 23%
Investment adviser: Warburg Pincus Counsellors
Portfolio manager: Richard King

Returns
One-year: 61.8% thru 1/31/94
Three-year: 22.5% thru 1/31/94

Representative Major Holdings

COMPANY	INDUSTRY	HQ
Telecom Argentina	Telecomm.	Argentina
Astra AB	Pharmaceut.	Sweden
Fletcher Challenge Ltd.	Div./forest/con.	New Zeal.
Banco De Santander	Banking	Spain
Woodside Petroleum Ltd.	Oil & gas	Australia

Investment Strategy. Warburg Pincus International Equity had an outstanding year in 1993, posting a return in excess of 51 percent. Indeed, the fund has been a stellar performer since its inception in 1989.

Portfolio manager King not only invests in developing countries such as Korea and Thailand, but also ferrets out value in emerging markets such as Chile, China, and Mexico. He has strengthened his holdings in the Latin American region, gaining bigger positions in Argentina and Mexico through firms in the telecommunication, banking, and construction industries.

King tempers his fund's exposure to the volatile international market diversification breadth. The top 10 holdings account for less than 20 percent of portfolio assets, and no single investment totals more than 3 percent of assets.

Closed-end Funds

Here's what Thomas J. Herzfeld, President and founder of Thomas J. Herzfeld Advisors, Inc. in Miami, Florida, has to say on the subject:

> Closed-end funds have been a major vehicle of choice for overseas investments for decades. Today there are over 40 emerging market country closed-end funds. Examples of closed-end fund performance for 1993 include the Turkish Investment Fund (+170 percent), First Philippine Fund (+131 percent), Templeton Emerging Markets (+100 percent), and Brazilian Equity Fund (76 percent).

Herzfeld also is editor of *The Thomas J. Herzfeld Encyclopedia of Closed-End Funds*, publisher of *The Closed-End Fund Research Report* and *The Investor's Guide to Closed-End Funds*, and author of *Herzfeld's Guide to Closed-End Funds* (McGraw-Hill, 1993). To inquire about or order a subscription to Herzfeld's *Research Report*, contact Thomas J. Herzfeld Advisors, Inc., The Herzfeld Building, P.O. Box 161465, Miami, Florida 33116, 305-271-1900.

To be sure, investing in overseas markets and closed-end funds can be volatile. For example, the Turkish and Philippine markets, which performed exceptionally well in 1993, were down over 55 and 17 percent, respectively, in the first quarter of 1994.

Herzfeld advises us, when investing in closed-end funds, to avoid purchasing closed-end funds that trade at a premium.

☆ 61 SWISS HELVETIA ☆

THE SWISS HELVETIA
   FUND, INC.
630 Fifth Avenue
New York, New York 10111
212-332-7930

Year begun: 1987
Assets: $185 million
Stock exchange: NYSE
Ticker symbol: SWZ

Investment adviser: Hottinger Capital Corp.
Portfolio manager: Georges L. de Montebello

Representative Major Holdings

COMPANY	INDUSTRY	HQ
Roche Holding AG	Pharmaceut.	Switz.
Nestle AG	Food	Switz.
Union Bank of Switz.	Banking	Switz.
Sandoz AG	Pharmaceut.	Switz.
Brown Boveri	Machinery	Switz.

Investment Strategy. Investment is in equity and debt securities of Swiss-based companies, with international exposure for long-term capital appreciation. The fund's largest sector holdings include pharmaceuticals (23 percent), banking (19 percent), machinery and metals (14 percent), food and beverages (12 percent), and insurance (10 percent).

"The Swiss Helvetia Fund's holdings read like a Who's Who of the world's largest and world-class companies. The fund's investment team has proven to be competent money managers," says George Cole Scott, publisher of the closed-end-fund investment newsletter, *The Scott Letter: Closed-End Fund Report,* and coauthor with Dr. Albert Fredman of "Investing in Closed-End Funds: Finding Value and Building Wealth" (New York Institute of Finance, 1991). For information on Scott's closed-end fund newsletter, contact *The Scott Letter,* Box 17800, Richmond, Virginia 23226, 800-356-3508.

According to Scott, The Swiss Helvetia Fund earned a total return in excess of 45 percent in 1993. The fund is expanding its holdings in smaller cyclical firms with good long-term-growth potential. As an indication of hidden value, the Swiss stock market has one of the lowest price-earnings multiples in Europe, with one of the highest expected earnings growth rates for its large multinational companies.

Special Situation

Cuba may soon reenter the world of nations. The country has been devastated by the collapse of communism worldwide and the loss of significant aid from the former Soviet Union. It lies in the heart of the Caribbean, and is only a half-hour flight from Southern Florida.

In the near future, Castro will yield to pressure to open up his country to trade with the West. Likewise, the United States will remove trade embargoes to help Cuba return to the family of nations. This will open up immediate investment opportunities, and eventually could lead to Cuba's admission as a full NAFTA trade partner. In fact, the wheels are already in motion. During the second quarter of 1994, a congressional subcommittee began hearings on normalizing trade relations with Cuba.

☆ 62 HERZFELD CARIBBEAN BASIN FUND ☆

Getting a jump on others, Thomas J. Herzfeld & Company, Inc. launched The Herzfeld Caribbean Basin Fund, Inc. in late 1993, and had completed subscription of 1.7 million shares at $5.20 per share by the end of March 1994. The fund began trading on NASDAQ in late May 1994, under the symbol CUBA.

Herzfeld has targeted investments in publicly traded companies anticipated to do well when the U.S. trade embargo is lifted. For example, Florida East Coast Industries (NYSE: FLA), a Florida railroad, should receive a boost in shipments resulting from cargo being shipped in and out of Florida to Cuba.

Other investments will include stakes in Cuban-American-owned and/or -managed businesses with intentions to expand to post-embargo Cuba, investment in major U.S. corporations seeking business in post-embargo Cuba, and companies specifically exempted from the current trade embargo under the Torricelli Amendment, which exempts postal and telecommunications firms.

Bonus List: More Mutual Funds. The following bonus list highlights additional mutual funds with good prospects of outperforming the market into the twenty-first century.

MUTUAL FUND	SECTOR	TYPE	TELEPHONE #
Alliance Gro. Fund B.	Growth	Open	800-227-4618
Emer. Mkts. Telecommun.	Telecomm.	Closed	212-832-2626
FBL Growth Common Stk.	Growth	Open	800-247-4170
Fidelity Dynatech Ser.	Technology	Open	800-342-5236
Fidel. Low-Priced Stk.	Low-price	Open	800-544-8888
Gabelli Global Telecomm.	Telecomm.	Open	800-422-3554
GT Worldwide Growth	Growth	Open	800-824-1580
Growth Fund of Spain	Spain growth	Closed	800-621-1148
IAI Emerging Growth	Emerging gr. co.	Open	800-945-3863
Latin Amer. Equity	Latin Amer.	Closed	212-832-2626
Oakmark International	Underval for. co.	Open	800-476-9625
T. Rowe Price Intl. Stk.	Intl. growth	Open	800-638-5660
Princor Emerg. Growth	Emer. companies	Open	800-247-4123
Scudder Global Sml. Co.	Glob. emer. co.	Open	800-225-2470
Thompson Oppor. B	Small-cap	Open	800-227-7337

Keep abreast of new mutual fund opportunities, both domestically and abroad. Investigate before you invest, then make the move to diversify wisely.

8

Terra Firma: Real Estate Investments

"Location, location, location!" used to be the rallying cry for real estate investors. While location still remains a dominant force in the selection of real estate investments, other critical factors also come into play when one is investing in real estate for the twenty-first century. These include cashflow, diversification, liquidity, and safety.

No matter how attractive a specific piece of property may be, unless it generates enough cashflow to service the debt load and prevent default, it's not a good investment. Likewise, a real estate investment must generate the cashflow you require for income.

Diversification in real estate holdings, like diversification in your overall portfolio, makes good investment sense, for it keeps you from getting overweighted in one real estate sector.

After disastrous losses in real estate in the eighties and early nineties, investors are seeking real estate investments that offer a greater amount of liquidity.

Finally, investors have taken a more cautious stance in real estate investing, seeking realistic returns without assuming unnecessarily high risks. As Will Rogers, who accumulated large land holdings in California (now the Will Rogers State Park), once said, "I'm more interested in the return *of* my money than the return *on* my money."

Like all investments, real estate runs through different cycles that make it more or less attractive than other investment alternatives depending on a variety of factors, such as interest rates, economic activity, tax legislation, and availability of capital.

There are a lot of reasons to consider real estate investing. First of all, despite recent hikes in the discount rate, interest rates are still near their lowest levels in over 20 years. Second, a lot of properties are available at bargain-basement prices. Third, as the various countries' economies and the overall world economy pick up steam, real estate holdings, assuming that they are in the right location and are the right type of property, should rise substantially in value and deliver above-average returns.

Keys to success in evaluating any real estate investment include investigating cashflow; obtaining appraisals on the property under consideration and appraisals on similar properties in comparable locations; assessing replacement cost, to determine if it makes more sense to purchase land and build new; considering tax consequences and potential negative tax legislation; and the advantages and risks of using various amounts of leverage.

Other considerations include the aforementioned liquidity, potential value appreciation, repairs and maintenance, property management, occupancy rates, competing properties, and functional obsolescence. Only after these items have been addressed and evaluated should the serious discussions over price and terms begin.

In addition to considering individual properties for purchase on your own, you can put up a stake in other real estate investment forms.

For example, fortunate clients of Gries Financial Corporation in Cleveland, Ohio, had the opportunity to invest in the Ravenna Woods Limited Partnership, a residential real estate partnership serving a market that did not have much direct competition in Twinsburg, Ohio.

In 1986, sixteen partnership units sold for $45,000 each. Near the end of 1993, the apartments were nearly 100 percent occupied, and the investment has been paying out increasing cashflow distributions, at an attractive double-digit level, over its life.

Via tax savings and cashflow, the project was returning an after-tax return in excess of 15 percent for 1993, with an average annual rate of return of over $11\frac{1}{2}$ percent from 1986 through 1993.

Another option is a real estate fund or partnership encompassing a variety of properties. To be sure, the disastrous real estate markets of the eighties, and the collapse of the savings-and-loan industry, decimated the ranks of real estate sponsors. Out of 150 real estate sponsors who exhibited at the 1985 International Association for Financial Planning Convention, only one was still exhibiting at the 1992 and 1993 conventions, Wells Real Estate Funds.

☆ 63 WELLS REAL ☆ ESTATE FUND

Asked to explain his firm's success, Leo F. Wells, President of Wells Capital, points to several strategies that help to guard his investors' principal and work to ensure attractive cashflows and returns:

> Our first concern is preserving safety of principal. We structure our investments with that preservation in mind. All funds are handled by a custodial trustee, NationsBank. NationsBank must obtain an independent appraisal before any property purchase or sale. Next, we only engage in all-cash ownership of properties. This debt-free status lowers our break-even occupancy to the 20 percent level, and prevents the properties ever being taken away due to mortgage default.

There are other key safety valves built into the Wells Real Estate Funds. Lease payments are guaranteed under contracts with *Fortune* 500 tenants. Lease payments are operating expenses, and will be paid before bondholder interest and stockholder dividends in the event the tenant company encounters financial difficulty.

Finally, Wells insists on four-quadrant diversification, meaning that each real estate fund diversifies with four to six different properties in four to six different geographic locations to four to six different *Fortune* 500 tenants operating in four to six different industries.

"You need all four quadrants to be properly diversified and preserve the principal," says Wells.

Adding an additional cushion of safety, all Wells's leases are negotiated as "triple net leases," requiring the tenants to pay expenses such as taxes, insurance, utilities, and maintenance.

The Wells Real Estate Funds (WREF) target investors with at least a $45,000 net worth and $45,000 annual gross income, or a $150,000 net worth. Minimum investment is a low $1000. According to Wells Real Estate Funds statistics, cashflow for WREF III started at 5.5 percent in 1989 and grew to 7.8 percent in 1993. The expected holding period is 8 to 10 years.

Don't worry if the current fund is already fully subscribed—the company typically offers a new fund following the closure of its predecessor. Properties are located around the United States in good economic environments, and preleased to *Fortune* 500 tenants. For example, in December 1993 WREF V and VI purchased a $6.9 million, four-story,

71,000-square-foot building leased to Hartford Fire Insurance Company south of Hartford, Connecticut. Terms include a 10-year lease with two consecutive 5-year options. The investment return to the partnership is estimated to be 10.1 percent.

Wells Real Estate Funds are located at 3885 Holcomb Bridge Road, Norcross, Georgia 30092, and may be contacted for information at 800-448-1010.

The Reit Route

"If investors are looking for more liquidity, the proliferation of real estate investment trusts (REITs) provides another option," says Sally Gries, President and founder of Gries Financial Corporation.

Real estate has long been considered for investment due to several important characteristics—its inflation-hedging capabilities, anticipated long-term cashflows and total returns—and as an effective way to diversify a portfolio.

Since over 50 percent of the world's value is tied up in real estate, it only makes sense that investors should include real estate in their investment strategies.

"REITs represent a logical choice for real estate ownership. They offer liquidity via publicly traded shares, provide diversification in property type as well as geographical location, deliver attractive yields tracking 10-year Treasuries, possess significant upside potential as they attract more investor attention, and are a good vehicle for raising additional capital," says David L. Millstein, National REIT partner with the accounting and consulting firm of Coopers & Lybrand in San Francisco, California. Coopers & Lybrand has published a book focusing on the opportunities for real estate investment trusts, entitled *REITs: The Future Is Now*.

Just what is a REIT? A real estate investment trust, or REIT, is a corporation or trust that combines the capital of many investors so as to acquire or provide financing for all types of real estate. In that respect, it operates much like a mutual fund for real estate. Its shares are traded on major stock exchanges, thus providing the liquidity that traditional real estate investments lack.

An important distinction between REITs and the average corporation lies in the tax law. A qualifying REIT does not pay any corporate income tax to the federal government, meaning that more capital and earnings can be reinvested in income-generating properties and paid out to investors. As a general rule, REITs are exempt from income taxes if they distribute 95 percent of income to the shareholders.

According to Mark O. Decker, President and Chief Executive Officer of the National Association of Real Estate Investment Trusts (NAREIT), an industry trade association headquartered in Washington, D.C., over the past 22 years REITs have significantly outperformed the S&P 500, direct real estate ownership, utilities, and government and corporate bonds. (See Fig. 8-1, Average Annualized Rates of Return.)

"REITs represent the main player in the real estate industry, with the drying up of other real estate capital sources such as savings-and-loans and banks," says David L. Brandon, Director REIT Advisory Services with Coopers & Lybrand in Washington, D.C.

Brandon points to some real estate sectors that promise to do well in the future. For example, in many areas of the country there has been little apartment construction over the past decade. Likewise, the trend toward factory outlet centers also opens up new investment opportunities.

Of course, as with any investment, there are some caveats here. The proliferation of new REITs means that there will inevitably be some bad REITs coming to market, along with the promising ones. In addition, the flood of investors into the REIT market sector could cause

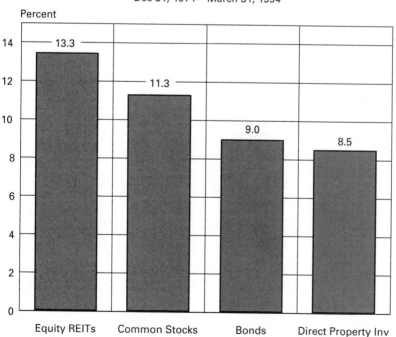

Figure 8-1. Average annualized rates of return. *(Source: NAREIT, S & P 500, Lehman Brothers, Evaluation Associates, and NCREIF.)*

price volatility. Also, rising interest rates may make some real estate projects less feasible than they were under lower-interest-rate scenarios. Again, investigate before you invest, in order to uncover those REITs best situated to perform well.

REITs were among the best-performing market sectors in 1993, despite a fourth-quarter drop that trimmed the annual gain. For the entire year, the Investor's Business Daily Finance-Equity REIT Index rose 20.8 percent.

Among the reasons to consider REITs now are the relatively high yields they offer and the fact that real estate prices often are at or below 25-year lows. Also, as REITs elicit more institutional investor interest, rising demand should drive the share prices of well-performing REITs higher.

In 1993 alone, more than $9 billion in REIT IPOs (initial public offerings) hit the streets. That figure nearly equals the value of REIT IPOs during the previous 10-year period. Today there are an unprecedented variety of REITs to choose from, with real estate investments in health-care facilities, medical office facilities, hotels, traditional retail, industrial, warehouse, office, residential properties, manufactured homes and communities, motels, factory outlets, and even golf courses.

"Today the REIT industry consists of some $60 billion in assets. I foresee the industry's market capitalization growing to $200 billion in 5 to 10 years, and $500 to $700 billion in 20 years," says NAREIT's President, Mark O. Decker.

According to Decker, today's REITs differ from their historical counterparts, which typically hired a real estate gun without an ownership interest. Today, the average REIT company management also maintains an average 15 percent ownership stake.

With the hundreds of REITs to choose from, how do you go about selecting an appropriate REIT for your portfolio? Here are some key points to consider in the decision-making process.

- Look at the underlying asset value of the real estate.
- Evaluate the prospects for the real estate sector (health care, factory outlet, etc.) the REIT operates in.
- Consider the impacts (both positive and negative) of the geographical location of the REIT's properties.
- Seek out firms with management ownership between 10 to 20 percent.
- Check out the REIT's market liquidity, in terms of shares exchanging hands on a regular basis.

- Compare yields and the additional risk associated with higher yields.

- Assess the leverage or risk posture of the REIT, to see if it coincides with your own risk posture.

- Look at management's expertise or track record in similar real estate ventures.

The following list of REITs represents a number of firms from a variety of real estate sectors. They range from large to small companies, from firms in the business for years to relatively new IPOs. This should give you an idea of the breadth and variety of the REIT sector.

For additional information on REITS, the following resources may prove helpful: *Realty Stock Review,* Charter Financial Publishing, 179 Avenue at the Common, Second Floor, Shrewsbury, New Jersey 07702, 908-389-8700, and *Pharus Realty Stock Report,* 121 W. 27th Street, Suite 303, New York, New York 10001. *Barron's* also carries a regular column, "The Ground Floor," on real estate and REITS.

REIT	INDUSTRY SECTOR
Center Point Properties Corp.	Indl./warehouse
Crown American Realty Trust	Enclosed shop. malls
G&L Realty	Medical office
Horizon Outlet Centers	Factory outlet
Jameson Company	Motels
National Golf Properties, Inc.	Golf courses
Omega Healthcare Investors, Inc.	Health care
Post Properties	Apartments
RFS Hotel Investors, Inc.	Hotels
ROC Communities, Inc.	Mfd. home comm.
Royale Investments, Inc.	Retail
Shurgard Storage Centers	Mini storage
Spieker Properties, Inc.	Indl./off./retail
The Town and Country Trust	Multifamily
Urban Shopping Centers, Inc.	Regional malls

Remember that these REITs may also be diversified by location. Some may concentrate on a specific region of the country (such as Post Properties, with 70 percent of its properties near its Atlanta, Georgia, headquarters), while others may target the whole country as their market. The market may be further segmented by the type of tenant attracted. (For instance, Post Properties seek upscale renters for its apartments, and provides the amenities and furnishings they desire.)

Not all of the REITs perform equally well in the market. A 1993 IPO, Manufactured Home Communities, ranked as the top-performing REIT

IPO that year with a 67 percent price surge, while Mark Centers Trust, a shopping center REIT, garnered the dubious honor of being the worst-performing REIT IPO of 1993, with a better than 25 percent drop in its per-share price.

The following well-managed REITs appear to be positioned to prosper in the years ahead.

REIT	INDUSTRY SECTOR
Kimco Realty Corporation	Shopping centers
New Plan Realty	Shopping centers/apts.
Tanger Factory Outlet Centers, Inc.	Factory outlet
United Dominion Realty Trust, Inc.	Apts./shopping centers
Washington Real Estate Investment Trust	Diversified r.e.

☆ 64 KIMCO REALTY ☆

KIMCO REALTY CORPORATION
1044 Northern Boulevard
Roslyn, New York 11576
516-484-5858

Stock Exchange: NYSE
Ticker symbol: KIM
DRIP program: Yes
Ownership:
  Institutional: 40%
  Insiders: 24%

Company Profile.   Kimco Realty Corporation owns the nation's largest publicly-traded portfolio of neighborhood and community shopping centers, with over 135 properties throughout more than 23 states.

Founded in 1966, Kimco Realty possesses extensive real estate experience across the country. The company went public in 1991. The turnaround year was 1993, with operations earning a profit of $1.25 per share, versus combined losses totaling nearly $5 per share for the three years ended December 31, 1991 (Kimco changed to a calendar year in 1992). Earnings improved again in 1993, with a jump to $1.76 per share.

Kimco's strategy is to be the low-cost provider to retail tenants, thus helping to ensure the acquisition of long-term leases with predictable income flows.

Management Talent.   Chairman Milton Cooper is a founding member of the company, while President David M. Samber joined the firm as an attorney in 1974, having previously served as Senior Vice President, Acquisition and Finance, from 1983 to 1991.

Financial Status. The company has been improving its balance sheet through the payoff of more than $60 million in high-cost, long-term debt, and by using the proceeds from a $75 million offering of perpetual preferred stock with an annual dividend rate of $7\frac{3}{4}$ percent. In addition, $100 million of 10-year unsecured notes at $6\frac{1}{2}$ percent interest allowed for the replacement of higher-cost, variable-rate, long-term debt.

DRIP Details. The Kimco Realty Corporation DRIP permits additional purchases of company shares with cash amounts ranging from $100 to $25,000 per quarter, at no administrative or commission cost to the plan participant. For information, contact American Stock Transfer & Trust Company, Attn: Dividend Reinvestment Department/Kimco, 40 Wall Street, 46th Floor, New York, New York 10005, 212-936-5100.

Particular Strengths. Kimco possesses long-term expertise in the shopping center market, top-quality management, and a proven track record of acquiring underutilized shopping centers and turning them around through renovations and other improvements.

Financial statistics (figures in millions, except per-share amounts):

For fiscal year ended December 31*	1990	1991	1992	1993
Revenues	$73	$48	$79	$99
Net income (loss)	(16)	(2)	19	35
Earnings (loss)/share	(2.52)	(.27)	1.25	1.76
Dividend/share	—	—	1.48	1.88
Long-term debt	366	266	258	200
Stock price range/share:				
High	—	$21\frac{1}{2}$	$31\frac{1}{8}$	$39\frac{1}{4}$
Low	—	$19\frac{1}{4}$	$21\frac{1}{8}$	$30\frac{1}{2}$

*Fiscal year 1991 ended April 30, the year 1991 covering 8 months with the conversion to a calendar fiscal year.

Investment Assessment. Kimco Realty Corporation yields around 5.5 percent, and boosted its dividend payout over 6 percent in early 1994. The company possesses a unique franchise of purchasing underperforming shopping centers and substantially improving their occupancy rates, cashflows, and profitability. Lower debt costs, and proceeds from recent equity offerings, will lower the cost of financing operations, provide more financial stability, and open up new opportunities for Kimco.

☆ 65 NEW PLAN REALTY ☆

NEW PLAN REALTY TRUST
1120 Avenue of the Americas
New York, New York 10036
212-869-3000

Stock exchange: NYSE
Ticker symbol: NPR
DRIP program: Yes
Ownership:
   Institutional: 15%
   Insiders: 7%

Company Profile.   The granddaddy of REITs, New Plan Realty has been around as a publicly traded company for many decades. It ranks as the second-largest publicly traded REIT in the nation, with over $1.2 billion in market capitalization. The company has paid dividends 51 out of its 52 years of existence. New Plan Realty dividends have risen for 15 consecutive years and yields over 6 percent, at a quarterly payout of 33 cents per share.

The company specializes in self-administering and company-managed shopping centers and apartments, concentrated in the Middle Atlantic region of the country. Overall, it owns in excess of 110 properties in 18 states.

Management Talent.   The Newman family has owned and operated the company since its founding back in 1942, and the family still controls just under 7 percent of the outstanding shares. Long-time industry veterans William Newman and Arnold Laubich serve as Chairman and Chief Executive Officer and President and Chief Operating Officer, respectively.

Financial Status.   One of the most financially stable and conservative firms in the industry, New Plan Realty's long-term debt is a paltry $20 million, or only about 1 percent of total capital.

DRIP Details.   Participants in the New Plan Realty DRIP may purchase additional shares of company stock for cash amounts ranging from $100 to $20,000 per quarter. As a bonus, the shares are purchased at a 5 percent discount below the average high and low sales prices for shares on the cash distribution payment date. For information, contact New Plan Realty Trust, 1120 Avenue of the Americas, New York, New York 10036-6783, 212-869-3000.

Particular Strengths. New Plan Realty has put its cash store to work, with the purchase of additional properties that will generate revenues in the years ahead. The company searches out quality properties in decent locations, which can be upgraded to improve operating results.

The company's financial prowess will open up opportunities not available to more cash-strapped or debt-laden REITs. Its low-debt posture gives it plenty of operating flexibility.

Financial statistics: (figures in millions, except per-share amounts):

For fiscal year ended July 31	1991	1992	1993	1994 (est.)
Revenues	$57	$65	$76	$90
Net income (loss)	40	49	43	55
Earnings (loss)/share	1.05	1.08	.89	1.15
Dividend/share	1.15	1.23	1.29	1.35
Long-term debt	19	18	20	20
Stock price range/share:				
High	24½	26⅛	26⅜	
Low	16⅛	19⅝	21½	

Investment Assessment. Concerns over rising interest rates and New Plan Realty's high dividend payout are overblown. The decline in the firm's fiscal 1993 earnings stemmed from an overly cautious cash position. In fact, rental revenues increased substantially in 1993, but interest and dividend income more than offset the earnings from new rentals. That cash hoard has now been put to work to generate higher total earnings.

Over the past 10 years, shareholders have earned a better than 17 percent total return. New Plan Realty is one of the best-managed and most financially strong companies in the industry. The company's stock trades not far above its 52-week trading low of $20 3/8 per share. (See Fig. 8-2, New Plan Realty Trust stock chart.) Look for a solid rebound.

NEW PLAN REALTY NYSE-NPR | **RECENT PRICE** 20 | **P/E RATIO** 17.4 (Trailing: 18.9 / Median: NMF) | **RELATIVE P/E RATIO** 1.20 | **DIV'D YLD** 6.8% | **VALUE LINE** 1177

TIMELINESS 3 (Relative Price Perform-ance Next 12 Mos.) Average

SAFETY 1 Highest (Scale: 1 Highest to 5 Lowest)

BETA .75 (1.00 = Market)

1997-99 PROJECTIONS

	Price	Gain	Ann'l Total Return
High	35	(+75%)	20%
Low	30	(+50%)	16%

Insider Decisions

Institutional Decisions

Target Price Range 1997 1998 1999

Relative Price Strength

Shaded areas indicate recessions

Options: ASE

	1978	1979	1980	1981	1982	1983	1984	1985	1986	1987	1988	1989	1990	1991	1992	1993	1994	1995	© VALUE LINE PUB., INC.	97-99
	.89	1.28	1.40	1.45	2.37	2.49	3.44	3.66	4.40	5.98	6.03	7.90	7.95	9.83	10.46	10.22	10.74	10.65	Book Value per sh	12.60
	.31	.30	.39	.40	.54	.59	.71	.80	.85	.84	.89	.98	1.01	1.03	.97	1.02	1.27	1.45	Funds from Ops per sh B C	1.95
	.31	.21	.31	.31	.46	.50	.60	.70	.74	.73	.70	.87	.91	.92	.86	.87	1.04	1.18	Earnings per sh A B	1.60
	.22	.25	.30	.34	.39	.51	.57	.65	.73	.81	.89	.97	1.05	1.13	1.21	1.28	1.32	1.36	Div'ds Decl'd per sh ■ a	1.60
	2.43	2.10	1.94	2.05	1.73	2.40	2.53	2.68	3.47	2.93	3.46	3.61	4.36	3.90	6.28	7.64	11.32	13.20	Loans & Real Est per sh	15.00
	7.61	9.20	9.91	9.96	12.83	13.25	16.62	17.26	20.67	26.64	26.85	34.71	35.15	44.49	48.38	48.96	52.59	53.00	Common Shs Outst'g E	60.00
	188%	135%	121%	166%	85%	194%	129%	163%	170%	157%	135%	104%	114%	81%	105%	131%	115%	160%	Premium over Book	160%
	12.0	14.1	9.9	12.5	14.5	14.5	12.8	13.8	30.9	21.0	20.4	18.4	18.7	19.3	25.0	27.2	22.3	20.0	Avg Ann'l P/E Ratio	20.0
	8.4	10.0	7.9	9.7	8.1	12.3	10.9	12.0	14.0	18.4	16.0	15.9	16.8	17.3	22.2	23.1	18.2	17.0	Avg Ann'l P/FFO Ratio	17.0
	8.6%	8.3%	10.0%	9.7%	8.9%	7.0%	7.4%	6.8%	6.2%	5.3%	6.2%	6.2%	6.1%	6.4%	5.6%	5.4%	5.7%	5.0%	Avg Ann'l Div'd Yield	5.0%
							17.3	19.7	21.9	26.2	28.5	33.8	38.0	41.4	47.6	65.3	96.4	125	Rental Income ($mill) A	180
							4.8	6.6	9.5	9.2	8.9	9.8	16.1	16.0	17.1	11.0	4.6	2.0	Other Income ($mill)	5.0
							64.3%	67.0%	70.2%	64.3%	62.4%	69.0%	68.4%	71.4%	71.0%	67.2%	64.3%	63.5%	Operating Margin	67.5%
							8.5	11.8	14.9	16.5	18.7	25.0	31.8	35.1	39.4	42.3	51.3	62.0	Net Profit ($mill)	93.0
							38.3%	44.8%	46.2%	46.0%	50.1%	57.4%	58.3%	60.7%	60.9%	55.4%	50.8%	48.8%	Net Profit Margin	50.1%
							.3	.7	1.5	2.2	2.2	4.8	3.3			.9	1.0	Nil	Capital Gains	Nil
							42.1	46.3	71.7	78.2	92.6	125.5	160.3	173.5	304.1	374.2	595.1	700	Loans & Real Est ($mill)	900
							47.0	44.3	96.3	96.3	22.5	22.7	22.7	18.6	17.5	23.3	28.1	125	Long-Term Debt ($mill)	150
							57.2	63.1	90.9	159.4	161.9	274.2	279.5	437.2	506.3	500.6	565.5	750	Net Worth ($mill)	750
							80.6%	81.3%	86.1%	96.7%	100.0%	98.7%	103.5%	109.3%	125.2%	125.4%	103.9%	94%	% Div'ds Decl'd to FFO	83%
							8.6%	8.0%	6.2%	5.9%	7.5%	6.6%	5.7%	11.8%	4.7%	4.7%	6.3%	6.5%	% Expenses to Assets	6.5%
							14.7%	15.1%	14.1%	11.6%	13.8%	14.5%	12.4%	11.8%	10.7%	8.6%	9.7%	10.0%	% Earned Total Cap'l	12.0%
							20.8%	19.7%	18.4%	15.2%	14.6%	15.3%	12.4%	12.0%	10.7%	8.6%	9.8%	11.0%	% Earned Net Worth	13.0%

BUSINESS: New Plan Realty Trust is a self-administered and managed, equity-oriented real estate investment trust specializing in the ownership of income-producing shopping malls and apartments. Investment locations are concentrated in states east of the Mississippi. Portfolio breakdown as of 7/31/94: real estate (historical cost basis), 95%; cash and marketable securities, 2%; mortgage and other loans receivable, 3%. Has about 11,894 shareholders; 318 employees. The Newman Family controls 5.9% of common stock. Merchant Navy Officer's Pension Fund, 8.6%; ABP, 9.5% (694 Prospectus). Org'd: Mass. Chrmn. & C.E.O.: William Newman. President: Arnold Laubich. Address: 1120 Avenue of the Americas, NY, NY 10036. Telephone: 212-869-3000.

Figure 8-2. New Plan Reality Trust stock chart. (Copyright 1994 by Value Line Publishing Inc. Reprinted by permission; all rights reserved.)

☆ 66 TANGER FACTORY ☆ OUTLET

TANGER FACTORY
  OUTLET CENTERS, INC.
1400 West Northwood Street
P.O. Box 29168
Greensboro, North Carolina 27408
910-274-1666

Stock exchange: NYSE
Ticker symbol: SKT
DRIP program: No
Ownership:
  Institutional: 48%
  Insiders: 40%

Company Profile.   A May 1993 REIT IPO, Tanger was one of the top-performing REITs, with a nearly 28 percent rise in its per-share price in 1993. While Tanger is a newcomer to publicly traded stocks, the Tanger family has been developing real estate properties since 1981.

The company specializes in building in mostly rural areas, away from major-department-store competition. Tanger administers and manages its 20 factory outlet centers located in 14 states. All of its properties have been originally developed by Tanger.

Management Talent.   Chairman, President, Chief Executive Officer, and founder of the company, Stanley K. Tanger created the factory outlet concept in 1981. Prior to that he served as President and Chief Executive Officer of the family-owned apparel-manufacturing business for 30 years. Executive Vice President Steven B. Tanger, son of Stanley, has worked for Tanger enterprises for nearly 20 years. He is responsible for all phases of project development, including site selection and land acquisition and development. The Tanger family owns approximately 40 percent of the company's outstanding shares.

Financial Status.   The company's debt-to-equity ratio is less than 10 percent, and the company plans to maintain that ratio under the 40 percent level. Revenues and earnings are both increasing dramatically, as the company expands its operations.

DRIP Details.   Tanger shareholders may acquire additional shares of company stock through dividend reinvestment or direct purchase of shares. For information, contact The First National Bank of Boston, Investors Relations Department, P.O. Box 644, Mail Stop 45-02-16, Boston, Massachusetts 02102, 617-575-2900.

Particular Strengths.   The company has successfully grown its base of operations from 10 factory outlet centers at the end of 1990 to 20 currently. With less than 300 factory outlet centers accounting for under 2 percent of retail sales in the United States, there's plenty of room for growth.

The factory outlet segment has been one of the fastest-growing segments of the retailing industry, drawing significant numbers of customers. Factory outlet retail revenues grew at an estimated 12.2 percent pace in 1992, versus only 4.1 percent for all retail centers.

By utilizing the company's own construction managers, Tanger keeps construction schedules and costs under control. Its site-selection criteria pay particular attention to both current and potential competition from other outlet and retail centers.

Financial statistics (figures in millions, except per-share amounts):

For fiscal year ended December 31	1990	1991	1992	1993
Revenues	$10	$13	$18	$29
Net income (loss)				5*
Earnings (loss)/share				.90*
Dividend/share				.535
Long-term debt	19	18	20	20
Stock price range/share:				
High	—	—	—	30
Low	—	—	—	22½

*Before effects of early extinguishment of debt amounting to $2.7 million or 55 cents per share.

Investment Assessment.   At least for the coming decade, the factory outlet concept is on track to experience exceptional growth. As one of the premier players in this retail and real estate segment, Tanger looks for continued growth in revenues and net income.

The high level of institutional ownership, combined with the number of shares owned by the Tanger family, translate into an effective small float. As Tanger posts strong gains, the demand for the firm's stock will push the price sharply higher.

☆ 67 UNITED ☆
DOMINION REALTY

UNITED DOMINION
   REALTY TRUST, INC.
10 South Sixth Street, Suite 203
Richmond, Virginia 23219-3802
804-780-2691

Stock exchange: NYSE
Ticker symbol: UDR
DRIP program: Yes
Ownership:
   Institutional: 38%
   Insiders: 6%

Company Profile.   United Dominion Realty Trust was formed in 1972 and came through the eighties without incurring any deficit years. It is now in the process of rebuilding its earnings, which fell to 16 cents per share in 1984 and again to 29 cents per share in 1991.

The firm is a self-administered equity REIT, specializing in apartment complexes (85 percent) and shopping centers (14 percent) and with a small foothold in the office/industrial building segment (1 percent). Its properties are located in the southeastern United States.

Management Talent.   President and Chief Executive Officer John P. McCann has served in those positions since 1974. Other top managers have extensive real estate experience with the company and/or in the real estate operations of major financial institutions. Management's strategy of concentrating its properties in one geographic region allows the company to regularly inspect each property and to closely monitor local real estate market developments as they evolve.

Financial Status.   A $78 million stock offering, in late 1993, allowed United Realty to pay off all of its $35 million in short-term debt and use the balance for property acquisitions. There are no significant debt maturities facing management in the short term, and the company takes a conservative stance toward the heavy use of variable-rate debt.

DRIP Details.   The United Dominion Realty DRIP Program permits company shareholders to purchase additional shares of stock at no commission or administrative cost in cash amounts ranging from $50 to $5000 per quarter. For information, contact United Dominion Realty Trust, Inc., Att: Secretary, 10 South Sixth Street, Suite 203, Richmond, Virginia 23219-3802, 804-780-2691.

Particular Strengths. United Dominion Realty has been enlarging its stake in the apartment segment, boosting the number of apartments owned by over 65 percent during the past several years. With no new apartment construction anticipated for a number of years, the company is well insulated from new competition.

Occupancy gains and rising rents in its core properties spell improved revenues, cashflow, and earnings. The geographic focus on the southeastern United States has worked well for the company.

Financial statistics (figures in millions, except per-share amounts):

For fiscal year ended December 31	1990	1991	1992	1993
Revenues	$44	$51	$63	$89
Net income (loss)	5	4	6	11
Earnings (loss)/share	.19	.15	.18	.29
Dividend/share	.62	.63	.66	.69
Long-term debt	118	168	181	229
Stock price range/share:				
High	$9\frac{1}{8}$	$10\frac{1}{2}$	$12\frac{3}{4}$	$16\frac{7}{8}$
Low	$12\frac{1}{4}$	$7\frac{1}{8}$	$9\frac{3}{4}$	$11\frac{7}{8}$

Investment Assessment. A rebounding southeastern U.S. economy; improving property mix with more apartment complexes; and the company's proven success at purchasing older properties and rehabilitating—all these make for a successful mix. The move to raise the apartment portion of its real estate portfolio promises higher returns in the coming years.

United Dominion Realty's talented management team and strong finances makes the company a good total-return candidate with solid dividend growth potential. Trading at around $13\frac{3}{8}$ per share, down from its 52-week high of $16\frac{7}{8}$ per share, the stock yields 5.8 percent. United Dominion Realty has paid out cash dividends every year since 1973, and has raised the dividend rate consecutively for the past 18 years.

☆ 68 WASHINGTON ☆ REAL ESTATE

WASHINGTON REAL
  ESTATE INVESTMENT TRUST
4936 Fairmont Avenue
Bethesda, Maryland 20814
301-652-4300

Stock exchange: AMEX
Ticker symbol: WRE
DRIP program: Yes
Ownership:
  Institutional: 13%
  Insiders: 3%

Company Profile. Washington Real Estate Investment Trust is a diversified, self-administered, real estate investment trust, serving the metropolitan Washington, D.C., region. It maintains a balanced portfolio mix, consisting of office buildings (36 percent), shopping centers (35 percent), apartment complexes (16 percent), and business centers (13 percent).

In business since 1960, Washington Real Estate has long been a survivor through good times and bad. The company has one of the best track records in the business. On average, cashflows have increased over 12 percent annually since 1973. The company maintains a low debt posture, and over the past 20 years compounded annual total return has exceeded 15 percent.

Management Talent. Chairman and President B. Franklin Kahn cofounded the company in 1960. He is a former Governor of the National Association of Real Estate Investment Trusts, has taught case-study seminars and real estate finance courses at the Wharton School of Finance (University of Pennsylvania) for over 40 years, and is a member of the New York Society of Security Analysts.

Financial Status. Washington Real Estate consistently keeps long-term debt at below the 10 percent level. Indeed, since early 1993 this conservative and financially strong company has been completely free of long-term debt. For decades, Kahn and team have delivered strong operating and financial performances.

Cashflow has improved every year since 1978, and in 1993 earnings per share tied a record high of 82 cents per share. The future looks even brighter.

DRIP Details.   The Washington Real Estate Investment Trust DRIP program allows additional cash investment in company shares in amounts of $100 to $25,000 per year. For information, contact the American Stock Transfer & Trust Company, 40 Wall Street, New York, New York 10005, 800-937-5449.

Particular Strengths.   Consistent performance by a top industry real-estate-management team, through all types of economic scenarios, provides a high degree of safety. Occupancy rates in the mid-nineties, coupled with strong growth prospects for the metropolitan Washington, D.C., area, will bolster future revenues and earnings. Over 95 percent of the company's properties are within an hour's drive of its headquarters.

A program of continually upgrading its property portfolio places Washington Real Estate in the premier category of real estate investors and keeps occupancy rates high. Its diversified real estate portfolio reduces the financial risk of any one market sector going sour.

Financial statistics (figures in millions, except per-share amounts):

For fiscal year ended December 31	1990	1991	1992	1993
Revenues	$30	$33	$34	$39
Net income (loss)	16	18	20	23
Earnings (loss)/share	.69	.74	.76	.80
Dividend/share	.73	.79	.84	.89
Long-term debt	12	11	1	—
Stock price range/share:				
High	12⅞	18½	21¼	24¾
Low	9⅛	10⅞	14⅞	18⅝

Investment Assessment.   Washington Real Estate Investment Trust is a premier industry company, with solid long-term management experience in its market area. Safety and total return are the investment keys for shareholders of this A-1 company.

Dividends have risen 27 times during the past 23 years, rising 10 percent in 1993 alone. With nearly $20 million in cash revenues and no long-term debt on the books, Washington Real Estate stands ready to expand its holdings with quality income-producing properties, to drive up rental revenues and earnings.

The stock is a bargain at its present trading range of around $18 per share, down from its all-time high of $24¾ per share. (See Fig. 8-3,

WASHINGTON R.E.I.T. ASE-WRE

| RECENT PRICE | 17 | P/E RATIO | 20.0 (Trailing: 20.7 / Median: NMF) | RELATIVE P/E RATIO | 1.38 | DIV'D YLD | 5.6% | VALUE LINE | 1183 |

TIMELINESS 4 (Relative Price Perform-ance Next 12 Mos.)

SAFETY 1 (Scale: 1 Highest to 5 Lowest)

BETA .65 (1.00 = Market)

1997-99 PROJECTIONS

	Price	Gain	Ann'l Total Return
High	25	(+45%)	14%
Low	20	(+20%)	9%

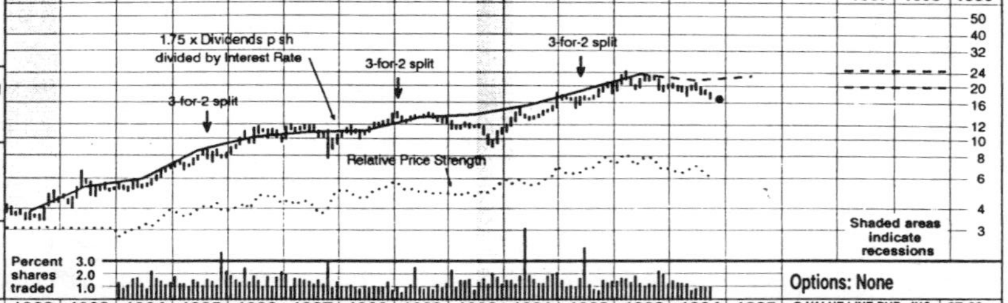

Target Price Range 1997 1998 1999

Options: None

© VALUE LINE PUB., INC. — column 97-99:

	97-99
Book Value per sh	5.65
Funds from Ops per sh	1.25
Earnings per sh A	1.05
Div'ds Decl'd per sh B a	1.10
Loans & Real Est per sh	5.80
Common Shs Outst'g C	31.00
Premium over Book	265%
Avg Ann'l P/E Ratio	21.0
Avg Ann'l P/FFO Ratio	18.0
Avg Ann'l Div'd Yield	5.1%
Rental Income ($mill)	62.0
Other Income ($mill)	Nil
Operating Margin	64.5%
Net Profit ($mill)	31.5
Net Profit Margin	50.8%
Capital Gains ($mill)	Nil
Loans & Real Est ($mill)	210
Long-Term Debt ($mill)	50.0
Net Worth ($mill)	175
% Div'ds Decl'd to FFO	88.0%
% Expenses to Assets	9.5%
% Earned Total Cap'l	15.5%
% Earned Net Worth	18.5%

BUSINESS: Washington Real Estate Investment Trust is a self-administrated, regional real estate investment trust, with an emphasis on investing in and developing income-producing properties. As of 6/30/94, the investment portfolio (based on cost) by property type included: shopping centers, 32%; office buildings, 43%; apartment buildings, 13%; business centers, 12%. The trust has typically used a very low amount of debt in property financing. Real estate investments are concentrated in and around the Washington, D.C. area. Has 29,000 shrhldrs. Insiders own 2.4% of stock (3/94 Proxy). Organized: District of Columbia. Pres. and Chmn. of the Board of Trustees: B. Franklin Kahn. Address: 10400 Connecticut Ave, Concourse Level, Kensington, MD 20895. Tel: 301-929-5900.

Figure 8-3. Washington Real Estate Investment Trust stock chart. (Copyright 1994 by Value Line Publishing Inc. Reprinted by permission; all rights reserved.)

Washington Real Estate Investment Trust.) Unlike other companies trading at a lofty 22 times earnings, Washington Real Estate Investment Trust has proven itself through long-term performance.

With its yield of around 5 percent and great earnings prospects, investors looking for total return from a solid company should snap these shares up. It is the oldest real estate investment trust in the nation, and intends to stay around for a lot longer.

The Mutual-Fund Road

An alternative to picking out your own individual REIT or basket of REIT holdings is to seek out quality, well-performing mutual funds specializing in this real estate sector. The Templeton Real Estate Securities Fund has an impressive track record.

☆ 69 TEMPLETON ☆ REAL ESTATE SECURITIES FUND

TEMPLETON REAL ESTATE
   SECURITIES FUND
Franklin/Templeton
   Distributors, Inc.
700 Central Avenue
St. Petersburg, Florida 33701-3628
800-292-9293
Ticker symbol: TEMRX
Objective/style: Long-term capital growth
Portfolio turnover: 20%
Investment adviser: Templeton Investment Counsel
Portfolio manager: Jeffrey Everett

Year begun: 1989

Assets: $75 million
Min. investment: $100
Load: 5.75% max.
Annual exp. ratio: 1.68%

One-year: 8.1% thru 3/31/94
Three-year: 12.1% thru 3/31/94

Representative Major Holdings

COMPANY	INDUSTRY	HQ
Empresas Ica Sociedad Contoladora SA	Construc. & housing	Spain
Revenue Properties Co. Ltd.	Real estate devel.	Canada
Rouse Company	Real estate devel.	U.S.
Nationwide Health Prop.	REIT/health care prop.	U.S.
Weyerhouser Company	Forest/bldg. products	U.S.

Investment Strategy. Templeton Real Estate Securities Fund provides an exposure to real estate with several twists. Not only does it invest in other than pure real estate developers, it also adds an international flavor to its portfolio.

For example, investments in companies such as Georgia-Pacific, Oriental Hotel Ltd., Schuler Homes, and Masco Corporation diversify its portfolio into forest products, leisure and tourism, housing construction, and building materials; all tied to the real estate industry or with extensive real estate holdings. Likewise, investments in foreign companies in Canada, Chile, Italy, and Spain provide a broad geographical diversification. The fund does not invest directly in real estate properties.

Overall, approximately 54 percent of the fund's holdings are located in the United States, with 22 percent deriving from Asia, nearly 19 percent from Europe, and the balance from other areas of the world such as Latin America, Australia, and New Zealand.

Templeton's bargain-hunting nature and contrarian strategy carry over, with its predictable good results, from its other funds to the Templeton Real Estate Securities Fund. (See Fig. 8-4, Templeton Real Estate Securities chart.)

Other Real Estate Mutual-Fund Options

The following list provides you with a number of mutual fund options, and with a variety of tactics for benefiting from real estate investments in one form or another.

FUND	TYPE	LOAD	800 #
Cohen & Steers Real.	Open	None	437-9912
Cohen & Steers Real. Inc.	Closed	—	437-9912
Columbia R.E. Eq.	Open	None	547-1037
DFA R.E. Secur.	Open	None	395-8005
Evergreen Global R.E.	Open	None	235-0064
Fidelity R.E.	Open	None	544-8888
Franklin R.E. Secur.	Open	Yes	437-9912
PRA R.E. Secur.	Open	None	435-1405
Pioneer Winthrop R.E.	Open	Yes	225-6292
United Services R.E.	Open	None	873-8637

IPLETON REAL ESTATE SECS   TEMRX

INV. OBJECTIVE	YIELD	NAV	ASSETS($MIL)	VALUE	852
Other Specialty	1.5%	13.49	117.0	LINE	

FUND DESCRIPTION: Templeton Real Estate Securities Fund seeks long-term capital growth, with current income as a secondary objective. Under normal conditions, at least 65% of its assets are invested in U.S. or foreign issues of companies engaged in the real-estate industry. The fund may invest the balance of its assets in the securities of non-real-estate businesses. Debt security holdings may not be rated lower than A.

ISSUE DATE
11/1/94

EXPENSE STRUCTURE
Management Fee 0.75%

12b-1 Fee	0.24%
1st Yr. Red. Fee	None

Sales Load	Pct.
Maximum	5.75
at $25K	5.75
at $100K	3.50
at $500K	2.00
Minimum	0.00

Total Return
Performance of $10K Investment
Initial Investment 9/30/89: $9,425.
Value at 9/30/94: $14,965.
— Fund
— S&P 500
Bottom Graph is Relative Strength of Fund Versus Peer.
Shaded areas indicate recessions.

Rising Line – Stronger Than Peer

Declining Line – Weaker Than Peer

HISTORICAL ARRAY

	1990	1991	1992	1993	1994	1995	1996	1997	1998	1999	1990	1991	1992	1993	9/94
Bid Price (NAV)										9.93	8.16	10.45	10.52	13.76	13.49
Dividends ($)										0.08	0.37	0.48	0.35	0.22	0.00
12-Mo. Div. Yield (%)										0.75	4.22	4.32	3.13	1.50	1.53
Cap. Gains ($)										0.00	0.09	0.00	0.00	0.00	0.00
Expense Ratio (%)										-	1.25	1.25	1.69	1.68	1.48
Exp. Ratio Rel. to Peer										-	0.64	0.64	0.92	0.95	0.85
Turnover (%)										-	10	25	32	20	21
Net Assets ($Mil.)										-	10.1	32.8	37.0	83.9	117.0
Total Return (%)										-	-13.1	34.4	4.2	33.0	-2.0
+/- S&P 500 (%)										-	-9.9	22.9	-3.6	22.9	-3.3
+/- to Peer (%)										-	-2.2	4.9	-5.2	15.2	-0.5
Quartile Perf. Rel. to Peer										3	3	4	2	2	2

Figure 8-4. Templeton Real Estate Securities Fund chart. (Copyright 1994 by Value Line Publishing Inc. Reprinted by permission; all rights reserved.)

Bargain Hunters

A number of firms specialize in building their real estate fortunes from the misfortunes of others, by purchasing depressed properties or partnership units from real estate partnerships that have soured since the eighties.

☆ 70 KENSINGTON ☆ INVESTMENT GROUP

"Real estate is coming off a bowl-shaped bottom which reduces the downside risk," says John Kramer, president of the Kensington Investment Group in Orinda, California.

Kensington seeks to earn above-average returns by purchasing limited partnerships with quality assets that are performing well. Due to market inefficiencies, Kramer anticipates purchasing $1.25 worth of real estate assets for every $1 invested.

"The trick is to stay out of the way of the elephants. We're seeking markets ignored by the major players," says Kramer.

The minimum investment in the Kensington Select Real Estate Income Fund is $40,000. For information, contact your financial planner, or call Kensington Investment Group at 510-253-2949.

"Real estate investments are more than a means to diversify your portfolio. Right now there are some real bargains out there," stresses Lewis Walker, a Certified Financial Planner and founder of Walker Capital Management Corporation in Norcross, Georgia.

Investigate the listed real estate investment alternatives, to determine which will best help you to achieve your investment objectives while fitting in with your risk posture. Seek out the best opportunities to ground your portfolio in a firm foundation of quality properties, partnerships, real estate investment trusts, or mutual funds.

9

Beating Inflation with Precious Metals

Precious metals have been an effective store of value since ancient times. Inflation fears, political instability, world economic crisis, armed conflict, and imbalances in precious metals' demand and supply combine to push metal prices higher.

For example, in the high inflationary years of the 1970s and early 1980s, gold prices surged, hitting a 200-year peak in 1980 at $850 per ounce. (See Fig. 9-1, Gold Prices, for recent price history.)

Gold Prices			
YEAR	HIGH	LOW	AVERAGE
1983	$510	$373	$424
1984	405	307	360
1985	341	282	317
1986	443	327	368
1987	502	389	447
1988	487	392	437
1989	419	356	382
1990	425	346	394
1991	403	341	363
1992	362	328	345
1993	414	325	361
1994	397	374	386 (thru May)

Figure 9-1. Gold price chart.

In addition to their great usefulness as hedges against calamity, many precious metals possess characteristics that make them attractive for both industrial and ornamental purposes. For example, as well as being used extensively in jewelry, gold is used by many high-tech man-ufacturers in the production of consumer products, covering every-thing from cellular phones to VCRs, and industrial products, ranging from telecommunication satellites to sophisticated military equipment.

Following the historic price rise in precious metals during the seven-ties and eighties, their prices have steadily drifted lower, with some brief spikes upward. Through most of the late eighties and early nineties the price of gold languished between $325 and $425, hitting a seven-year low in March 1993 of $325 per ounce.

In the fall of 1993, my article on gold investments appeared in the October/November issue of *Your Money*. Among the factors listed there that could bring a resurgence to gold and other precious-metal prices were a return to an inflationary environment, a loss of confidence in the world's central banks, a currency crisis, and the outbreak of wars.

Since then the Federal Reserve Bank has hiked up the discount rate three times, and continued hostile outbreaks in the former Yugoslavia and political unrest in South Africa have dominated front-page head-lines.

Gold funds were the hottest-performing group in 1993. A top gold fund, Lexington Strategic Investments Fund, rose over 247 percent in 1993. While the immediate past may not be a good indicator of gold and other precious-metal performance in the future, the underlying fundamentals strongly suggest that precious metals will perform well during the inflationary and politically unstable periods we will undoubtedly encounter from time to time as we move into the twenty-first century.

Here's what Vahid Fathi, senior metals analyst with Kemper Securities in Chicago, has to say on the subject:

> The fundamental supply/demand relationship is supportive of higher gold prices for the foreseeable future, at least through 1994 and 1995. The worldwide aggregate supply of gold has been flattening out, after the tremendous new capacity added in the 1980s. There's been continued strong demand, despite half of the world's economy being mired in a recession. Finally, Russia has disposed of the majority of its excess gold reserves, so it will no longer be a depressing factor on the price of gold.

With all that in mind, the following companies represent the best ways to invest in precious metals, and some bright prospects for sub-stantial gains as world economic and political circumstances drive pre-cious-metal prices higher.

North American Gold Mining Companies

By far the best-financed, most stable gold mining companies are based in North America. While there are numerous South African gold-mining companies with substantial reserves, the political unrest in that part of the world, and the risks associated with that unrest, outweigh the possible investment gains. The following companies are well positioned to benefit from a rise in the price of gold.

☆ 71 AMERICAN ☆ BARRICK

AMERICAN BARRICK
   RESOURCES CORPORATION
24 Hazelton Avenue
Toronto, Ontario, Canada M5R 2E2
416-923-9400

Stock exchange: NYSE
Ticker symbol: ABX
DRIP program: No
Ownership:
   Institutional: 38%
   Insiders: 20%

Company Profile. American Barrick Resources Corporation is a Canadian-based, low-cost gold mining company with reserves in excess of 27 million ounces. Its low-cost gold production allows the company to make money on gold prices as low as $275 per ounce. Its large reserves rank it number one in North America, and among the world's largest gold mining companies. The company has been a consistent performer since its founding in 1983.

Production is estimated to rise to 2 million ounces by 1995, up nearly 33 percent from 1993's production rate. The company has increased its reserves by nearly 50 percent in the past five years. Major gold-producing properties and reserves include the Goldstrike Mine in the rich Carlin Trend region of Nevada; the Holt-McDermott Mine in northern Ontario; the Meikle Mine in Nevada; and the Mercur Mine in Utah. The company also maintains offices in Mexico and Chile, and actively seeks to develop new mining operations around the world.

American Barrick engages in an active hedging program, designed to allow the company to benefit from the upside potential in gold prices while taking a conservative approach and providing downside gold-price protection. The company uses spot-deferred contracts that may be rolled forward for 10 years.

It works like this. If the spot price declines below the contract price, the company can deliver gold to satisfy the contract. On the other hand, if the spot price rises above the contract price, the company can sell gold on the spot market and roll the contracts forward for future delivery. Thus American Barrick is covered on both sides of the market.

Management talent. Executive Director and Chairman Gregory C. Wilkins leads a talented team with considerable gold mining expertise. Expanding its management depth, Neil MacLachlan, with extensive experience in Asia, has been appointed Managing Director, Asia, and Alexander Davidson has joined the firm as Vice President, Exploration.

Financial Status. Strong earnings growth has boosted both cashflow and the company's overall financial strength. Cashflow has more than doubled, to $1.10 per share in 1993 from 50 cents per share in 1991. Likewise, long-term debt has decreased substantially, to around $225 million from over $400 million in 1989. Look for this scenario to continue to improve, as operating cashflow more than covers planned capital expenditures and cash dividends.

Particular Strengths. Higher gold production, low-cost operations, and a successful hedging strategy will keep American Barrick in the ranks of the premier gold companies for many years to come. The company is well protected on the downside, and stands to benefit as the price of gold rises with increased demand.

Financial statistics (figures in millions of US$, except per-share amounts):

For fiscal year ended December 31	1990	1991	1992	1993
Revenue	$283	$369	$554	$681
Net income (loss)	58	92	175	213
Earnings (loss)/share	.23	.34	.62	.75
Dividend/share	.04	.04	.065	.08
Long-term debt	363	311	322	225
Stock price range/share:				
High	12⅜	13⅞	16⅜	30⅜
Low	7⅝	9⅛	11⅛	13⅝

Investment Assessment.   American Barrick's financial strength and improving operations will provide it with considerable flexibility to take advantage of new gold mining opportunities as they arise. The stock represents a solid, conservative play in gold mining stocks. A rise in the price of gold will reward shareholders handsomely. In the meantime, American Barrick represents a quality growth company. With the pullback in the price of gold in the early part of 1994, the share price of American Barrick dropped from a 52-week high of $31 per share to the $23½-per-share level. The bottom line: a good long-term holding for those turbulent times ahead.

☆ 72 ECHO BAY MINES ☆

ECHO BAY MINES LTD.
10180 101st Street
Edmonton, Alberta, Canada T5J 3S4
403-496-9704

Stock exchange: AMEX
Ticker symbol: ECO
DRIP program: No
Ownership:
Institutional: 25%
Insiders: 2%

Company Profile.   Canadian Echo Bay Mines Ltd. explores for gold in both Canada and the United States, and operates four mining operations: McCoy/Cove Mine in Nevada; Lupin, in Canada's Northwest Territories; Round Mountain in Nevada; and Kettle River in Washington. The company also has several properties in development stages in Alaska.

Echo Bay also represents a silver play, since its McCoy/Cove deposit ranks as the largest North American silver-producing mine and one of the three largest in the world. In 1993 it produced 12.5 million ounces of silver.

Management Talent.   The Echo Bay management team consists of industry veterans, including Chairman Robert F. Calman, President and Chief Executive Officer Richard C. Kraus, and Chief Operating Officer and Executive Vice President Robert C. Armstrong. Past strategic mistakes, such as the investments in the Muscocho Group (written down in 1990), are now history.

Financial Status.   Echo Bay has worked down its long-term-debt position to $210 million, from over $340 in 1989. More importantly, its cash and investments in U.S. Treasury notes and other short-term investments now exceed its long-term debt. Operating cashflow increased by 45 percent in 1993, to a record $110 million plus.

Particular Strengths.   "Echo Bay has good reserves, decreasing production costs, and rising production. It's a fallen star as far as Wall Street is concerned, due to past mistakes, but those are behind them now. The company should do well in this cycle," observes Vahid Fathi, senior metals analyst with Kemper Securities in Chicago.

Financial statistics (figures in millions of US$, except per-share amounts):

For fiscal year ended December 31	1990	1991	1992	1993
Revenue	$339	$316	$312	$367
Net income (loss)	(60)	7	(27)	14
Earnings (loss)/share	(.60)	.07	(.30)	.03
Dividend/share	.07	.08	.08	.08
Long-term debt	336	268	246	210
Stock price range/share:				
High	21¼	10⅛	8¼	14½
Low	7⅛	6⅝	4⅜	4⅛

Investment Assessment.   Higher production, decreasing costs, and major developmental projects in the wings portend better financial times ahead for Echo Bay. The fact that Wall Street is down on the company only serves to make it undervalued, in light of the firm's promising future. The present positives here far outweigh past negatives. Purchase for strong gains. The company trades at just over a third of its 1989 high of $30⅛ per share, and 50 percent below its 52-week trading-range high. Wall Street will come around with higher stock prices, as gold and silver prices rise and Echo Bay cashes in with higher earnings. (See Fig. 9-2, Echo Bay Mines Ltd. stock chart.)

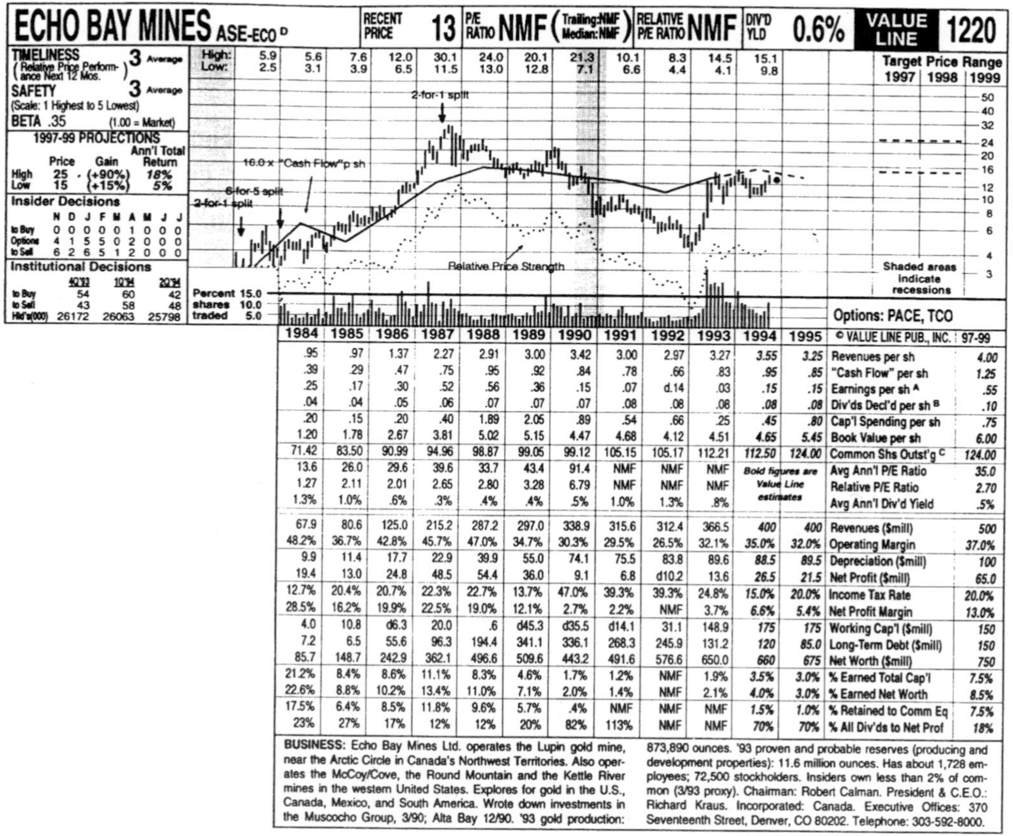

ECHO BAY MINES ASE-ECO ᴰ | **RECENT PRICE** 13 | **P/E RATIO** NMF (Trailing:NMF Median:NMF) | **RELATIVE P/E RATIO** NMF | **DIV'D YLD** 0.6% | **VALUE LINE** 1220

TIMELINESS 3 Average (Relative Price Perform- ance Next 12 Mos.)	High:	5.9	5.6	7.6	12.0	30.1	24.0	20.1	21.3	10.1	8.3	14.5	15.1
	Low:	2.5	3.1	3.9	6.5	11.5	13.0	12.8	7.1	6.6	4.4	4.1	9.8

Target Price Range 1997 | 1998 | 1999

SAFETY 3 Average
(Scale: 1 Highest to 5 Lowest)
BETA .35 (1.00 = Market)

1997-99 PROJECTIONS

	Price	Gain	Ann'l Total Return
High	25	(+90%)	18%
Low	15	(+15%)	5%

Insider Decisions

	N	D	J	F	M	A	M	J	J
to Buy	0	0	0	0	1	0	0	0	0
Options	4	1	5	5	0	2	0	0	0
to Sell	6	2	6	5	1	2	0	0	0

Institutional Decisions

	4Q'93	1Q'94	2Q'94
to Buy	54	60	42
to Sell	43	58	48
Hld's(000)	26172	26063	25798

Percent 15.0
shares 10.0
traded 5.0

2-for-1 split
16.0 x "Cash Flow" p sh
6-for-5 split
2-for-1 split
Relative Price Strength
Shaded areas indicate recessions

Options: PACE, TCO

© VALUE LINE PUB., INC.

1984	1985	1986	1987	1988	1989	1990	1991	1992	1993	1994	1995		97-99
.95	.97	1.37	2.27	2.91	3.00	3.42	3.00	2.97	3.27	3.55	3.25	Revenues per sh	4.00
.39	.29	.47	.75	.95	.92	.84	.78	.66	.83	.95	.85	"Cash Flow" per sh	1.25
.25	.17	.30	.52	.56	.36	.15	.07	d.14	.03	.15	.15	Earnings per sh ᴬ	.55
.04	.04	.05	.06	.07	.07	.08	.08	.08	.08	.08	.08	Div'ds Decl'd per sh ᴮ	.10
.20	.15	.20	.40	1.89	2.05	.89	.54	.66	.25	.45	.80	Cap'l Spending per sh	.75
1.20	1.78	2.67	3.81	5.02	5.15	4.47	4.68	4.12	4.51	4.65	5.45	Book Value per sh	6.00
71.42	83.50	90.99	94.96	98.87	99.05	99.12	105.15	105.17	112.21	112.50	124.00	Common Shs Outst'g ᶜ	124.00
13.6	26.0	29.6	39.6	33.7	43.4	91.4	NMF	NMF	NMF	Bold figures are Value Line estimates		Avg Ann'l P/E Ratio	35.0
1.27	2.11	2.01	2.65	2.80	3.28	6.79	NMF	NMF	NMF			Relative P/E Ratio	2.70
1.3%	1.0%	.6%	.3%	.4%	.4%	.5%	1.0%	1.3%	.8%			Avg Ann'l Div'd Yield	.5%
67.9	80.6	125.0	215.2	287.2	297.0	338.9	315.6	312.4	366.5	400	400	Revenues ($mill)	500
48.2%	36.7%	42.8%	45.7%	47.0%	34.7%	30.3%	29.5%	26.5%	32.1%	35.0%	32.0%	Operating Margin	37.0%
9.9	11.4	17.7	22.9	39.9	55.0	74.1	75.5	83.8	89.6	88.5	89.5	Depreciation ($mill)	100
19.4	13.0	24.8	48.5	54.4	36.0	9.1	6.8	d10.2	13.6	26.5	21.5	Net Profit ($mill)	65.0
12.7%	20.4%	20.7%	22.3%	22.7%	13.7%	47.0%	39.3%	39.3%	24.8%	15.0%	20.0%	Income Tax Rate	20.0%
28.5%	16.2%	19.9%	22.5%	19.0%	12.1%	2.7%	2.2%	NMF	3.7%	6.6%	5.4%	Net Profit Margin	13.0%
4.0	10.8	d6.3	20.0	.6	d45.3	d35.5	d14.1	31.1	148.9	175	175	Working Cap'l ($mill)	150
7.2	6.5	55.6	96.3	194.4	341.1	336.1	268.3	245.9	131.2	120	85.0	Long-Term Debt ($mill)	150
85.7	148.7	242.9	362.1	496.6	509.6	443.2	491.6	576.6	650.0	660	675	Net Worth ($mill)	750
21.2%	8.4%	8.6%	11.1%	8.3%	4.6%	1.7%	1.2%	NMF	1.9%	3.5%	3.0%	% Earned Total Cap'l	7.5%
22.6%	8.8%	10.2%	13.4%	11.0%	7.1%	2.0%	1.4%	NMF	2.1%	4.0%	3.0%	% Earned Net Worth	8.5%
17.5%	6.4%	8.5%	11.8%	9.6%	5.7%	.4%	NMF	NMF	NMF	1.5%	1.0%	% Retained to Comm Eq	7.5%
23%	27%	17%	12%	12%	20%	82%	113%	NMF	NMF	70%	70%	% All Div'ds to Net Prof	18%

BUSINESS: Echo Bay Mines Ltd. operates the Lupin gold mine, near the Arctic Circle in Canada's Northwest Territories. Also operates the McCoy/Cove, the Round Mountain and the Kettle River mines in the western United States. Explores for gold in the U.S., Canada, Mexico, and South America. Wrote down investments in the Muscocho Group, 3/90; Alta Bay 12/90. '93 gold production: 873,890 ounces. '93 proven and probable reserves (producing and development properties): 11.6 million ounces. Has about 1,728 employees; 72,500 stockholders. Insiders own less than 2% of common (3/93 proxy). Chairman: Robert Calman. President & C.E.O.: Richard Kraus. Incorporated: Canada. Executive Offices: 370 Seventeenth Street, Denver, CO 80202. Telephone: 303-592-8000.

Figure 9-2. Echo Bay Mines Ltd. stock chart. *(Copyright 1994 by Value Line Publishing Inc. Reprinted by permission; all rights reserved.)*

☆ 73 HOMESTAKE ☆ MINING

HOMESTAKE MINING COMPANY
650 California Street
San Francisco, California 94108-2788
415-981-8150

Stock exchange: NYSE
Ticker symbol: HM
DRIP program: Yes
Ownership:
    Institutional: 43%
    Insiders: 8%

Company Profile.   The San Francisco-based Homestake Mining Company is an international gold mining company with major interests in Canada, the United States, and Australia, as well as smaller interests in Chile and Mexico. It also is part owner of a large sulphur deposit in the Gulf of Mexico. The company operates its namesake Homestake Mine in South Dakota, and the McLaughlin Mine in California.

A long-term player in the gold mining industry, the company was founded in 1877 and its stock has traded continuously on the New York Stock exchange since 1879.

In 1992 the company made its single largest acquisition, with the purchase of International Corona Corporation, a large Canadian gold producer. The move added approximately 600,000 ounces of annual and boosted Homestake's gold reserves by more than 5.4 million ounces.

Management Talent.   Chairman and Chief Executive Officer Harry M. Conger and President and Chief Operating Officer Peter Steen possess nearly three-quarters of a century combined mining experience as mining engineers and company executives. Other Homestake top managers have extensive mining experience, with both the company and other industry firms.

Financial Status.   Homestake's assets total more than $1.1 billion. The company sports cash and short-term investments in excess of $100 million, and carries a low debt-to-equity ratio of .4 to 1. Cashflow is healthy, and more than adequate for anticipated capital requirements.

DRIP Details.   The company's DRIP program allows for additional cash investments in company stock in amounts from $25 to $5000 per quarter. For information on the dividend reinvestment program, contact The First National Bank of Boston, Shareholder Services Division, P.O. Box 644, MS 45-02-07, Boston, Massachusetts 02102-0644, 800-442-2001.

Particular Strengths. Lowered expenses and improved operating efficiencies have slashed Homestake's cash operating costs to the $230-per-ounce level. The merging of the Corona and Homestake operations also seeks to slash some $25 million from annual administrative and exploration expenses. Homestake will be a leaner, more efficient operation from here on out. Another plus is the 1.2 million ounces of added gold reserves from the Eskay Creek project, as a result of the feasibility study completed in late 1993.

Financial statistics (figures in millions, except per-share amounts):

For fiscal year ended December 31	1990	1991	1992	1993
Revenue	$794	$672	$684	$722
Net income (loss)	12	(262)	(176)	53
Earnings (loss)/share	.08	(1.98)	(1.31)	.38
Dividend/share	.20	.20	.20	.10
Long-term debt	460	365	293	283
Stock price range/share:				
High	$23\frac{5}{8}$	$19\frac{5}{8}$	$16\frac{5}{8}$	$22\frac{7}{8}$
Low	$15\frac{1}{4}$	$13\frac{7}{8}$	10	$9\frac{5}{8}$

Investment Assessment. Homestake, as one of the world's largest gold mining operators and with geographically diverse proven and probable gold reserves in excess of 17 million ounces, will be a major beneficiary of rising gold prices as the supply/demand relationship falls into periodic deficits as economies expand.

Now behind Homestake are the years of recent losses due to restructuring charges, discontinued uranium and oil and gas operations, and other write-downs. The future glitters like the gold the company mines. With the stock trading over 25 percent below its 52-week high, Homestake has plenty of room to rebound as the price of gold rises. A good sign of things to come: The company also doubled its quarterly dividend payout to 5 cents per share.

☆ 74 PEGASUS GOLD ☆

PEGASUS GOLD INC.
601 West First Avenue, Suite 1500
Spokane, Washington 99204
509-624-4653

Stock exchange: AMEX
Ticker symbol: PGU
DRIP program: No
Ownership:
  Institutional: 45%
  Insiders: 1%

Company Profile. Pegasus Gold Inc. produces gold, silver, lead, and zinc from its mining operations in Idaho, Montana, and Nevada. The company also owns 61 percent of Zapapan N. L. in Australia, and recently entered into an agreement with Goldbelt Resources to develop the Leninogorsk tailings project in the Republic of Kazakhstan, assuming that the political and financial risk can be successfully underwritten by a third party such as the World Bank.

Other international expansion moves include the acquisition of two Chilean gold properties and possible participation in an Emerging Markets Gold Fund to finance gold projects in Third World countries. Although headquartered in Spokane, Washington, Pegasus gold is officially a British Columbia, Canada, company.

Management Talent. Management, under the leadership of President and Chief Executive Officer Wemer G. Nennecker, is committed to excellence, as evidenced by its corporate mission statement. Nennecker took over the company's top post when former President and Chief Executive Officer John Wilson left to assume a position with Placer Dome Inc. (see Placer Dome management discussion, following). Previously, Nennecker held positions as Executive Vice President and Director of Sante Fe Pacific Minerals Corporation and President of Sante Fe Pacific Gold Corporation.

Financial Status. Cash and short-term investments in excess of $110 million more than doubles long-term debt of $52 million. Solid cashflow permits capital expenditures, exploration, and property acquisition, in line with management's aggressive expansion strategy.

Particular Strengths. Pegasus is a rapidly growing mining company, with gold production expanding from less than 285,000 ounces in 1988 to nearly 400,000 ounces in 1993. Gold production is estimated to surge another 75 percent to 700,000 ounces in the next several years, as new projects come on-line and Pegasus acquires new properties. The firm carries on both conventional open-out mining operations and the innovative heap-leaching extraction process.

Financial statistics (figures in millions, except per-share amounts):

For fiscal year ended December 31	1990	1991	1992	1993
Revenue	$171	$156	$182	$215
Net income (loss)	(38)*	10	(6)*	10
Earnings (loss)/share	(1.55)*	.37	(.22)*	.30
Dividend/share	.10	.10	.10	.10
Long-term debt	48	65	42	52
Stock price range/share:				
High	16⅛	14⅛	18½	28⅛
Low	9⅛	11⅜	11⅜	12⅝

*Includes property write-down in the amount of $24.6 million or 84 cents per share in 1992, and $35.1 million or $1.42 per share in 1990.

Investment Assessment.   Pegasus's stock price had a nice run-up in late 1993, rising to an all-time high of $28⅛ per share. Since then its market price has trended steadily downward in the wake of lower gold prices, a $35 million charge against earnings in 1994, and concerns over environmental problems at the company's Zortman/Landusky Mine in Montana. The stock hit a new 52-week low (under $14 per share) in July 1994.

Record gold production, promising properties, and higher gold prices make this medium-sized gold producer an attractive investment in the gold mining stock sector. The environmental concerns are overblown, and with the stock sinking to new 52-week lows, Pegasus is a classic undervalued company.

☆ 75 PLACER DOME ☆

PLACER DOME, INC.
1055 Dunsmuir Street, Suite 1600
P.O. Box 49330
Vancouver, British Columbia,
  Canada V7X 1P1
604-661-1991

Stock exchange: NYSE
Ticker symbol: PDG
DRIP program: No
Ownership:
  Institutional: 35%
  Insiders: 1%

Company Profile. Placer Dome, Inc. operates worldwide mining facilities, with gold and silver mines in Australia, Chile, New Guinea, and North America. Copper and other metals also are produced in Canada, The Philippines, and Mexico. In late 1993, Placer Dome acquired a 70 percent interest in the promising Las Cristinas property in Venezuela.

Management Talent. Chairman Robert M. Franklin and President and Chief Executive Officer John M. Wilson (previously President and CEO of Pegasus) lead a management team with many years' experience in all facets of the mining industry, both with Placer and with other firms. Management's five-year plan targets gold production of 2.5 million ounces per year, up from approximately 1.8 million ounces in 1993.

Financial Status. The company's cash reserve of in excess of $700 million dwarfs its approximately $250 million in long-term debt. Cashflow has been steadily improving with lower operating costs. Cash production costs have consistently come in at around $190 per ounce, making the company an industry low-cost operator.

Particular Strengths. Placer's ability to seek out and find new, quality gold reserves is one of its aces in the hole. In 1993 alone, the company took on significant value via its worldwide exploration and acquisition programs. Its financial strength will keep these programs intact, and reserves growing.

The firm's 50 percent–owned copper project in northern Chile represents an earnings kicker as the world economy rebounds and copper prices rise. The property is estimated to have 250 million tons of high-grade copper reserves, with an estimated production cost of 52 cents per pound. The mine is scheduled for start-up in 1995.

Financial statistics (figures in millions of US$, except per-share amounts):

For fiscal year ended December 31	1990	1991	1992	1993
Revenue	$931	$969	$1,020	$917
Net income (loss)	165*	(236)*	111	107
Earnings (loss)/share	.27*	(1.02)*	.47	.45
Dividend/share	.26	.26	.26	.26
Long-term debt	310	250	69	243
Stock price range/share:				
High	21½	16⅞	12⅜	25⅝
Low	13⅜	9⅝	9	11¼

*Includes write-down of mining interests totaling $344 million or $1.45 per share in 1991, and $34 million or $.14 per share in 1990.

Investment Assessment. Placer enters into strategic joint-venture mining operations so as to extend its production and property acquisition capabilities. For example, during the third quarter of 1993 the company and Kennecott Corporation forged an agreement to combine adjacent properties in a 70/30 joint venture (Placer 70 percent), with an estimated reserve of 1.3 million ounces of gold.

Placer will expand its innovative approaches to gold exploration and development, and in the process lower costs. The firm's diverse mining base (both geographically and in terms of metals) adds a degree of stability to earnings.

As the price of gold rises, the value of Placer Dome's 18 million ounces of gold will rise substantially, as will its stock market price.

☆ 76 THE RTZ CORP. ☆

THE RTZ CORPORATION PLC	Stock exchange: NYSE
6 St. James's Square	Ticker symbol: RTZ
London, England SW1Y 4LD	DRIP program: No
(071) 930 2399	Ownership:
American Depositary Receipt	Institutional: 12%
U.S. Contact: 212-921-1060	Insiders: 10%

Company Profile. RTZ Corporation PLC ranks as a world leader in international mining, with interests in a wide variety of natural resources and industrial minerals such as copper, gold, iron ore, aluminum, lead, zinc, silver, coal, uranium, borax, titanium, talc, and diamonds.

The firm's operations derive 72 percent of profits from mining and metals and 28 percent from industrial minerals. Geographically, 45 percent of profits come from North America, 36 percent from Australia/ New Zealand, 13 percent from Africa, and the balance from other areas.

Management Talent. Chairman Sir Derek Birkin and Chief Executive Robert Wilson lead a seasoned team of world-class managers and engineers, with decades of experience in all phases of international mining operations.

Financial Status. The company boasts solid finances that allow it to pour more than $200 million into exploration activities, about a quarter of which is targeted toward precious metals such as gold and silver. The firm sports around $1 billion in working capital. Dividends have been paid every year since 1962, and the stock yields around 1 percent.

Particular Strengths. RTZ's worldwide presence and strong finances afford it ample opportunity to seize promising properties when they arise. In mid-1993, RTZ acquired Nerco's Montana/ Wyoming coal interest for a combined $1.1 billion in cash and acquired debt. It subsequently sold off the Nerco oil and gas interests for $600 million, making RTZ a major player in the U.S. coal industry for $500 million.

Acquisitions of and expansions at copper, coal, and gold operations in 1993 and 1994 will boost production capacity substantially. RTZ prides itself on being a low-cost producer.

Financial statistics (figures in millions of US$, except per-ADR amounts):

For fiscal year ended December 31	1990	1991	1992	1993
Revenue	$7,531	$6,684	$4,957	$4,710
Net income (loss)	978	575	377	452
Earnings (loss)/ADR	3.960*	2.32*	1.50	1.60
Dividend/ADR	1.512	1.662	1.31	1.301
Long-term debt	2,659	2,465	2,058	1,980
Stock price range/ADR:				
High	41¾	41½	48½	49¼
Low	30	31½	35½	37⅝

*Before special charges of 78 cents per share in 1991, and credits of 23 cents per share in 1990.

Investment Assessment. "RTZ has been taking advantage of its solid finances and depressed mineral and mining markets to strengthen its hand for the future. It's the world's most diversified mining company, and the largest and/or lowest-cost producer of numerous commodities either worldwide or regionally," says Louis A. Moscatello, CFA and President of American Investment Services, a registered investment adviser headquartered in Great Barrington, Massachusetts.

As the economy heats up and commodity prices rebound, RTZ's profits should increase dramatically.

☆ 77 SANTA FE ☆ PACIFIC CORP.

SANTA FE PACIFIC CORPORATION
1700 East Golf Road
Schaumburg, Illinois 60173
708-995-6000

Stock exchange: NYSE
Ticker symbol: SFX
DRIP program: Yes
Ownership:
    Institutional: 68%
    Insiders: 1%

Company Profile. Santa Fe Pacific Corporation represents another diversified way to play the precious metals market. In addition to owning and operating the Atcheson, Topeka and Santa Fe Railway company, the firm also maintains interests in precious metals operations and pipelines. In July 1994, Santa Fe and Burlington Northern agreed to merge, forming the largest U.S. railroad network with $7 million in revenues and 33,000 track miles.

Management Talent. Chairman, President, and Chief Executive Officer Robert D. Krebs has been skillfully redefining the company. In 1993, Santa Fe Pacific exchanged its coal and aggregate mining assets for two California and Nevada gold-mine properties of Hanson Natural Resources Company. The move more than doubled Santa Fe's gold production capacity and substantially increased reserves, making it the nation's sixth-largest gold producer.

Financial Status. A better than $5 billion company, Santa Fe Corporation's earnings from continuing operations have steadily improved on a growing revenue base. This has helped to reduce debt leverage and improve cashflow.

DRIP Details. The Santa Fe Pacific Corporation DRIP program allows for additional cash purchases of stock in amounts from $10 to $1000 per month. For information on the dividend reinvestment plan, contact First Chicago Trust Company–NY, P.O. Box 3506, New York, New York 10008, 800-526-5678.

Particular Strengths. Sharply rising gold reserves, low-cost gold production, and higher gold prices promise to boost Santa Fe Pacific's bottom line in the years ahead. In the railroad segment, a greater emphasis on customer service and a more pronounced shift toward the intermodal market spell higher rail revenues and profits.

Financial statistics (figures in millions, except per-share amounts):

For fiscal year ended December 31	1990	1991	1992	1993
Revenue	$2,297	$2,360	$2,496	$2,726
Net income (loss)	(112)	96	(105)	339
Earnings (loss)/share	(.62)*	.54	.34*	1.81
Dividend/share	.10	.10	.10	.10
Long-term debt	1,801	1,630	1,246	1,185
Stock price range/share:				
High	23⅛	14	14⅛	22½
Low	6	5⅛	10⅝	12¾

*Excludes 91 cents per share for extraordinary charge and effects of accounting change in 1992, and extraordinary charge of 7 cents per share in 1990.

Investment Assessment. Santa Fe increased its gold reserves over 25 percent in 1993, and anticipates that it will boost gold production 50 percent in 1994 to 900,000 ounces. Coupled with rising gold prices and improved rail efficiency, the future looks on-track to post record revenues and profits in the years ahead.

Santa Fe completed an IPO of its gold unit in June at $14 per share. It retains 86 percent of Santa Fe Pacific Gold's outstanding shares, which are expected to be spun off to shareholders later. Such a move could make the value of Santa Fe Pacific Corporation shareholders' positions increase in value. Look for the spinoff of the rest of its stake in Santa Fe Gold to shareholders. You'll then *own* two quality companies.

A Silver Play

Like its gold counterpart, silver has enjoyed a resurgence of interest after years of neglect. In February 1993, spot silver prices drifted to a 19-year contract low price of $3.53 an ounce. By mid-1994, silver prices rose to above $5 an ounce.

"There's the same demand/supply imbalance for silver as gold is experiencing. The replacement rate is not offsetting the depletion of reserves, therefore silver prices will trend higher," says Vahid Fathi, senior metals analyst with Kemper Securities in Chicago.

☆ 78 HECLA MINING ☆

HECLA MINING COMPANY	Stock exchange: NYSE
6500 Mineral Drive	Ticker symbol: HL
Box C-8000	DRIP program: No
Coeur d'Alene, Idaho 83814	Ownership:
208-769-4100	Institutional: 43%
	Insiders: 1%

Company Profile. Hecla Mining Company is a diversified mining company with operations in gold, lead, industrial minerals, and silver. Currently over 25 percent of company revenues come from silver operations. Unfortunately, the low price of silver in recent years has made the silver operations unprofitable. In fact the company's last profitable year was 1990, when it earned 11 cents per share.

Management Talent. Chairman, President, and Chief Executive Officer Arthur Brown and top vice presidents have extensive company and industry experience, through both good and tough times. Management has positioned the company as a low-cost producer, poised to turn the company profitable as market conditions improve. Having been in business for over 102 years, the company has staying power.

Financial Status. Despite four years of deficits, Hecla has pared down long-term debt and improved its working capital position.

Particular Strengths. Hecla has in excess of 140 million ounces of silver and over 3 million ounces of gold reserves to support future production. The company recently made a move to expand its operations overseas. The firm's Sonora, Mexico, La Choya gold operations came on-stream in late 1993.

Financial statistics (figures in millions of US$, except per-share amounts):

For fiscal year ended December 31	1990	1991	1992	1993
Revenue	$163	$120	$113	$85
Net income (loss)	7	(15)	(49)	(16)
Earnings (loss)/share	.22*	(.51)*	(1.60)*	(.48)
Dividend/share	.05	—	—	—
Long-term debt	70	77	70	49
Stock price range/share:				
High	16⅛	12½	12	15¼
Low	6⅞	6¾	7⅜	7⅜

*Includes extraordinary charges of 91 cents per share in 1992 and 17 cents per share in 1991, and an extraordinary credit of 8 cents per share in 1990.

Investment Assessment. "Hecla represents a proxy on the silver market," says Fathi. As silver and gold prices rebound, Hecla's fortunes are due to improve. Since silver prices have been more depressed than gold, there's more potential for a dramatic price rise.

Hecla's stock price has languished near the bottom of its 52-week price range. A turn toward profitability could more than double Hecla's market price in future years, as the twenty-first century unfolds.

☆ 79 PLATINUM ☆

Platinum Possibilities

Platinum retained a surplus demand/supply relationship in 1993 due to a number of factors including increased South African production, rising exploration activities, and lackluster worldwide automobile sales (platinum is used in automobile catalytic converters). Most analysts see this surplus running at least through 1995.

"Platinum has the most compelling long-term supply/demand fundamentals. There are no massive above-ground stocks held by central banks, it has many essential and often irreplaceable applications, and over 95 percent of the world's production comes from politically uncertain countries such as South Africa and Russia," says Bernard Savaiko, senior precious metals analyst with Paine Webber in Weehawken, New Jersey.

"I find platinum attractive due to an expected sharp rise in world auto production and an increased use of platinum as more countries require the installation of catalytic converters," says James Steele, research department head for Refco in New York City.

The scarcest among the precious metals, platinum rose from under $340 per ounce in March 1993 to a peak of $419 per ounce in August 1993, based mainly on supply-interruption concerns in South Africa.

The metal still remains a solid play against future supply disruptions, as the economic and political upheavals in South Africa and the former Soviet Union play themselves out. An international economic rebound, and rising automobile production, could also turn platinum's current surplus status into a deficit in short order. This is important because, as illustrated in Fig. 9-3, platinum prices tend to outperform gold when annual demand exceeds new supply.

According to Nina A. Lipton, director of market research for the Platinum Guild International (USA) Inc. in New York City, the most popular way to invest in platinum is to purchase it in pure form, either as bars or coins.

Probably the easiest and most convenient method is to purchase legal-tender coins, such as the Australian Koala, the Canadian plat-

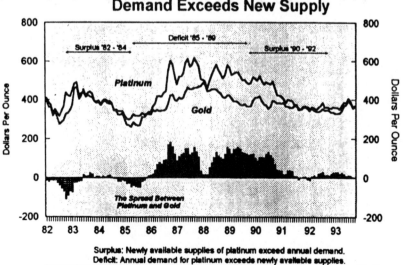

Platinum Prices Tend To Outperform Gold When Annual Demand Exceeds New Supply

Surplus: Newly available supplies of platinum exceed annual demand.
Deficit: Annual demand for platinum exceeds newly available supplies.
Source: Platinum Guild International and Johnson Matthey (Nearby Contract; Avg Monthly Close)

Figure 9-3. Platinum vs. gold price performance chart.

inum Maple Leaf, and the Isle of Man Noble. The price of the coins is the spot price of platinum, plus a premium to offset the cost of production and sales. Their weight and purity are authenticated, and each coin receives the full backing and assurance of the issuing nation.

A stake in platinum makes sense, given the long-term prospects for demand outstripping supply and the political factors that could disrupt supply and dramatically drive up the price of platinum.

Precious-metal Mutual-fund Options

The following precious-metal mutual funds deserve consideration, as precious-metal supply/demand relationships promise to achieve an imbalance likely to drive up precious metal prices.

☆ 80 LEXINGTON ☆ STRATEGIC INVESTMENTS FUND

LEXINGTON STRATEGIC
   INVESTMENTS FUND, INC.   Year begun: 1974
Park 80 West, Plaza Two   Assets: $85 million
P.O. Box 1515   Min. investment: $1,000
Saddle Brook, New Jersey   Load: 5.75% max.
   07662-5812   Annual exp. ratio: 2.78%
800-526-0056
Ticker symbol: STIVX
Objective/style: Long-term capital growth
Portfolio turnover: 4.80% (varies widely from year to year)
Investment adviser: Lexington Management Company
Portfolio manager: Caesar M. P. Bryan

Returns
One-year: 247.23% thru 12/31/93
Three-year: 5.14% thru 12/31/93
Five-year: 1.54% thru 12/31/93

Representative Major Holdings

COMPANY	HQ
Beatrix Mines, Ltd.	S. Africa
Deelkraal Gold Mining Co., Ltd.	S. Africa
Doornfontein Gold Mining Co., Ltd.	S. Africa
Durban Roodeport Deep, Ltd.	S. Africa
East Rand Gold & Uranium Co., Ltd.	S. Africa

Investment Strategy. Lexington Strategic Investments Fund concentrates its holdings in shares of companies engaged in the exploration, mining, processing, fabrication, and distribution of natural resources such as minerals, metals, and precious metals. A large percentage of the fund's assets is located in the Republic of South Africa, the major gold and precious-metals mining region of the world.

The fund will retain at least 25 percent of its value in such securities, unless unusual and adverse conditions exist in the natural resource industry. Typically, 80 percent of the fund's gross income will derive from assets outside of the United States.

With the political risk of South Africa come opportunities for substantial gains. Lexington Management Corporation has managed financial assets since 1938, and it has been adept at scoring big returns when their assessment of the situation has proven correct.

☆ 81 LEXINGTON ☆
STRATEGIC SILVER FUND

LEXINGTON STRATEGIC
SILVER FUND, INC.
Park 80 West Plaza Two
P.O. Box 1515
Saddle Brook, New Jersey
07662-5812
800-526-0056
Ticker symbol: STSLX
Objective/style: Capital appreciation
Portfolio turnover: 18.58% (varies widely from year to year)
Investment manager: Lexington Management Corporation
Portfolio manager: Caesar M. P. Bryan

Year begun: 1986
Assets: $36 million
Min. investment: $1000
Load: 5.75% max.
Annual exp. ratio: 2.60%

Returns
One-year: 76.5% thru 12/31/93
Three-year: 10.1% thru 12/31/93
Five-year: 1.0% thru 12/31/93

Representative Major Holdings

COMPANY	HQ
Coeur d'Alene Mines Corporation	U.S.
Hecla Mining Company	U.S.
Corporation San Luis A2	Mexico
TVX Gold Inc.	Mexico
Grupo Mexico	Mexico

Investment Strategy.   Lexington Strategic Silver Fund invests in securities of companies involved in the exploration, mining, processing, fabrication, and/or distribution of silver. Since there are no real pure silver plays, many of the companies also engage in other mining activities such as copper, gold, lead, and zinc. In fact, the major part of the company's operations is more than likely the production of other precious or base metals, with silver as a secondary operation.

The fund can invest up to 25 percent in any two companies. Its two largest positions at the end of 1993 accounted for over 19 percent of fund assets: Coeur d'Alene Mines Corporation (11.5 percent) and Hecla Mining Company (7.9 percent). At least 80 percent of the fund's assets must be invested in silver-related companies that have been in business more than three years.

Since Bryan started managing the fund, he has expanded its portfolio dramatically to include many more companies. He also has added an international flavor, with the addition of Mexican mining companies such as Corporation San Luis, Grupo Mexico, and Industrias Peñoles, as well as the Australian mining company MIM Holdings, Ltd., all large silver producers. MIM Holdings alone account for around 10 percent of Western U.S. silver production. Four percent of the fund's assets are invested in MIM Holdings, Ltd. Bryan also is considering investing in Peruvian mining companies.

Taking a conservative approach, Bryan has avoided the financially troubled Sunshine Mining Company, even though the largest percentage of its revenues come from silver operations.

Other precious-metal mutual funds that have performed well during periods of inflation, economic and political instability, and rising demand include those in the following list.

FUND	800 #	PERFORMANCE, 3/93–3/94
Bull & Bear Gold investors	847-4200	34.0%
Lexington Goldfund	526-0056	41.6%
Pioneer Gold Shares	225-6292	43.3%
Scudder Gold	225-2470	43.5%
United Services World Gold	873-8637	50.3%
Vanguard Spec. Gold & Precious	662-7447	42.9%

Each fund tackles precious metals in different ways. Some gravitate toward North American mining stocks, others are more concentrated in South African mining stocks, and still others take a heavier position in bullion. But regardless of which way you decide to invest in precious metals, do your homework first, and understand clearly what potential risks and rewards are involved.

10

Gushing Profits: Oil and Gas Investments

The stage is set. Oil prices plunged to near eight-year lows at the end of March 1994, in the wake of OPEC's (Organization of Petroleum Exporting Countries) inability to come to agreement on production cutbacks. Between June 1993 and the end of March 1994, oil prices plunged from over $20 a barrel to just under $14 a barrel.

However, the dark cloud that has surrounded oil and gas investments over the past decade is finally beginning to dissipate. OPEC itself has projected an increase in worldwide oil demand by as much as 15 percent after the year 2000, with improvement in the world economy. The twin engines of population growth and the continued industrialization of the developing world will drive oil and gas usage in the twenty-first century.

Near-term, the Houston, Texas–based oil advisers Randall & Dewey, Inc., forecast sharply rising oil prices in 1995 and 1996, based on its survey that crude oil prices stabilized during the first quarter of 1994.

Likewise, the American Gas Association estimated that natural gas consumption in 1994 would improve by as much as 2.4 percent over 1993's usage. With the Clinton administration's push toward cleaner fuels, gas usage should only increase in the decades ahead. Adding impetus to natural gas's growth potential, the United States Department of Energy released a 49-point plan citing natural gas as the fuel that will aid the country in shedding its dependence on imported oil while helping to improve the nation's environment.

Investors staking out quality investments in the oil and gas sector, before the turnaround takes full effect, should be able to earn substantial overall returns.

Drilling for Dollars: Oil and Gas Partnerships

When you decide to invest in a drilling operation, oil and gas limited partnerships are the way to go. Make sure you know the past performance of the drilling company and the risks involved. For most investors, the limited partnership makes sense from a risk standpoint. Steer clear of drilling programs that subject the participants to unlimited liability for a variety of risks, including violations of environmental regulations, costs from blowouts, stuck drill pipes, and other operational liabilities that can obligate you for costs significantly exceeding your initial partnership investment.

With the collapse of oil prices in the eighties, a lot of companies that had sponsored limited oil and gas partnerships fell by the wayside. In addition, many of the companies still in the business curtailed drilling programs and partnerships dramatically. Public oil and gas drilling programs raised only around $29 million in 1993, down 60 percent from the $73 million raised in 1992 and far below the $2.1 billion experienced in the drilling boom of 1981.

An independent oil and gas company that has successfully put together drilling and income partnerships for years is the Swift Energy Company in Houston, Texas.

"Swift Energy partnership programs have come out on top, in terms of cash paid out to date, of all the companies we track," says Nancy Schabel Mahon, Vice President with the Shrewsbury, New Jersey–based Robert A. Stanger & Company, Inc., publisher of *The Stanger Report*, a newsletter that tracks limited partnerships.

"The oil and gas industries follow roughly 15-year cycles peak to peak, with both of them peaking out in the early to mid-eighties. We should be in the early phases of an up cycle in the energy markets," says A. Earl Swift, Chairman, President, and Chief Executive Officer of Swift Energy Company.

In the natural gas sector, Swift views the excess overhang in the demand/supply relationship as disappearing. With four to five years required to develop proven reserves, increased demand quickly translates into higher prices.

The following partnership program seeks to benefit from the return to higher oil and gas prices as the energy cycle unfolds.

☆ 82 SWIFT ☆
DEPOSITARY RECEIPTS

SWIFT DEPOSITARY RECEIPTS
Swift Energy Marketing Company
16825 Northchase Drive, Suite 540
Houston, Texas 77297
713-874-2820, 800-45-SWIFT

Min. investment: $5000
IRAs & Keoghs: $2000
Load: None

Under the Swift Depositary Receipt Program, the Managing Partner assumes all selling and offering expenses, and uses the proceeds of the partnership offering to acquire property. All other costs, cash distributions, and sales proceeds are split 85 percent to partnership investors and 15 percent to the General Manager before payout (return of original investment), and 75 percent to the partnership investors and 25 percent to the General Manager after payout.

The partnership contains a liquidation feature that anticipates liquidating the oil and gas properties beginning in the fifth year of operations and winding up in the ninth year. This feature allows the Managing Partner to take advantage of favorable cyclical prices.

All properties will be acquired on a cash basis, and there will be no additional assessments to partners. Providing additional protection, the partnership acquires interests only in a diversified number of proven producing oil and gas properties.

Another way to take part in the fortunes of Swift Energy Company is to invest directly in its stock.

☆ 83 SWIFT ENERGY ☆
COMPANY

SWIFT ENERGY COMPANY
16825 Northchase Drive, Suite 400
Houston, Texas 77060
713-874-2700
800-777-2412

Stock exchange: NYSE
Ticker symbol: SFY
DRIP program: No
Ownership:
  Institutional: 28%
  Insiders: 17%

Company Profile.   Swift Energy Company engages in the acquisition, development, operation, and exploration of oil and gas properties. The company has increased its reserves every year since 1985, and in the past five years reserves have grown at a compound rate exceeding 40 percent. Swift Energy finances most of its acquisition activities via public offerings of oil and gas partnerships. A little over 63 percent of company reserves are located in Texas, nearly 15 percent in Oklahoma, over 11 percent in Louisiana, and the balance in 14 other states.

Management Talent.   Chairman, President, and Chief Operating Officer A. Earl Swift is well regarded in the oil and gas industry. Not your typical oil industry rigger, Swift is an engineer as well as an attorney armed with an MBA. He manages his company through a strategic planning process, with specific targeted goals.

Financial Status.   Swift Energy issued $29 million in long-term debt in June 1993, consisting of 6.5 percent Convertible Subordinated Debentures maturing on June 30, 2003. The proceeds were used to fund the advance purchase of producing oil and gas properties for affiliated partnerships. The company has working capital of $10 million and an improving cashflow.

Particular Strengths.   Rising reserves, strong finances, and a proven track record in acquiring producing properties are Swift Energy's strong suits. Since 1984, the firm has raised over $400 million through the sale of oil and gas partnerships.

Financial statistics (figures in millions, except per-share amounts):

For fiscal year ended December 31	1990	1991	1992	1993
Revenue	$20	$15	$19	$24
Net income (loss)	7	3	4	5
Earnings (loss)/share	1.49	.52	.73	.82
Dividend/share	—	—	—	—
Long-term debt	—	—	—	29
Stock price range/share:				
High	$12\frac{7}{8}$	11	$9\frac{1}{2}$	14
Low	$8\frac{3}{8}$	$5\frac{1}{4}$	$5\frac{5}{8}$	$8\frac{5}{8}$

Investment Assessment.   Swift Energy continues to rapidly expand its reserves, and has taken an international approach to its operations. In 1993, the firm signed an agreement with a Russian joint-stock company to provide technical and managerial assistance for the development and production of oil and natural gas in Siberia. The contract calls for Swift Energy to receive a net-profits interest of at least 5 percent, from the sale of oil and gas from the two fields under development. In addition, through its wholly owned subsidiary, Swift Energy de Venezuela, C.A., Swift is investigating opportunities in that country.

From 1991 to 1993, earnings per share rose over 57 percent, to 82 cents. Despite this good performance and increasing reserve potential, the firm's stock price trades 21 percent below its 52-week and all-time high of $14 per share. If you're betting on the resurgence of oil and gas prices, Swift Energy is the right place to do so.

☆ 84 BURLINGTON ☆ RESOURCES

BURLINGTON RESOURCES INC.
999 Third Avenue
Seattle, Washington 98104-4097
206-467-3838

Stock exchange: NYSE
Ticker symbol: BR
DRIP program: No
Ownership:
    Institutional: 70%
    Insiders: 1%

Company Profile.   Burlington Resources was spun off from Burlington Northern in 1988. Its own spinoff of its natural gas pipeline subsidiary (El Paso Natural Gas), in 1992, transformed the firm into a pure oil and gas exploration, development, and production company.

Since coming out from beneath the umbrella of Burlington Northern, Burlington Resources has generated over $1.4 billion from the sale of nonstrategic real estate and mineral and forest-product assets. These funds have been reinvested in domestic oil and gas reserves, which have been growing at a 10 percent annual rate.

Management Talent.   Chairman and Chief Executive Officer Thomas H. O'Leary carried over an experienced management team from the Burlington Northern spinoff. By streamlining and refocusing the company's assets, he has made Burlington Resources a premier diversified energy company.

Financial Status.   The company has substantially reduced its debt load since 1991, paying off nearly $500 million. With a debt shelf registration of $500 million, and another $900 million in unused credit facilities, the company has plenty of operating maneuverability to purchase additional reserves and make strategic acquisitions.

Particular Strengths. Burlington Resources has exceptional financial strength with which to fund its heavy development and reserve acquisition expenditures, which totaled more than $500 million in 1993, up dramatically from the $315 million spent in 1992.

The firm's costs to locate and produce gas are running at around half the industry average, giving it a competitive edge.

Financial statistics (figures in millions, except per-share amounts):

For fiscal year ended Dec. 31	1990	1991	1992	1993
Revenue	$1,025	$1,036	$1,141	$1,249
Net income (loss)	150*	103*	218*	256
Earnings (loss)/share	.87*	.75*	1.44*	1.95
Dividend/share	.70	.70	.60†	.65
Long-term debt	529	1,298	1,003	819
Stock price range/share:				
High	50⅛	43¾	43⅝	53⅞
Low	36⅞	32⅞	33	36½

*Excludes income from discontinued operations of $105 million or 74 cents per share in 1990, $105 million or 79 cents per share in 1991, and $68 million or 51 cents per share in 1992.

†In 1992 the company reduced the dividend to reflect the spinoff of El Paso Natural Gas.

Investment Assessment. In mid-September 1994, Burlington Resources traded near its 52-week low of around $37 per share, in the wake of lower earnings. Making its shares even more attractive, the company has repurchased over 23 million of them since 1988. The company represents a solid rebound play on expected higher oil and gas prices.

☆ 85 ENERGEN CORP. ☆

ENERGEN CORPORATION
2101 Sixth Avenue North
Birmingham, Alabama 35203-2784
205-326-2700

Stock exchange: NYSE
Ticker symbol: EGN
DRIP program: Yes
Ownership:
    Institutional: 44%
    Insiders: —%

Company Profile. Energen Corporation operates two major business segments: natural gas distribution, and oil and gas exploration. Its Algasco subsidiary serves more than 435,000 gas customers in central and north Alabama. Energen increased its natural gas customer base 1.7 percent in 1993. The Taurus Exploration subsidiary conducts exploration efforts off U.S. shores, and possesses extensive coalbed methane experience. In 1993 this business segment more than doubled net income, on a 20 percent rise in revenue.

Management Talent. Chairman and Chief Executive Officer Rex J. Lysinger and President and Chief Operating Officer Wm. Michael Warren Jr. have guided Energen into an expansion of its oil and gas operations, with acquisitions of producing properties even as it has continued to grow its natural-gas-distribution customer network.

Financial Status. Record earnings for the third straight fiscal year delivered a return on equity of 13.1 percent in 1993. Net cashflow provided by operations has been steadily increasing, providing ample capital for operations and expanded oil and gas activities. The Board of Directors boosted the cash dividend payout by 4 percent in 1993.

DRIP Details. The Energen DRIP program allows for the purchase of additional company shares in cash amounts between $25 and $5000 per quarter. There are no commission or administrative costs to the shareholder. As a bonus, the stock is purchased at a 5 percent discount. Information on the dividend reinvestment program may be obtained by contacting the company's Investors' Relations Department at 2101 Sixth Avenue North, Birmingham, Alabama 35203-2784, 205-326-2634 or 800-654-3206.

Particular Strengths. Energen has a number of things going for it. It serves a growing market area with its gas distribution network. Its coalbed methane consulting and operating fees are expanding as new contracts are inked. Its Taurus subsidiary has more than tripled its proved gas reserves since 1991.

Financial statistics (figures in millions, except per-share amounts):

For fiscal year ended September 30	1990	1991	1992	1993
Revenue	$325	$326	$332	$357
Net income (loss)	11	14	16	18
Earnings (loss)/share	1.15	1.42	1.54	1.77
Dividend/share	.895	.955	1.01	1.05
Long-term debt	83	78	91	86

Stock price range/share:	1990	1991	1992	1993
High	21½	20	18⅞	26¾
Low	16	16	15	17⅝

Investment Assessment. Accelerating earnings, backed by a more diverse revenue mix, bode well for Energen Corporation. The company's cash dividend currently yields an attractive 5 percent. Energen trades nearly 20 percent below its all-time high of $26¾ per share, reached in 1993. A great stock to own while you wait for higher natural gas prices to unfold.

☆ 86 QUESTAR CORP. ☆

QUESTAR CORPORATION
P.O. Box 45433
Salt Lake City, Utah 84145-0433
801-534-5000

Stock exchange: NYSE
Ticker symbol: STR
DRIP program: Yes
Ownership:
    Institutional: 78%
    Insiders: —%

Company Profile. Questar Corporation is a $1.5 billion, integrated gas holding company, operating three business segments: retail gas distribution; gas and oil exploration, production, and marketing; and interstate gathering, transportation, and storage.

Questar's Mountain Fuel Supply company serves over 550,000 customers in Utah, southwestern Wyoming, and southeastern Idaho. The company's exploration and production group engages in activities mainly in the Rocky Mountain and Midcontinent regions. Questar Pipeline operates a 2500-mile, interstate, natural gas gathering-and-transmission system in Colorado, Wyoming, and Utah.

Management Talent. Chairman, President, and Chief Executive Officer R. D. Cash has held the Questar reins since 1985. Top management's decades of industry experience paid off when it guided Questar to six straight years of higher net income and earnings-per-share.

Financial Status. Several key performance benchmarks show Questar to have been an industry leader between 1989 and 1993. Its total return to shareholders hit 29.9 percent in 1993, return on equity came in at 14.5 percent, and the cash dividend rose 20 times in 21 years.

DRIP Program. The Questar Corporation dividend reinvestment program permits additional cash purchases of company stock in amounts between $50 and $15,000 per quarter. There are no commission or administrative charges to the shareholder for DRIP purchases. For information on the program, contact Shareholder Services at Questar Corporation, P.O. Box 11150, Salt Lake City, Utah 84147, 801-534-5885.

Particular Strengths. Questar has strong investment opportunities, as the Rocky Mountain region develops into a primary gas-supply area. Questar Corporation targets 1994 capital expenditures totaling nearly $300 million, 77 percent higher than 1993's level. In the first quarter of 1994 it has already spent $100 million for two significant oil and gas reserve acquisitions.

Financial statistics (figures in millions, except per-share amounts):

For fiscal year ended December 31	1990	1991	1992	1993
Revenue	$532	$624	$591	$660
Net income (loss)	57	64	74*	82
Earnings (loss)/share	1.45	1.63	1.79*	2.03
Dividend/share	.97	1.01	1.04	1.09
Long-term debt	328	354	365	372
Stock price range/share:				
High	19⅞	24¾	27½	44
Low	16⅜	16⅝	18½	25⅜

*Excludes credit of $9.3 million or 23 cents per share, for cumulative effect of change in accounting for income taxes.

Investment Assessment. Look for solid total-return prospects. A steadily rising dividend, higher revenues and earnings, and expanding reserves promise to keep Questar's industry-leading total-return-to-shareholders track record intact. The stock has plenty of upside potential, trading 25 percent below its all-time high of $44 per share and yielding 3.4 percent.

☆ 87 SEAGULL ENERGY ☆

SEAGULL ENERGY CORPORATION
1001 Fannin Street, Suite 1700
Houston, Texas 77002-6714
713-951-4700

Stock exchange: NYSE
Ticker symbol: SGO
DRIP program: No
Ownership:
  Institutional: 82%
  Insiders: 3%

Company Profile. Seagull Energy Corporation operates in three natural gas market segments: exploration and production, pipeline and marketing, and transmission and distribution. This $1 billion company owns extensive gas reserves, and in late 1993 it made an acquisition in Canada, a growing presence in the North American gas market. The company conducts exploration activities off the shores of Texas and Louisiana in the Gulf of Mexico, and onshore in Arkansas, Oklahoma, Louisiana, Texas, and western Canada. The transmission and distribution operation serves the greater metropolitan Anchorage area. Between 1991 and 1993, Seagull Energy went through a period of explosive growth.

Management Talent. Chairman, President, and Chief Executive Officer Barry J. Galt managed that growth, as a firm with just over $600 million in assets became one with over $1.3 billion in less than three years. In the presence, Galt increased the company's proved oil and gas reserves two and a half times, to over 1 Tcfe.

Financial Status. Seagull Energy boosted its capitalization with the February 1993 issuance of five million shares, netting $164 million. Proceeds were used to pay off acquisition debt. Strong cashflow will be used to further pay down long-term debt and to acquire property.

Particular Strengths. Substantial gas and oil reserves and rapidly expanding production allow Seagull to take advantage of market opportunities. The Canadian purchase gives the firm a foothold in that important North American supply market.

Financial statistics (figures in millions, except per-share amounts):

For fiscal year ended December 31	1990	1991	1992	1993
Revenue	$210	$249	$239	$377
Net income (loss)	21	5	7	27
Earnings (loss)/share	1.11	.23	.26	.76
Dividend/share	—	—	—	—
Long-term debt	49	219	608	460
Stock price range/share:				
High	$16\frac{7}{8}$	$15\frac{3}{4}$	$16\frac{7}{8}$	$32\frac{7}{8}$
Low	$9\frac{1}{16}$	$10\frac{1}{2}$	$10\frac{7}{8}$	$14\frac{7}{8}$

Investment Assessment. Seagull's revenues and earnings surged in 1993 and are poised to do the same in 1994 and beyond, as additional producing properties are brought into the company fold. Higher gas and oil prices can only improve Seagull Energy's prospects. Earnings for the first six months of 1994 nearly doubled the already impressive results for 1993's similar period.

Trading at around the midpoint of its 52-week trading range of $32\frac{7}{8}$ to $21 per share, Seagull Energy stock has ground to regain as the market recognizes its tremendous potential.

☆ 88 TRANSTEXAS ☆ GAS CORP.

TRANSTEXAS GAS CORPORATION
363 North Sam Houston Parkway East
Suite 1900
Houston, Texas 77060
713-447-3111

Stock exchange: NASDAQ
Ticker symbol: TTXG
DRIP program: No
Ownership:
   Institutional: 7%
   Insiders: 93%

Company Profile. TransTexas Gas Corporation came public in March 1994, with an initial public offering of 5 million shares priced at $14 per share. The company is engaged in the exploration and development of gas located primarily in South Texas. While a newcomer to the stock market, TransTexas has drilled, since 1973, more than 1200 wells producing over 2 Tcf of natural gas. It's the third-largest producer of natural gas in Texas, on a gross basis. TransTexas' pipeline system connects to seven intrastate and six interstate pipeline systems, providing access to all major markets in the continental United States and parts of Mexico.

Management Talent.   Director and Chief Executive Officer John R. Stanley founded TransAmerican 35 years ago and expanded it from a single gas station to a large integrated company. President and Chief Operating Officer Arnold H. Brackenridge came to the company in 1993, having previously served as President and Chief Executive Officer of Wintershall Energy, a BASF company. He is an industry veteran of 35 years.

Financial Status.   Not an investment for the risk-adverse, TransTexas uses significant leverage. In August 1993 the company issued $500 million in senior-secured notes, in exchange for certain assets transferred by TransAmerican to TransTexas. TransAmerican had previously filed for bankruptcy in 1975 and 1983. Another bankruptcy filing by TransAmerican could result in a claimant attempting to consolidate the assets of both companies, making the assets of TransTexas Gas Corporation subject to the claims of creditors.

Particular Strengths.   TransTexas has over 20 years' drilling experience in the South Texas region, and it has recently doubled its drilling rate. Over 95 percent of the company's reserves are in natural gas, which is expected to turn up before oil. Its more than 200,000 undeveloped acres are expected to sustain more than 25 years of drilling inventory. TransTexas runs a low-cost operation, its operating cost structure substantially below the industry average.

Financial statistics (figures in millions, except per-share amounts):

For fiscal year ended July 31	1991	1992	1993	1994*
Revenue	$226	$258	$326	$170
Net income (loss)	41	51	55	24†
Earnings (loss)/share†	—	—	.75	.34
Dividend/share	—	—	—	—
Long-term debt	100	105	83	500
Stock price range/share:‡				
High			14⅛	
Low			10	

*For first nine months of fiscal 1994.

†Includes charges for non-operating expenses of $9 million for litigation expenses, and $35 million in interest expense on notes.

‡Initial public offering in March 1994. Price range from March to mid-September 1994.

Investment Assessment. TransTexas Gas Corporation has the potential to be a real winner in the gas arena. It has proven itself a savvy driller, and has ample undeveloped acreage for future drilling and production. Yet the financial risks, given its highly leveraged position, have kept many investors at bay. Since it came to market at an offering price of $14 per share, the stock has traded as low as $10 per share before rebounding to the $12-per-share level.

With more than 90 percent of the firm's shares in the hands of TransAmerican (owned by John Stanley), the stock's float is thin. But that can work both ways. An aggressive drilling program, combined with higher gas prices, could send TransTexas's profits soaring and its stock price gushing to lofty heights.

Going the Professional Management Route

Investors looking for a proxy for the natural gas industry would be wise to give the American Gas Index Fund, Inc. a look.

☆ 89 AMERICAN GAS ☆ INDEX FUND

AMERICAN GAS INDEX
   FUND, INC.
4922 Fairmont Avenue
Bethesda, Maryland 20814
301-657-1517
800-621-7874
Ticker symbol: GASFX

Year begun: 1989
Assets: $272 million
Min. investment: $2500
IRA & Keoghs: $500
Load: None
Annual exp. ratio: 85%

Objective/style: Index to natural gas industry performance
Portfolio turnover: 21.5%
Investment adviser: Money Management Associates
Portfolio manager: Richard J. Garvey

Returns
One-year: 16.6% thru 12/31/93
Three-year: 10.3% thru 12/31/93

Representative Major Holdings

COMPANY	INDUSTRY SEGMENT
Enron Corp.	Pipeline
Panhandle Eastern Corp.	Pipeline
Consolidated Natural Gas Comp.	Diversified/integrated
Pacific Gas & Electric Comp.	Nat. Gas & Elec. Util.
Occidental Petroleum Corp.	Diversified/integrated

Investment Strategy.   As its name implies, the American Gas Index Fund is structured to match the performance of the natural gas industry. It's the only natural resources mutual fund that invests in the approximately 100 publicly traded natural gas distribution and transmission companies headquartered in the U.S. and belonging to the American Gas Association.

It represents a convenient way to play the natural gas industry without worrying about how to avoid picking the wrong stock. Since its inception the fund has earned over 11 percent, and its most recent one-year performance (ended December 31, 1993) earned its shareholders 16.56 percent despite a fourth-quarter pullback.

Now it's time for you to energize your portfolio returns with quality oil and gas investments. To help you keep abreast of upcoming investment opportunities in the energy field, the coupon at the end of this book makes it possible for you to order *Utility & Energy Portfolio* at a discount.

11

Stacking
Your Profits
with Coins

Rare and Bullion Coins

Coins, like other hard-asset investments, go through cycles, during which economic factors such as rising interest rates and fears of inflation impact on prices. The most recent market top occurred back in 1989. Through the early 1990s, coin prices have ratcheted downward.

"The rare-coin market is around 10 percent above its absolute bottom, trading around 25 cents on the dollar from the last peak in June 1989," says Mike Goss, of Jefferson Coin & Bullion in Houston, Texas.

For example, a review of *The Certified Coin Dealer Newsletter* of June 2, 1989, reflected a realized price of $13,200 for an 1881-CC (Carson City mint mark) Morgan Dollar with a PCGS-67 grade (see the discussion on coin grades, following). The January 1994 bid price for that same coin stood at only $3600, about 27 percent of its former value.

The last three major bull markets in rare coins took place between 1987 and 1989, 1983 and 1986, and 1976 and 1980. According to Goss, over the past 40 years, each new peak in the coin market has surpassed the level of the previous peak. Fig. 11-1 illustrates the price action of a representative rare coin, the $5 Liberty MS-63, from its peak in 1989 to early 1994.

Over the long term, coins have proven themselves to be an attractive investment vehicle, especially during inflationary times. Not surpris-

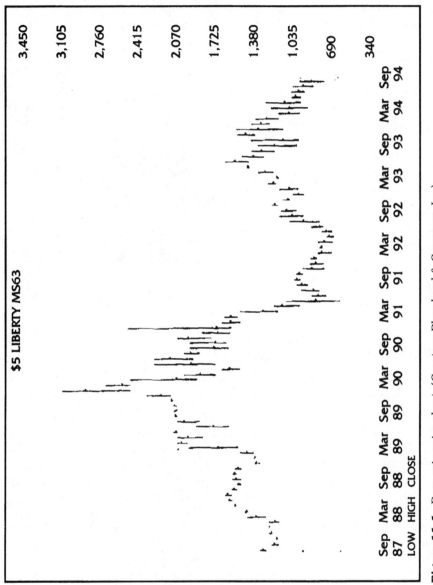

Figure 11-1. Rare coin price chart. (*Courtesy Blanchard & Company, Inc.*)

ingly, rare-coin bull markets are accompanied by higher gold and silver prices, and it's not unusual for rare coins to outperform both gold and silver.

With that in mind, what are the prospects for rare coins today? As indicated earlier, many coins trade at far below their 1989 highs. Since it's impossible to pinpoint a market bottom, the current price level for entry into coin investments looks reasonable, from a long-term investment perspective.

The precious-metals scenario has already been discussed in Chapter 9, Beating Inflation with Precious Metals. Suffice it to say, here, that the rise in interest rates by the Federal Reserve Board sparked inflation fears in 1994 and ignited activity in the precious-metals markets, driving gold and silver prices higher.

Crucial to investing in the rare-coin market is finding and dealing with a reputable firm. Mike Fuljenz, Vice President of Jefferson Coin & Bullion in Houston, Texas, provides the following handy checklist for selecting your rare-coin dealer:

- Do they have their clients' respect?
- Do they have their peers' respect?
- Do they stress client education?
- Are they seasoned market participants?
- Are they major participants at coin conventions?
- Do they respond knowledgeably and confidently, when you ask about the performance of their recommendations?
- Will they work on a percentage over cost basis on large orders?
- Do they have their own inventory?
- Are they willing to fax coin availability and pricing?
- Do they strive to better their profession?
- Are they able to recommend a certified coin in several categories, so that you can compare price and value?

Fuljenz challenges rare-coin investors to "Dare to Compare" before they purchase, in order to ensure that they receive the best prices.

Professional coin dealers recommend sticking with coins graded and independently certified either by PCGS (Professional Coin Grading Service) or NGC (Numismatic Guaranty Corporation). That way, you know the quality of coin you are receiving. Typically, coins graded by other services are less liquid, and trade at a discount to PCGS and NGC coins.

Coin Grades

In order to be a successful coin investor, it is imperative that you thoroughly understand the grading system. Along with rarity (the number of coins minted and remaining), the coin's grade ranks as one of the major determinants of its value.

The following American Numismatic Association grading descriptions are intended to apply to the entire range of U.S. coins. For more coin-specific grading of individual coin types, refer to the official ANA coin-grading guide. While you are not expected to become an expert coin grader just in order to invest in rare coins, you will need to know what each grade means in terms of potential coin value. As indicated above, the safest route is to purchase only PCGS- and NGC-graded coins, to ensure accuracy of grading.

A grade is the classification of a coin to a position in an ordered ranking scale, ranging from MS-70 Perfect Uncirculated to AG-3 About Good. It is advised that investors not purchase coins below grade MS-60, staying in the MG-grade grouping for maximum safety. Coins in this range tend to be more in demand, and therefore more liquid when you desire to sell.

MS-70 Perfect Uncirculated.   The perfect coin. This coin has very attractive sharp strike and original luster of the highest quality for the date and mint mark. No contact marks are visible under magnification. There are absolutely no hairlines or scuff marks or defects. Attractive and outstanding eye appeal. Copper coins must be bright, with full original color and luster.

MS-69.   This coin must possess very attractive sharp strike and full original luster for the date and mint. There must be no more than two small nondetracting contact marks or flaws. No hairlines or scuff marks can be seen. Has exceptional eye appeal. Copper coins must be bright, with full original color or luster.

MS-68.   This coin has attractive sharp strike and full original luster for the date and mint, with no more than four light, scattered contact marks or flaws. No hairlines or scuff marks showing. Exceptional eye appeal. Copper coins must have lustrous original color.

MS-67.   This coin possesses full original luster and sharp strike for date and mint. May have three or four very small contact marks, and one more noticeable but not detracting mark. On comparable coins, one or two small single hairlines may show under magnification, or one or two partially hidden scuff marks or flaws may be present. Eye appeal is exceptional. Copper coins must have lustrous original color.

MS-66. This coin must have above-average quality of strike and full original mint luster, with no more than two or three minor but noticeable contact marks. A few very light hairlines may show under magnification, or there may be one or two light scuff marks showing on frosted surfaces or in the field. The eye appeal must be above average, and very pleasing for the date and mint. Copper coins must display full original or lightly toned color.

MS-65. This coin shows an attractive high quality of luster and strike for the date and mint. A few scattered contact marks or two larger marks may be present, and one or two patches of hairlines may be present under magnification. Noticeable light scuff marks may show on the high points of the design. Above-average overall quality and pleasing overall eye appeal. Copper coins must have full luster, with original or darkened color.

MS-64. This coin has at least average luster and strike for the type. Several small contact marks in groups, as well as one or two moderately heavy marks may be seen. One or two patches or hairlines may show under low magnification. Noticeable light scuff marks or defects may be seen within the design or in the field. Attractive overall quality, with a pleasing eye appeal. Copper coins may be slightly dull.

MS-63. This coin has mint luster that may be slightly impaired. Numerous small contact marks and a few scattered heavy marks may be noticeable. Small hairlines are visible without magnification. Several detracting scuff marks or defects may be present throughout the design or in the fields. The general quality is about average, but overall the coin is rather attractive. Copper coins may be darkened or dull.

MS-62. This coin exhibits a dull or impaired luster. Clusters of small contact marks may be present throughout, with a few large marks or nicks in prime focal areas. Hairlines may be very noticeable. Large, unattractive scuff marks may be seen on major coin features. The strike, rim, and planchard quality may be noticeably below average. Overall eye appeal is generally acceptable. Copper pieces show a diminished color and tone.

MS-61. This coin may show diminished mint luster or be notably impaired. The surface shows marks and hairlines. Overall eye appeal is generally acceptable.

MS-60. This coin may have heavy marks in all areas. This represents the final level of recommended investment quality. Coins below this grading level should be collected for numismatic purposes only.

In order to fully understand coin grades, the investor must also know the meaning of various numismatic terms. The following glossary provides you with the basics of numismatics terminology:

ANA: American Numismatic Association.

Abrasion: Light rubbing or marking on coins, caused by friction.

Alloy: A mixture of two metals to provide a durable coin.

Blank: A sized and weighted metal disk, from which coins are minted. See *planchet*.

Brilliance: Term used to describe various degrees of brightness or clarity in the grading process.

Circulated: A coin that has been in the general circulation or trade channels.

Die Defect: A flaw in a coin die that transfers to the struck coin. The numismatic value of a coin with a die defect depends on the number of coins released and the coin's condition.

Double Strike: A visible coin defect, created when the die strikes a slightly offset blank or planchet more than once.

Field: A coin surface on which there is no date, design, inscription or motto.

Flyspecks: Oxidation spots on the coin surface caused by moisture, perspiration, or some other means.

Frosted Proof: U.S. proof coins minted prior to 1936, with a frosted or dull design and an inscription that contrasts sharply with the mirror-like finish of the field.

Hairlines: Tiny scratches and lines that may be the result of cleaning, polishing, or wiping.

High Points: The parts of the coin with the highest design relief. These high points receive the most wear.

Inscription: The lettering, legend, or motto, stamped or engraved on a coin.

Legend: The primary inscription on a coin.

Lint Marks: Minute incise marks (not scratches or hairlines) on a proof-coin surface, caused by pieces of lint, thread, hair, or some other substance.

Luster: The coin's original mint sheen, which can become affected over time by use and exposure to the elements. Proper packaging and storage are advised, to retain the mint sheen.

Mint Condition: The condition of a coin when it leaves the mint. The mint condition of a proof coin will vary substantially from the mint condition of a business-strike coin issued for general circulation.

Mint Mark: The small identification mark or symbol, struck on a coin to indicate where it was minted. In some cases the *absence* of a mint mark designates a particular mint.

Mint State: Coins that have never been circulated. Also called *uncirculated.*

Mirror Finish: Highly brilliant, reflective finish on the field of a coin.

Nick: A small mark on a coin, in which metal is displaced but not removed.

Planchet: A weighted and sized metal disk, from which coins are struck. See *blank.*

Proof: A coin with a special, high-quality surface, and mirrorlike finish. Proofs are not intended for general circulation.

Relief: The part of a coin's design that is raised above the field or coin surface.

Scratch: A line or groove on a coin created by a sharp instrument.

Strike: Terms such as *sharp, weak,* etc., used to describe the characteristics or quality of a coin strike.

Wear: Removal of metal from the surfaces of a coin, by abrasion, cleaning, or handling.

Mike Fuljenz's Coin Picks

"Rare coins should be part of a balanced investment strategy but should comprise no more than 10 percent of the overall portfolio, nor any more than one-half of the precious metal portion of the holdings. A suggested precious metal split is one-third bullion, one-third gold mining stocks, and one-third rare coins," advises Fuljenz.

It's important to note that all legitimate dealers sell to the public at their cost plus a markup of 10 to 30 percent over replacement costs of coins, depending on market situations.

Fuljenz prefers high-grade gold coins, because they tend to outperform their lower-grade counterparts. Proof coins are the most popular, and thus often elicit the most demand. He advises staying with high-grade coins but not going over MS-66, because these grades carry too high a premium to make sense as an investment.

☆ 90 ☆

1901 $20 Liberty Gold (MS-65)

Only 111,526 of these 1901 Liberties were minted—less than 0.2 percent of the 1940 Liberty mintage. In 1994, the 1901 sold at $1160, less than one-third of its 1989 bid of $3800. This coin could more than double and still not hit its previous high.

☆ 91 ☆

American Gold Eagle (1-ounce Bullion Coin)

"The American Eagle still represents the number-one bullion pick, with a 75 percent share of the bullion coin purchases. It carries the cheapest buy/sell spread of all bullion coins, making it easier to turn a profit. An added bonus: It can be purchased for IRA accounts," says Fuljenz.

Other benefits: It is easily recognizable and liquid, and broker reporting is not required as it is on other bullion coins such as Krugerrands or Canadian Maple Leafs.

Fuljenz advises that we watch the spot price of gold and not pay more than 5 percent over spot for bullion gold eagles.

☆ 92 ☆

Proof-65 Morgan Silver Dollars

The price of proof-65 Morgan silver dollars soared from $625 in December 1976 to hit a peak of $10,000 in June 1989. The recession of the early nineties had dropped their prices to $3250 by the end of 1993.

Taking a look at the connection between rare-coin prices and gold prices, Fuljenz considers the gold price of $425 an ounce as a watershed point. "It will take gold breaking above $425 an ounce in order for rare-coin prices to really take off," says Fuljenz.

With gold testing the $400-an-ounce price barrier, the time to take positions in quality rare coins is before the $425-an-ounce threshold gets broken.

Blanchard & Company Coin Recommendations

Russell Augustin, Director of Numismatics for the New Orleans–based Blanchard & Company, the nation's largest retailer of PCGS- and NGC-certified rare coins, provides the following Blanchard proof-gold-coin recommendations for consideration by investors.

☆ 93 ☆

Proof Gold Dollars, 1854-1879, Grade Proof 64 or Higher

There are only 155 certified examples of these coins accounted for, out of an original mintage of 971 for this period, or less than 12 percent of the original mintage (see Fig. 11-2). Traditionally these coins trade for a premium over more common-date Proof Gold Dollars, but this premium is at its lowest level since 1973.

Figure 11-2. Proof Gold Dollar. (*Courtesy Blanchard & Company, Inc.*)

☆ 94 ☆

Liberty Half Eagles, 1860-1879, Grade Proof 64 or Higher

Demand is especially intense for these coins minted during the War Between The States (1861-1865). Proof mintages of the Liberty Half Eagle (see Fig. 11-3) ranged from 4 to 230. Only a tiny fraction are known to survive today. PCGS and NGC report only 569 examples in all grades, or just 13 percent of the original mintage of 4167.

Figure 11-3. Liberty Half Eagle. (*Courtesy Blanchard & Company, Inc.*)

☆ 95 ☆

Proof Liberty Quarter Eagles, Grade Proof 65 or Higher, Especially Proof 67

Proof Liberty Quarter Eagles represent some of the great rarities in American numismatics, due to their low mintages and low survival rates (see Fig. 11-4). Original mintages ranged from 2 to 223. Today, 1005 investment-grade examples have been examined by PCGS and NGC.

Figure 11-4. Liberty Quarter Eagle. (*Courtesy Blanchard & Company, Inc.*)

☆ 96 ☆

Proof Saint-Gaudens Double Eagles, Grade Proof 64 or Higher

Regarded as the most beautiful of all numismatic coins, the High Relief Saint-Gaudens Double Eagle comes complete with an interesting story (see Fig. 11-5). This coin apparently was struck in proof, although Congress did not authorize this act. Most likely they were struck for dignitaries and politicians, and have only recently begun to trade in the numismatic community.

Figure 11-5. Saint-Gaudens Double Eagle. (*Courtesy Blanchard & Company, Inc.*)

Only 689 Proof Saint-Gaudens Double Eagles were minted from 1980 to 1915, with only 233 surviving in all grades. Of these, only 36 have been graded Proof 64 or higher.

☆ 97 ☆

Proof Indian Eagles, Graded Proof 66 or Higher

Out of an original mintage of 822 coins from 1908 to 1915, only 189, or 22 percent, survive today.

☆ 98 ☆

Pattern Coins

Tim Benford, founder of Benford Associates in Mountainside, New Jersey, considers pattern coins to be one of the sleepers in the rare-coin world. Benford, who writes extensively on numismatics, says

> Pattern coins defy the rare-coins rules. Typically, the lower the mintage and the higher the grade, the more valuable the coin. However, patterns are extremely rare but have yet to command the premium prices of other similarly rare coins.

Just what *are* pattern coins? Simply put, patterns are just that. They were patterns or prototypes of coins that were being considered for circulation. They were struck to illustrate for members of Congress and other government officials a potential new design or denomination, new coin sizes, mottoes, or different metal alloys.

As patterns, they experienced limited mintage runs, mainly used to provide various samples of the proposed coinage. Pattern mintages ranged from a single coin to just over a thousand, with the average running between a dozen to 100 pieces. Over 2000 different patterns have been struck from 1792 to the present.

Patterns were rejected for a variety of reasons, as for instance that the type of alloy could be counterfeited too easily, there was lack of agreement on artistic quality, or technical difficulties were encountered in the minting process.

According to Benford, patterns have so far remained off the beaten path of most coin collectors, and are for the most part totally unknown to investors. As a result, they remain substantially underpriced in the marketplace.

Benford's Pattern Picks

Liberty Head Nickel Patterns

First, a little background. The Liberty Head Nickel was officially struck as a regular U.S. Mint coin from 1883 to 1912. However, five examples of the 1913 Liberty Head Nickel were struck before the Mint received word that the Buffalo Nickel would be the officially sanctioned five-cent coinage for 1913. If you are fortunate enough to own one of the 1913 Liberty Head Nickels, it commands between $750,000 and $1 million. Not bad, for a coin that is *neither* a regular-issue coin *nor* a pattern!

In anticipation of a new nickel design, the mint started to produce various patterns in 1881. Several of these nickel patterns had very low mintages of under 30 pieces each, and were quite similar to the regular-issue 1883 Liberty Head Nickel. In high grades ranging from MS-60 to -65, they can be found at auctions for under $5000. A transitional 1882 Liberty Head Nickel pattern (identical to the regular issue of 1883 in all but date), of which less than 20 pieces exist, sold for under $8000 in 1993. That's a far cry from the up to $1 million for the bogus 1913 nickels.

According to Benford, collector interest in patterns is picking up, and prices have been rising as a result. Patterns that sold at auctions for under $500 as recently as six years ago are now being sold for $2000 and more.

No matter which types of coins you decide to invest in, it pays to investigate before you invest. Learn the different coin appearance grades, for they're a big factor in determining a coin's worth. For a novice coin investor, finding a reputable dealer is crucial, since you will have to depend on someone else's ability until you have gained a good feel for the coin market and coin values. Here's a list of coin information publications and reference sources, to help get you up to speed on investing in coins.

Coin Information Sources

American Numismatic Association, 818 N. Cascade Avenue, Colorado Springs, CO 80903 (publishes *The Numismatist*).

American Numismatic Society, Broadway & 155th Street, New York, NY 10032.

Auction Prices Realized, Krause Publications, 700 E. State Street, Iola, WI 54990.

Certified Coin Dealer Newsletter, Dept. CCDn, P.O. Box 7939, Torrance, CA 90504.

Coin Buyer's Guide, American Institute for Economic Research, Great Barrington, MA 01230.

Coin World, 911 Vandemark Road, Sidney, OH 45365.

Guide Book of United States Coins (Red Book), R. S. Yeoman.

"Numismatic News," Krause Publications (address above).

The Consumer's Guide to Coin Investing and Collecting, Blanchard and Company, P.O. Box 61740, New Orleans, LA 70161-1740.

United States Patterns and Related Issues, Bowers & Merena, Inc., Box 1224, Wolfboro, NH 03894.

12

Cruising to Profits with Antique and Classic Cars

Roadworthy Investments

As the owner of a 1936 Oldsmobile (driven from Wyoming to New York City and back in 1993; see photo on back-cover flap), I can vouch for the pleasures an antique car can provide over the years. But what about their investment possibilities? I personally know a friend who purchased a 1935 Ford V-8 Deluxe Model 48 Four-Door Sedan for $7000, enjoyed it for a few months, then turned around and sold it for $11,000 in 1991. According to the *Old Cars Price Guide* for June 1988, published by Krause Publications in Iola, Wisconsin, the value of that car should have been about $8500 in top condition. If my friend's 1935 Ford had been a convertible rather than a sedan, it would have been worth around $25,000 in mid-1994.

The key to successful antique-car investing is the same as in any other type of investing. Know the market, and take advantage of market opportunities when they arise. My friend bought low and sold high. As we saw with coins, automobile prices too have gone through cycles, last peaking in the late eighties and now beginning to show life again.

There's a collector car to fit every investor's pocketbook, from $750,000 Duesenbergs to Henry Ford's less expensive autos for the common man.

One caveat: Don't think you can purchase a fixer-upper and make money on it. I'll give ten-to-one odds that the expenses to restore a car, not to mention the time invested, will far outstrip your return. You're far better off attending an auction, bankruptcy sale, or antique automobile dealer, and purchasing the results of someone else's painstaking (and expensive) efforts. Remember, take advantage of market opportunities.

To be sure, the majority of cars produced over the past decades are not and never will be collector cars from an investment perspective. Sure, you may want to purchase that 1950 Dodge Sedan you took on your first date, but don't expect it to increase the diameter of your retirement nest egg. Enjoy it for the pleasure it gives you, but that's it. By the way, your new 1950 Dodge Sedan is worth around $7000 in top condition. Now, if you own a 1950 Dodge Series D34 Coronet Convertible, we can talk some money. According to estimated prices from the June 1994 *Old Cars Price Guide,* in prime condition the convertible would command approximately $20,000.

Just what is it, then, that makes a collector car a good investment? It's the same thing that makes any investment worthwhile: the old supply/demand relationship. While surely there is no big supply of 1950 Dodge Sedans around anymore, there's also no big demand for them, either. Thus there is no dramatic upward price pressure to achieve dramatic investment gains.

The elements that go into an investment-grade collector car include styling, engineering, performance, the high critical opinion of automotive specialists, popular opinion, rarity, mileage, and condition. Domestically, Fords and Chevrolets have drawn more collector interest than other manufacturers or product lines such as Chryslers or Oldsmobiles. There are also special-interest cars that have drawn the attention of collectors, such as the Ford Mustang ($15,000 to $75,000, depending on year and model) or the 1957 Chevrolet V-8, Bel Air two-door hardtop ($28,000) or convertible ($43,000).

However, specific model years, body styles, and other factors also can come into play to make a car more desirable than others in the same line or other lines. For example, the unique design concepts of the Chrysler Airflow make it far more valuable than its more traditional counterparts. The 1937 8-cylinder Chrysler Airflow Coupe commands around $23,000, while the standard 1937 6-cylinder Chrysler Business Coupe is worth only around $11,000. In fact, the 1937 Chrysler Convertible, Imperial Convertible, and Imperial Custom models are the only Chrysler automobiles from that year that are valued more highly than the Airflow. See Table 12-1 for pricing information for some of the 1937 Chrysler and Imperial line of automobiles.

It is obvious from Table 12-1 that a car's condition is extremely important. The 1937 Airflow Coupe is worth nearly two and a half times more in condition 1 as opposed to condition 3. If you don't possess the expertise to determine a car's condition yourself, it's wise to have the car appraised by an independent party experienced in the collector car field.

The *Old Cars Price Guide* uses a six-grade rating system, ranging from 6 (lowest) to 1 (highest). The condition code descriptions are as follows:

1. **Excellent** Restored to current maximum professional standards of quality in every area, or perfect original with components operating and appearing as new. A 95-plus-point show car that is not driven.

2. **Fine** Well restored, or a combination of superior restoration and excellent original. Also, an extremely well-maintained original showing very minimal wear.

3. **Very good** Completely operable original or "older restoration" showing wear. Also, a good amateur restoration, all presentable and serviceable inside and out. Plus, combinations of well done restoration and good operable components, or a partially restored car with all parts necessary to complete it and/or valuable NOS parts.*

*NOS refers to "New Old Stock" parts.

Table 12-1. 1937 Chrysler and Imperial Price Guide

CONDITION	3	2	1
ROYAL 6-cyl., 116" wb			
RS conv.	$10,000	$17,500	$25,000
Conv. sedan	11,200	19,600	28,000
Business coupe	4,400	7,700	11,000
RS coupe	3,950	7,000	12,000
Touring sedan	3,950	7,000	10,000
Airflow, 8-cyl., 128" wb			
Coupe	9,200	16,100	23,000
Four-door sedan	8,800	15,400	22,000
Imperial, 8-cyl., 121" wb			
RS conv.	11,200	19,600	28,000
Conv. sedan	12,000	21,000	30,000
Business coupe	6,000	10,500	15,000
RS coupe	6,400	11,200	16,000
Touring sedan	6,000	10,500	15,000
Imperial, 8-cyl., 140" wb			
Five-passenger sedan	10,000	17,500	25,000
Seven-passenger sedan	10,800	18,900	27,000
Sedan limo	15,200	26,600	38,000

Source: *Old Car's Price Guide,* June 1994.

4. **Good** A driveable vehicle needing no or only minor work to be functional. Also, a deteriorated restoration or a very poor amateur restoration. All components may need restoration to be "excellent," but the car is mostly usable as is.

5. **Restorable** Needs complete restoration of body, chassis, and interior. May or may not be running, but isn't weathered, wrecked, or stripped to the point of being useful only for parts.

6. **Parts car** May or may not be running, but is weathered, wrecked, and/or stripped to the point of being useful primarily for parts.

An excellent way to become savvy in the world of collector cars is to subscribe to several automobile publications. A list of some of the major ones is provided for your convenience at the end of this chapter. They provide listings of automobiles for sale, and advertisements for upcoming auctions. It's also a good idea to join a general automobile club, as well as a specialized one or two. Most clubs publish car newsletters on upcoming auctions, plus many have classified ads through which members are selling their cars.

Here's a partial list of addresses for car clubs in the United States:

Antique Automobile Club of
  America
501 West Governor Road
Hershey, PA 17033

Airflow Club of America
8554 Boyson Street
Downey, CA 90242

Buick Club of America
P.O. Box 898
Garden Grove, CA 92642

Chevrolet Club of America
P.O. Box 5387
Orange, CA 92667

DeSoto Club of America
1925 McGee
Kansas City, MO 64108

Dodge Brothers Club
4451 Wise Road
Freeland, MI 48623

Imperial Owners Club
  International
P.O. Box 991, Dept. KI
Scranton, PA 18503-0991

Lincoln & Cont. Owners Club
P.O. Box 68308
Portland, OR 97268-0308

Packards Intl. Motor Car Club
302 French Street
Santa Ana, CA 92701

The Early Ford V-8 Club
P.O. Box 2122
San Leandro, CA 90713

Thunderbirds of America
P.O. Box 2250
Dearborn, MI 48123

Tucker Automobile Club of Amer.
311 West 18th Street
Tifton, GA 31794

Willys Club
 509 West Germantown Park
 Norristown, PA 19403

  Dean Kruse, Chairman of the auto auctioneer Kruse International in Auburn, Indiana, offers seven pointers on how to be successful in investing in antique automobiles. Kruse also is a founder and board member of the National Automotive and Truck Museum of the United States, and a board member for the Auburn-Cord Duesenberg Museum.

1. Convertibles offer the best return and appreciation opportunities. When the top goes down, the price goes up.

2. Purchase cars at least 20 years old.

3. Purchase top-quality cars with a ranking of at least 90 points on a scale of 100.

4. When buying lower-priced cars outside of the Duesenberg class, purchase big-three products: Ford, General Motors, Chrysler.

5. Stay away from soft colors such as green and blue; stick to black, white, and red.

6. Keep your automobile in a heated garage, and drive it periodically.

7. Purchase either a restored automobile or one in very good original condition.

Dean Kruse's Low-priced Antique Automobile Picks

☆ 99 ☆

Early V-8 Fords (1935), Convertible

The Franklin Mint has just released a collector's edition of the 1932 Ford V-8, testifying to the immense popularity of this Ford series of cars.

☆ 100 ☆

1964½ Mustang 289 8-Cylinder Convertible

The thirty-year anniversary of Ford's introduction of the Mustang came in 1994. This car could be a hot item in the coming year. Estimated auction prices will range from $15,000 to $20,000 in 1994. The expected price increase will be 15 percent.

☆ 101 ☆

1955 Chevrolet Bel Air Convertible

A sporty new introduction to liven up the Chevrolet car lineup. The estimated auction price will be between $17,000 to $25,000 in 1994. The expected price increase will be 15 percent.

High-priced Picks

☆ 102 ☆

Duesenberg

Kruse likes Duesenbergs built from 1929 to 1937, the J Series, not the A Series. Desirable classics are selling from around $500,000 to $1,000,000 and up (add another $50,000 to $150,000 for a supercharged Duesenberg). One of the strongest cars ever built, it was a favorite with the stars. Gary Cooper owned a 1930 Duesenberg J Durham Tourster, while Clark Gable hit the Hollywood streets in his 1935 Duesenberg J. Perpetual bad guy James Cagney improved his image with his 1932 Duesenberg J Dietrich Convertible Berline.

Duesenberg was the first American car to win the Grand Prix at LeMans, France, in 1921. It also captured the Indianapolis 500 three times in the 1920s. Between 1929 and 1937, a mere 481 Model J's were crafted. More than 75 percent of all the Duesenbergs made still exist today, and an estimated 55 percent are still in operable mechanical condition. (See Fig. 12-1, 1930 Duesenberg SJ Murphy Convertible Coupe.)

Without a doubt, the Duesenberg represents the premier example of the high-speed luxury car ever built in America. The product of the German-born brothers, Frederick and August Duesenberg, the Duesenberg came closer to European styling than any other American car in history.

Ironically, the popular Duesenberg J came into being under the watchful eye of Lobban Cord, who purchased the Duesenberg Motor Company and brought it out of receivership in 1926, three years before the financial crisis that sank not only Wall Street share prices but also many automobile companies.

Cord instructed Duesenberg to construct the finest chassis possible, so as to deliver a car with exquisite performance wrapped in exquisite luxury. All the famous coachwork houses from both America and Europe competed for the right to build the ultimate coach for the project. The culmination of all this effort was the Duesenberg J, unveiled in 1928. In various forms, the Series J remained in production for nine years.

The chassis housed a powerhouse of an engine. The J was fitted with a straight-eight cylinder engine displacing a massive 420 cubic inches. Each cylinder had four valves, operated by twin overhead camshafts. Far ahead of its day, the Duesenberg J sported a mechanical computer that warned the operator of problems with the oil level or battery charge. The sleek car exhibited sheer power and speed, unmatched by anything of the day. It cruised at 115 miles per hour and topped out around 120 miles per hour. It could hit 110 miles per hour, in second gear, in a mere 21 seconds.

The chassis alone cost nearly $12,000 (in 1930s dollars) to build. Fine carriage cloths, soft leathers, and rare woods finished off the coach work, while many engine components were made of buffed and polished plated or stove-enameled metal.

Bids for J Duesenbergs at Kruse International auctions, as reported in the 1993 and 1994 editions of *Collectible Vehicle Auction Results & Collector's Guide* include the following.

Figure 12-1. 1930 Duesenberg SJ Murphy Convertible Coupe (*Courtesy of Kruse International.*)

YEAR/MODEL DESCRIPTION		BID PRICE
1929 J 103 LeBaron	8-cyl	$1,000,000
1929 J Durham Phaeton	ST 8	885,000
1929 J 103 LeBaron	ST 8	875,000
1929 J Murphy Conv.	ST 8	885,000
1930 J Murphy Conv.	ST 8	1,600,000
1930 J Murphy Conv. Coupe	ST 8	590,000
1931 J Murphy Conv.	ST 8	1,200,000
1931 J Murphy Conv.	ST 8	1,100,000
1931 J Rollston J Victoria	V-8	775,000
1934 J 555 Torpedo Phaeton	ST 8	1,000,000
1934 J Murphy Conv. Sedan	V-8	580,000
1935 J Bohman & Schwartz	ST 8	470,000

Duesenberg enthusiasts may join the Auburn-Cord-Duesenberg Club, Route 6, Box 482, Rome City, New York 13440.

☆ 103 ☆

Hispano Suiza

Kruse also likes another classic, Hispano Suiza (1919-1939). The Kruse International *Collectible Vehicle Auction Results & Collector's Guide,* 1993 and 1994 editions, include the following Hispano Suiza bids.

YEAR/MODEL DESCRIPTION		BID PRICE
1926 H6B	6-cyl	$140,000
1928 Suiza	V-8	150,000
1928 4-door Fernandez	6-cyl	127,000
1928 H6B	6-cyl	210,000
1930 Coupe	6-cyl	150,000
1937 K 6 Van Vorden	6-cyl	40,000
1937 Van Vorden Saloon	6-cyl	45,000

One of the world's great motor cars, the Hispano Suiza took on styling and engineering unique to its Spanish/Swiss heritage. The Barcelona, Spain–headquartered firm also established a manufacturing plant on the outskirts of Paris in 1911. The company also manufactured the famous V-8 "Hisso" aircraft engine that powered many of the best fighter planes in World War I.

The Spanish/Swiss connection came about when the Swiss-born Marc Birkit, an electrical engineer, founded his first plant in Barcelona in 1901 with funding supplied by Spanish financier Señor J. Castro.

The company produced some cars for entrance in the French Grand Prix in the early 1900s, but its first automobile for sale to the general public did not appear until 1904, and full-scale production did not begin in earnest until after World War I. The Hispano Suiza achieved perfection through the introduction of the 12-cylinder models prior to World War II.

Carrying over its knowledge gained from producing tough, lightweight aircraft engines, Hispano Suiza developed dependable automobile engines out of light alloys (aluminum). The company used its patented pressurized enameling process to make the upper half of the engine virtually corrosion-proof. The Hispano-Suiza was the choice of European royalty for its elegant styling. In fact, beginning in 1911, the company named its new Type 15-T model after the reigning Spanish monarch, Alfonso XIII.

The Hispano Suiza car club is located in the United States. It may be contacted by writing to the Hispano Suiza Society, 175 St. Germain Avenue, San Francisco, California 94114, or by calling 415-664-4378.

Other High-priced Picks

Other favorites that Dean Kruse feels have good appreciation potential include the V-16 Cadillac (1930-1938), 12-cylinder Packards (1933-1938), and the Rolls-Royce Silver Ghost (1907-1924).

A number of antique car shows and auctions are held across the country each year. The serious antique automobile collector will want to consult the following publications.

Collectible Vehicle Auction Results & Collector's Guide (current edition), Kruse International, P.O. Box 190, Auburn, IN 46706.

Collector Car Annual, 911 Vandemark Road, Box 482, Sidney, OH 45365.

Collector Car News, P.O. Box 5279, Long Beach, CA 90805.

Hemmings Motor News, Box 256, West Road, Route 9, Bennington, VT 05201.

Old Cars Price Guide, Krause Publications, 700 E. State Street, Iola, WI 54990-0001.

Old Cars Weekly News & Marketplace, Krause Publications (address above).

Standard Guide to Cars & Prices (current edition), Krause Publications (address above).

13
Other
Collectibles

The Art Angle

Art and other collectibles are quite different from other investments. For one thing, the beauty and therefore the desirability is often in the eye of the beholder. What appeals to one person may not appeal to another. Along the same lines, each object of art is fairly unique, and transactions for a specific piece occur infrequently.

How then does art fare as an investment? This question was recently evaluated by Professor Robert R. Ebert, holder of The Buckhorn Chair in Economics at Baldwin Wallace College in Berea, Ohio. His findings originally were reported in the Summer 1994 issue of *The Economy,* a newsletter sponsored by The Buckhorn Chair in Economics.

To summarize, Professor Ebert used Sotheby's art index numbers from 1975 through mid-1992. Art prices and the return on investment in art were on a general uptrend, but exploded in the late 1980s. This was followed by a severe contraction, from which the market has not recovered as of mid-1994.

According to Ebert, Japanese corporate collectors and art speculators were a factor in the run-up of art prices. With the onset of financial troubles in Japan, Japanese demand for art weakened substantially. Weakening European and U.S. economies also contributed to the drop in art demand. By late 1990, many contemporary works were failing to sell at auction. Likewise, sales of expressionist and modern art failed to meet expectations in the nineties.

Ebert also cites William Baumol, an economist at Princeton and New York Universities. Baumol says that returns on art investments are systematically lower than those in financial instruments. He also notes a nonmarket risk (theft, damage, and fire) involved in the ownership of art. Baumol concludes that paintings brought an average annual compounded real rate of return of 0.55 percent (in the 1760–1960 period) after adjustments for inflation.

Another study, by James Pesando of the University of Toronto, analyzed the auction market for modern prints in the 1977-1992 period. This study found that the annual real return on all modern prints averaged 1.51 percent over that 15-year period, versus 2.54 percent for long-term Treasury bonds and 8.14 percent for stocks.

Ebert concludes that only those who have no aversion to risk and are prepared to accept considerable market volatility should purchase art objects for speculative purposes.

It is imperative that those who choose to invest in the collectible arena understand the risk associated with such investments. Keeping that fact always in mind, the following areas look attractive given today's market climate.

☆ 104 ☆

Antique Stock and Bond Certificates

Ironically, many stock and bond certificates have more value as collectible items than they do as an investment in or debt issue of the corporation that originally issued them. For instance, a 1947 stock certificate for 10,000 shares in Tucker Corporation realized a sale price in excess of $2100 in the Seventh Annual Strasburg Stock & Bond Auction in early January 1994. (See Fig. 13-1, Tucker Corporation Class B stock certificate.) Likewise, an 1878 certificate for 100 shares of Standard Oil garnered nearly $9000. In 1989, a similar certificate with Rockefeller's signature was selling for $4500. (See Fig. 13-2, Standard Oil stock certificate.)

To be sure, the purchasers did not look at the traditional investment value of these stock certificates when they made their winning bids, for both certificates are worthless on any securities exchange. After all,

Figure 13-1. 1947 Tucker Corporation Class B Stock
Certificate (*Courtesy R.M. Smythe & Company, Inc.*)

Tucker went out of business decades ago, and the Standard Oil (now
part of British Petroleum) certificate was canceled long ago.

The attraction of these certificates resides in their historic significance
and rarity. The Tucker Corporation Class B Common Stock certificate
featured a stylized TUCKER logo on an elaborate blue underprint, and
was personally signed by Preston Tucker (unlike the relatively common Class A shares, with an engraved signature). This certificate is one
of only five known Class B Tucker Corporation certificates.

Figure 13-2. Standard Oil Stock Certificate (*Courtesy R.M.
Smythe & Company, Inc.*)

The Standard Oil certificate gains its value from having been personally signed by John D. Rockefeller as well as by Henry Morrison Flagler,
an oil magnate associated with Rockefeller. Flagler also organized the
Florida East Coast Railway and built lavish resort hotels in Miami. The
shares were issued to Jabez A. Bostwick, another instrumental figure in
the early affairs of Standard Oil, at the time the world's largest oil producer with a 90 percent share of the U.S. oil business.

Noted business figures are not the only area of scripophily (collection
of stock and bond certificates) receiving attention and high bid prices.
The field of interest is quite varied, covering a host of certificate issues:
automobile companies, railroads, telegraph firms, oil companies, gold
mining firms, motion picture studios, turnpikes, utilities, American
Philatelic Society, Pacific Coast Jockey Club, Kansas City Baseball Club,
and even the Francis Scott Key Memorial Association.

At the same January 1994 auction, an investor paid over $2000 for a
1921 certificate for five shares of Houdini Picture Corporation, signed
by the celebrated magician Henry Houdini.

Other factors besides noted signatures and historical significance also
come into play when determining the worth of a certificate. Intricate
engraving, design work, or unique art can add to the value of a certificate. For example, a United States Treasury War Finance Committee
certificate, signifying ownership of a War Bond, is adorned with 22
Disney characters in full color. This item carried a $250 price in early
1991 and $375 in early 1994.

Shares of the Ringling Bros.–Barnum & Bailey Combined Shows have
a multicolored inner border frame, consisting of acrobats, clowns, cir-
cus wagons, lions, and more.

As is true of most collectibles, one of the difficulties of dealing in
antique certificates is finding the markets and determining a fair price.
Since each certificate is unique and physical conditions can vary widely, comparison prices are hard to obtain. On the other hand if a number
of similar certificates exist, its rarity is greatly reduced, along with its
market value.

"The first priority for someone considering collecting antique certificates is to approach it because they like them and want to learn more
about them. They should enjoy what they own, and if the value rises all
the better," advises Stephen L. Goldsmith, Executive Vice President
with R.M. Smythe & Company, Inc., a New York City firm engaged in
securities research as well as certificate appraisal and auctioneering.

As in any collectible field, the key is to try to discern trends and
events that will impact pricing. The following guidelines will help you
to zero in on market segments that tend to outperform the rest of the
field.

Rarity   It's the old supply/demand relationship at work. Typically, the rarer an item, the higher price it can obtain in the market.

Condition   Well-preserved certificates tend to achieve higher prices than their worn counterparts. Likewise, certificates with cancellation holes tend to draw lower bids than do certificates canceled by red ink printed across the certificate and signatures.

Age   As a general rule, the older the certificate, the more it is worth. This ties in with the rarity of an issue. Older issues will likely have fewer "survivors" down through the years.

Signatures   As indicated earlier, the presence of the signature of a noted industrialist or other historically significant person, such as Thomas A. Edison, can dramatically increase the value of a certificate.

Historical event   A certificate tied to a historical event (for example, the War Bond issue described a moment ago, or the founding of a major company such as Coca-Cola or American Express) heightens a certificate's demand and value.

Subject   Some topics seem to generate more investor interest than others. Railroad certificates appear to be perennial favorites among investors.

Artistic quality   Intricate design, quality engraving and lithography, and unique and beautiful design and artwork—all these enhance the value of a certificate.

Personally, I like the one-of-a-kind certificates, which should increase in value more than the average certificate. One example is a 100-share certificate of Hudson & Manhattan Railroad stock. While other railroad certificates may sell for $259 to $350, this one sold for $825, over 60 percent more than its pre-auction estimated sales price. What made this particular Hudson & Manhattan Railroad stock certificate more valuable was its issuance to the 1926 undefeated world heavyweight boxing champion Gene Tunney—his signature is on the attached stub.

In addition to attending certificate auctions or visiting certificate dealers, there's another way to financially benefit from antique certificates. Uncanceled old securities can be worth a lot of money. The fact that the company is no longer listed on an exchange doesn't mean the certificate is worthless. It may have changed its name, merged with another firm, or even gone into bankruptcy.

R.M. Smythe & Company, Inc., and others, will research any certificate for a small fee. One of their clients brought in 100 shares of Alamito Company common stock. Research uncovered the fact that the

Arizona company merged in 1986 into Osceola Energy, Inc., for $165 cash for each share of common stock. The "worthless" certificates earned the client $16,500!

For more information on the art of collecting certificates, consult any or all of these three good reference sources:

Insider's Guide to Antique Securities, Haley Garrison
Scripophily: Collecting Bonds, Keith Hollender
The Stock & Bond Collectors Price Guide, Bill Yatchman

☆ 105 ☆

Buy the Book

Investing "by the book" takes on a different meaning in the world of rare books. According to Paul Melzer, owner of Paul Melzer Fine and Rare Books in Redlands, CA, two areas that have generated collector interest are modern first editions (from the turn of the century to date) and fine art books.

Two modern-era authors who have developed a good following are Ernest Hemingway and John Steinbeck. As in other collectible fields, rarity and condition come into play. Consider the following pricings of first editions of *For Whom The Bell Tolls* and *The Grapes of Wrath*.

	For Whom...	*Grapes of Wrath*
Without dust jacket	$25–50	$50–$100
With dust jacket—perfect	$600–$700	$2,500
Signed copy w/jacket	$3,000–$4,000	$4,500

By way of comparison, 20 years ago the Hemingway book with a dust jacket would have sold for $50 to $60 while the Steinbeck book with a dust jacket would have brought around $100.

"Art books have several things going for them. With an original issue price from $35 to $100 or more, a fair amount of money went to assure the quality of their publication. Second, the print run was usually quite limited, between 5000 to 10000 copies. Finally, many art books are not reprinted, further limiting their availability," says Melzer.

A classic example is Marc Chagall's *Jerusalem Windows*, published in the early 1960s. Originally it sold for $35 and had to be remaindered (sold at a fraction of the original sales price to clear out inventory). Chagall's windows were exhibited in Paris and New York before they were installed in the synagogue at the new Hadassah–Hebrew University Medical Center in the Judean Hills, west of Jerusalem, in February 1962. Chagall chose the Twelve Tribes of Israel as the theme for his stained-glass-window creations. Today, Chagall's *Jerusalem Windows* sells for between $1200 and $1500.

"Before you purchase any book, you need to educate yourself. Call around to several dealers and get price quotes. It pays to be cautious," advises Melzer.

Venturing into the collectible field is not for the fainthearted. After all, the collectible tin-can market is at 60 percent of the price level it was at in 1989, and baseball cards have dropped 20 percent in price from five years ago. Likewise, cigar-band prices have dropped considerably in recent years, as the generation that collected them has died off.

"It's important to realize that only several hundred people really make up the bulk of the market for a particular collection. In that group, there are about five real movers and shakers. Then it takes something to get the market moving, like a book, to generate enough attention for people to start building world-class collections," says Tony Hyman, collectible expert and author of *Trash or Treasure: A Guide to the Best Buyers of Antiques & Collectibles* ($29.95 published by Treasure Hunt Publications, Box 3000, Pismo Beach, CA 93448).

Hyman advises that it's quality, not quantity, that counts. Purchase the best you can afford, and in fine condition. He also strongly recommends that you watch trends, to decipher when the big boys have become interested in a particular collectible. Get in early, and get out before the big boys exit and the market for that collectible collapses.

Currently, Hyman is purchasing all the quality cigar boxes he can get his hands on. Forget Prince Edward, and look for quality.

"The top cigar boxes have terrific lithography and artwork. One with an 1872 aerial view of San Francisco is worth around $300 right now. I see cigar boxes being worth 10 to 30 times their current value in less than a decade," says Hyman.

There's plenty of food for thought in these pages. Properly structure your investment portfolio for the twenty-first century, and you may soon be driving that 1930 Duesenberg SJ down your main street.

Glossary

Accreted: The process of earning or growing gradually. For example, the interest on zero coupon bonds is accreted.

Adjustable Rate Preferred: A preferred security, with its dividend payment pegged to a specific index or indices.

American Depositary Receipt (ADR): A negotiable receipt for shares of a foreign corporation held in the vault of a U.S. depositary bank.

Annual Report: The Securities and Exchange Commission–required report, presenting a portrayal of the company's operations and financial position. It includes a balance sheet, income statement, statement of cashflows, description of company operations, management discussion of company financial condition and operating results, and any events that materially impact the company.

Asset Allocation: An investment strategy of reducing risk and increasing return by investing in a variety of asset types.

Asset play: A stock investment that value investors find attractive due to asset undervaluation by the market.

At the Money: The situation when the underlying security's market price equals the exercise price.

Basis Price: The cost of an investment used to determine capital gains or losses.

Bear Market: A period of time during which stock prices decline over a period of months or years.

Bond: A long-term debt security that obligates the issuer to pay interest and repay the principal. The holder does not have any ownership rights in the issuer.

Bond Ratio: The measure of a company's leverage comparing the firm's debt to total capital.

Bottom-up Investing: An investment strategy that starts with company fundamentals and then moves to the overall economic and investment environment.

Busted: A convertible whose underlying common stock value has fallen so low that the convertible provision no longer holds any value.

Call Option: A contract giving the holder the right to buy the underlying security at a specific price during a specified time period.

Call Provision: A provision allowing the security issuer to recall the security before maturity.

Cash Equivalent: An asset type with maturities of less than one year.

Cashflow: The flow of funds in and out of an operating business. Normally calculated as net income plus depreciation and other noncash items.

Cashflow/Debt Ratio: The relationship of free cashflow to total long-term indebtedness. This ratio is helpful in tracking a firm's ability to meet scheduled debt and interest payment requirements.

Cashflow/Interest Ratio: This ratio determines how many times free cashflow will cover fixed interest payments on long-term debt.

Cashflow per Share: Cashflow per share represents the amount earned before deduction for depreciation and other charges not involving the outlay of cash.

Cash Ratio: This ratio is used to measure liquidity. It is calculated as the sum of cash and marketable securities, divided by current liabilities. It indicates how well a company can meet current liabilities.

Closed-end Fund: An investment fund with a fixed number of shares outstanding and that trades on exchanges, like stock in regular companies.

Cluster Investing: A method of diversification that recommends investing in stocks from different clusters or groups.

Common and Preferred Cashflow Coverage Ratios: These ratios determine how many times annual free cashflow will cover common and preferred cash dividend payments.

Common Stock Ratio: The relationship of common stock to total company capitalization.

Contrarian: An investor seeking securities that are out of favor with other investors.

Convertibles: A security that is exchangeable into common stock at the option of the holder, under specified terms and conditions.

Covered Call: An option in which the investor owns the underlying security.

Cumulative: As it relates to preferred stock, any unpaid preferred dividends that accrue and must be paid prior to resumption of common stock dividends.

Current Ratio: A liquidity ratio calculated by dividing current assets by current liabilities.

Cycles: Repeating patterns of business, economic, and market activity.

Cyclical: Industries and companies that advance and decline in relation to the changes in the overall economic environment.

Debt-to-Equity Ratio: The relationship of debt to shareholder's equity in a firm's capitalization structure.

Defensive Investments: Securities that are less affected by economic contractions, thus offering downside price protection.

Diversification: The spreading of investment risk by owning different types of securities, investments in different geographical markets, etc.

Dollar-Cost Averaging: An investment strategy of investing a fixed amount of money over time, to achieve a lower average security purchase price.

Dow Jones Industrial Average: A market index consisting of 30 U.S. industrial companies. Used as a measure of market performance.

Dow Theory: An investment theory that the market moves in three simultaneous movements that help to forecast the direction of the economy and the market.

Drip: A dividend reinvestment plan, in which stockholders may purchase additional shares with dividends and/or cash.

Earnings per Share: Net after-tax income, divided by the number of outstanding company shares.

Economic Series: The complete cycle of types of economic periods, as from expansion to slowdown to contraction to recession/depression to increased activity back to expansion.

Economic Value: The economic value of a stock represents the anticipated free cashflow the company will generate over a period of time, discounted by the weighted cost of a company's capital.

Efficient Market: A market that instantly takes into account all known financial information and reflects it in the security's price.

Exercise Price: The price at which an option or futures contract can be executed. Also known as the *striking price*.

Expiration Date: The late day on which an option or future can be exercised.

Federal Reserve: The national banking system, consisting of 12 independent federal reserve banks in Atlanta, Boston, Chicago, Cleveland, Dallas, Kansas City, Minneapolis, New York, Philadelphia, Richmond, St. Louis, and San Francisco.

Fiscal Year: The 12-month accounting period that conforms to the company's natural operating cycle versus the calendar year.

Freddie Mac: The nickname of the Federal Home Loan Mortgage Corporation.

Free Cashflow: Free cashflow is determined by calculating operating earnings after taxes, then adding depreciation and other noncash expenses, less capital expenditures and increases in working capital.

Free Cashflow/Earnings Ratio: The percentage of earnings actually available in cash. It is the percentage of free cash available to company management for investments, acquisitions, plant construction, dividends, etc.

Fundamental Analysis: An investment strategy that focuses on the intrinsic value of the company, as evidenced by a review of the balance sheet, income statement, cashflow, operating performance, etc.

Gap: The occurrence of a trading pattern in which the price range from one day does not overlap the previous day's price range.

Global Depository Receipt (GDR): Similar to ADRs, these depositary receipts issued in the international community represent shares in a foreign company. Other designations include International Depository Receipt (IDR) and European Depository Receipt (EDR).

Growth Investments: Companies or industries with earnings projected to consistently outpace the market over the long term.

High-Tech Stock: Securities of firms in high-technology industries such as biotechnology, computers, electronics, lasers, medical devices, and robotics.

Hybrid Security: A security that possesses the characteristics of both stock and bonds, such as a convertible bond.

Indenture: The legal contract spelling out the terms and conditions between the issuer and bondholders.

Index: A compilation of performance for specific groupings of stocks or mutual funds, such as the Dow Jones Industrial Average, S&P 500, etc.

Indicator: A measurement of the economy or securities markets used by economists and investment analysts to predict future economic and financial moves and direction. Indicators are classified as *leading, coinci-*

dental, or *lagging.* Indicator examples include interest-rate changes, utility consumption, number of unemployment claims, etc.

IPO (Initial Public Offering): The first public offering of a company's stock.

Insider: Anyone having access to material corporate information. The term is most frequently used to refer to company officers, directors, and top management.

Institutional Investor: Investor organizations, such as pension funds and money managers, who trade large volumes of securities.

In the Money: The situation when the price of the underlying security is above the exercise price.

Intrinsic Value: The difference between the current market price of the underlying security and the striking price of a related option.

Junk Bonds: Bonds with ratings below investment grade.

Leading Indicator: An economic measurement that tends to accurately predict the future direction of the economy or stock market.

LEAPS: Long-term equity participation securities. Long-term options with maturities of up to two years.

Leverage: The use of debt to finance a company's operations. Also, the use of debt by investors to increase their return on investment from securities transactions.

Life-cycle Investing: Developing an investment strategy based on where you are in your life cycle.

Liquidity: The degree of ease with which assets can be turned into readily available cash.

Listed: Investment securities that have met the listing requirements of a particular exchange.

Maintenance Margin: The minimum equity value that must be maintained in a margin account. Initial margin requirements include a minimum deposit of $2000 before any credit can be extended. Current Regulation T rules require that maintenance margin equal at least 50 percent of the market value of the margined positions.

Margin: The capital (in cash or securities) that an investor deposits with a broker to borrow additional funds to purchase securities.

Margin Call: A demand from a broker for additional cash or securities, as collateral to bring the margin account back within maintenance limits.

Mutual Fund: An investment company that sells shares in itself to the investing public, then uses the proceeds to purchase individual securities.

NAFTA: North American Free Trade Agreement.

Naked Option: An option written when the investor doesn't have a position in the underlying security.

NASDAQ: National Association of Securities Dealers Automated Quotation System, providing computerized quotes of market-makers for stocks traded over-the-counter.

Net Asset Value: The quoted market value of a mutual-fund share. Determined by dividing the closing market value of all securities owned by the mutual fund, plus all other assets and liabilities, by the total number of shares outstanding.

Numismatics: The study, collecting, and investing in money and medals.

OPEC: The Organization of Petroleum Exporting Countries.

Obsolete Security: Security that is no longer actively traded on an exchange but has collector value.

Option: A security that gives the holder the right to purchase or sell a particular investment at a fixed price for a specified period of time.

Out of the Money: An option whose striking price is higher than the underlying security's current market price for a call option, or whose striking price is lower than the current market price for a put option.

Participating: As it relates to preferred stock, the preferred stock-holder shares in additional dividends as the earnings of the company improve.

Payout Ratio: The percentage of a company's profit paid out in cash dividends.

Portfolio: The investment holdings of an individual or institutional investor, including stocks, bonds, options, money market accounts, etc.

Preferred: A security with preference to dividends and a claim to corporate assets over common stock.

Price/Earnings Ratio: Determined by dividing the stock's market price by its earnings per common share. Used as an indicator of company performance, and in comparisons with other stock investments and the overall market.

Put Option: A contract giving the holder the right to sell the underlying security at a specific price over a specified time frame.

Quick Ratio: The quick ratio is used to measure corporate liquidity. It is regarded as an improvement over the current ratio, which includes the usually-not-very-liquid inventory. The quick-ratio formula is computed as current assets, less inventory, divided by current liabilities.

Range: The high and low prices over which the security trades during a specific time frame; day, month, 52 weeks, etc.

Rating: The independent ranking of a security with regard to risk and ability to meet payment obligations.

Rebalancing: The process of adjusting a portfolio mix so as to return to a desired asset-allocation level.

Relative Strength: A comparison of a security's earnings or stock price strength, in relation to other investments or indices.

Risk: The financial possibility (uncertainty) that the actual return will vary from the expected return. Risk factors include inflation, deflation, interest-rate risk, market risk, liquidity, default, etc.

Rule of Eight: A diversification strategy which contends that a minimum of eight stocks is necessary to properly diversify a portfolio.

Scripophily: The collecting of antique stock and bond certificates.

Secondary Market: A market where previously issued securities trade, such as the New York Stock Exchange.

Short against the Box: An investment strategy of selling short while holding a long position in the security.

Short Sale: The sale of a security not yet owned, in order to capitalize on an anticipated market price drop.

Short Squeeze: A rapid price rise that forces investors to cover their short positions. This drives the security price up even higher, often squeezing an even greater number of short investors.

Special Situation: An undervalued security with special circumstances—management change, new product, technological breakthrough, etc.—that favor its return to better operating performance and higher prices.

Spinning Off: The shedding of a corporate subsidiary, division, or other operation, via the issuance of shares in the new corporate entity.

Split: A change in the number of outstanding shares through board of directors' action. Shareholder's equity remains the same; each shareholder receives the new stock in proportion to their holdings on the date of record. Dividends and earnings per share are adjusted so as to reflect the stock split.

S&P 500: A broad-based stock index composed of 400 industrial, 40 financial, 40 utility, and 20 transportation stocks.

Striking Price: The price at which an option or future contract can be executed according to the terms of the contract. Also called the *exercise price.*

10K, 10Q: The annual and quarterly reports required by the Securities and Exchange Commission. They contain more in-depth financial and operating information than the annual and quarterly stockholder's reports.

Technical Analysis: An investment strategy that focuses on market and stock price patterns.

Top-down Investing: An investment strategy that starts with the overall economic scenario and then moves downward to consider industry and individual company investments.

Total Return: The return achieved by combining both the dividend/interest and capital appreciation earned on an investment.

Trading Range: The spread between high and low prices for a given period.

Turnaround: A positive change in the fortunes of a company or industry. Turnarounds occur for a variety of reasons—economic upturn, new management, new product lines, strategic acquisitions, etc.

Underlying Security: The security that may be bought or sold under the terms of an option agreement, warrant, etc.

Undervalued Situation: A security with a market value that doesn't fully represent its potential or the true value of the company.

Uptrend: An upward movement in the market price of a stock.

Volume: The number of units of a security traded over a given time frame.

Warrant: An option to purchase a stated number of shares at a specified price within a specific time frame. Warrants typically are offered as sweeteners, to enhance the marketability of stock or debt issues.

Working Capital: The difference between current assets and current liabilities.

Yield: An investor's return on investment from its interest- or dividend-paying capability.

Zero Coupon: A bond selling at a discount to maturity value, and earning interest over the life of the bond but paying it upon maturity.

Index

About the Author

Richard J. Maturi is a highly respected freelance writer specializing in the business and investment fields. He is the author of more than 900 articles that have appeared in such noted publications as *Barron's, The New York Times, Investor's Business Daily, Kiplinger's Personal Finance, Your Money, Institutional Investor,* and *Industry Week.* In addition, he publishes three newsletters: *Utility & Energy Portfolio, Gaming and Investments Quarterly, and 21st Century Investments.* His previous books include *Divining the Dow, Money Making Investments Your Broker Doesn't Tell You About, Wall Street Words, Stock Picking,* and *Main Street Beats Wall Street.* He is a member of Wyoming Media Professionals, American Society of Journalists and Authors, and The Denver Press Club.

The author of *The 105 Best Investments for the 21st Century* invites you to examine these three special offers:

- *Gaming & Investments Quarterly*
  Covers the gambling, hotel, and entertainment industries with in-depth analysis of unique common stock investment opportunities. Regular $75 annual subscription; special price, $25 annual subscription.

- *Utility & Energy Portfolio*
  Includes investment ideas, discussions of where to find higher yields and safety, plus coverage of major industry trends and key players. Regular $95 annual subscription; special price, $35 annual subscription.

BONUS   Either subscription entitles you to a free copy of *Wall Street Words: The Basics and Beyond*, a $14.95 value.

- *21st Century Investments*
  New investments newsletter covering investment opportunities positioned to perform well into the next century and beyond. Regular subscription $95, special six month trial offer for only $5.

------------------------------------- TEAR HERE -------------------------------------

Please send check or money order or order with your Discover® card:

R. Maturi Inc.
1320 Curt Gowdy Drive
Cheyenne, WY 82009
    ——— *Gaming & Investments Quarterly*   @$25.
    ——— *Utility & Energy Portfolio*   @$35.
    ——— *21st Century Investments*   @$5. six month trial offer

Name _____
                         PLEASE PRINT

Address _____
                        INCLUDE APT # IF APPLICABLE

City _____ State _____ Zip _____

Account No._____ Exp. Date _____